THE CARIBBEAN EXODUS

Contents

Preface

Migration processes are complicated human dramas. The actors include political exiles and refugees, people fleeing violence and terror, displaced persons who have lost home and occupation, economic migrants who are valued for their skills or for their willingness to do bottom-of-the-ladder work, and finally, an enormous army of illegal aliens who are in search of ways to better their lives even in the face of obstacles put before them. The actors come smack up against impersonal bureaucracies, racial and ethnic prejudice, occupational discrimination. And yet for all their agony and difficulties these dramas are ultimately stories of hope and enormous courage, the source of many productive human experiences.

Having said that, it is necessary to focus on the political and social problems attendant to migration. Both sending and receiving societies reveal a painful confusion and uncertainty as to how to deal with the apparently never-ending stream of refugees and migrants. In no recent phenomenon has this been so clear as it was during the massive migration to the United States by thousands of Haitians and Cubans. To understand those migrations, and others as well, it is necessary to locate them within the broader historical, cultural and geographic frameworks in which they developed.

The purpose of *The Caribbean Exodus* is to achieve a better knowledge and understanding of one of history's greatest migrations—that in the 20th century from the Caribbean—and to call attention to the vulnerable condition of thousands upon thousands of human beings—persons frequently considered surplus not only economically but politically, not only by the receiving societies but by the sending ones as well—and to attempt to delineate what may be the range of options available to the societies and governments involved.

THE CARIBBEAN EXODUS

Introduction

Barry B. Levine

Exodus has been a constant theme throughout human history. In Western history the Bible, the Odyssey, and other great books in our tradition are evidence of the fundamental nature of human flight and the search for roots. Contemporary America understands itself in terms of great migrations to its shores, first from Europe and today from elsewhere. This anthology deals with an important migration, that from the Caribbean. The idea for the anthology came about several years ago when the United States was in the throes of trying to understand the significance of the spectacular phenomenon of tens of thousands of Cubans and Haitians risking all kinds of dangers to get to our shores, through treacherous waters, often aboard rickety ships. One quite deliberate intention of this volume, however, is to divert discussion of the Caribbean migration away from narrow focuses that simply concentrate on Haitians and Cubans fleeing to Miami and to locate these movements within broader historical, cultural, and geographic frameworks. From different perspectives and employing various methodologies, the authors of the following chapters discuss emigration from Central America, Mexico, Puerto Rico, Cuba, Haiti, the Dominican Republic, and the West Indies, and immigration into Canada, France, Great Britain, Holland, and the United States. The purpose is to provide a wider perspective for discussions of the Caribbean exodus. This anthology had something of a previous life in the form of a special-topic issue of *Caribbean Review*, published under the same title (Winter 1982, Vol. XI, no.

1). Nine articles that appeared in that issue have been rewritten and much revised for this volume, and seven articles have been added to the collection, four of which have been written especially for inclusion here.

Framework for Understanding the Caribbean Exodus

Surplus Populations:
Economic Migrants and
Political Refugees

Barry B. Levine

In the United States in 1986, upon dialing (718)756-1441 one would be treated—at no charge beyond the fee for the telephone call—by a certain Mr. Compton Fairweather, formerly of Belize and now of Brooklyn, New York, to a prerecorded tape reporting on the latest news of concern to Belizeans. On any given tape—they changed every Tuesday morning—one might hear about the border dispute between Belize and Guatemala, about recent appointments made by the Belizean government, about fires in Belize City, about births, surprise birthday parties, marriages, and deaths of Belizeans "at home" (such as the two families in Belize City who attempted to settle a property dispute "with guns and machetes") and abroad (such as Church and community activities in Brooklyn—for example, the Grand Winter Dance, including instructions as to which subway to take to get there).

This example, among a whole array of others, is one that symbolizes the reconquest of the metropolitan powers by Caribbean peoples. If Europe sent migrants to America, and then imported non-European slaves and other indentured laborers to work the new lands, thus creating creole America, creole America is now "reconquering" the mainlands.[1]

These migration processes are complicated human dramas. The actors include political exiles and refugees, people fleeing violence and terror, displaced persons who have lost home and occupation, economic migrants who are valued either for their wealth and skills

5

or for their willingness to do bottom-of-the-ladder work, and, finally, an enormous army of illegal aliens who are in search of ways to better their lives even in the face of bureaucratic obstacles put before them.

But the migration dramas, for all their agonies and difficulties, are ultimately dramas of hope and of enormous courage. They pit migrating actors against impersonal bureaucracies, alien cultures and languages, racial and ethnic prejudice, and occupational discrimination. Against such odds the migrants attempt to recreate their lives with dignity and their dramas, more often than many observers care to recognize, are productive human experiences.

For the most part, migrants come with a less than total desire to destroy and obliterate their past. In the case of the Puerto Rican migration, for example, it is clear that in the original exodus from the island it was economic opportunity—even at the cost of social status—that drew the islanders to the mainland. Yet given the economic development of the island, many Puerto Ricans eagerly returned and willingly yielded economic gains to recover social status.[2] In a similar vein, those who flee for political and safety reasons do so with a definite hope to return—pinning their hopes either on the expectation of some divine plan for historic justice or, if need be, on conspiratorial activities that they themselves must engage in. It is this combination of roots in one place, and an on-going life in another, this conflict of cultures producing marginal men, that is the basis for the syncretic accretions and coalescences that form Caribbean ethnic subcultures throughout North America's metropolitan cities. Latin Miami, Haitian Brooklyn, Salvadoran San Francisco are culturally productive centers of excitement and vitality.

Having affirmed this, however, it is important to focus on the political and social problems attendant to migration. This is especially so, given the fact that both sending and receiving societies reveal a painful confusion and uncertainty as to how to deal with what appears to be a never-ending flow of refugees and migrants. If Lenin's assertion is right, that emigrants, like soldiers, "vote with their feet," then it is obvious that the sending societies no longer seem able to provide their citizens with a decent life, whether decency be defined as the absence of persecution or the provision of economic opportunities. Nor do receiving societies know how to deal with the migrants: they do not know how to regulate the flow; they do not know how to treat those who have come to their shores; they do not know what responsibilities they have toward—and what responsibilities they should demand from—the new arrivals. Receiving societies do not know what they may demand from sending societies; sending societies do not know what they owe their itinerant citizens.

In a certain sense migration is a problem beyond its own narrow definition, for it is a phenomenon that by its nature crystallizes and starkly illustrates the core of the relationship between the individual and the state. The state is the one social institution to which all persons must respond. One need not belong to a religious group, to a family, or even to an economic enterprise; yet one must belong to a state. In the political realm there is no equivalent to the voluntary status of being secular, single, or even unemployed; all humans need citizenship, somewhere. What migration demonstrates is the dependence of people on the goodwill of the state, for the state is the only institution that can protect the individual from a multitude of problems—paradoxically, but most importantly, including those generated by the state itself.

And in the case of migration—whether for economic or political reasons—if one state no longer wants or can provide for the *émigrés*, then the ticklish question arises as to who *will* protect them. The image of stateless people—people on boats, people who arrive on land often only to remain bureaucratically afloat—is a chilling one. Reports of piracy at sea only emphasize the phenomenon. Stated starkly, if nobody wants them, then nobody will protect them. Consider Colorado Governor Richard Lamm's lame statement that "America cannot become the lifeboat of all the excess population floating around."[3] Politically, to be an *apatride* means not so much to be deracinated as to be defenseless; to be stateless is to be rightless.[4] Migrants between two countries lead precarious lives.

In another context, Richard Rubenstein has applied the concept of "surplus population" to those groups of people who have become expendable; people who have become redundant not simply demographically, but also superfluous politically. In *The Cunning of History*[5] Rubenstein used "surplus population" to discuss the predicament of Jews subject to Hitler's bureaucratic cruelty. Interestingly, if not felicitously, he reminds us that before the "final solution" was adopted a previous one was aired: a forced expulsion of all Jews from Germany. In both cases the necessary precondition was a process of denaturalization and denationalization, stripping Jews of citizenship and of any recourse to German law to protect their political and civil rights. Recent resistance to attempts by South Africa's government to strip that country's blacks of South African citizenship in favor of some dubious form of citizenship in defenseless and debile homelands, again reminds us of the importance of citizenship for the protection of human rights—rights which must be translated into political or civil rights to be defensible at all.

The 1980 Cuban exodus from Mariel, including the Cuban government's creation of the nonperson, noncitizen category of *escoria* ("scum"), as well as their refusal to take back those few who migrated but who would rather have returned to the island, again demonstrates how easy it is to create "surplus population." But the surplus population phenomenon is also illustrated by economic migrations, for they underscore the sending country's inability to protect its citizens, abandoning to another state gladly released responsibilities. Chicano author José Antonio Burciaga has lamented that "Mexico sends workers to this country [the United States but] never bothers to insure their welfare. . . . We are the children of Sanchez whom Mexico never educated."[6] The only hope for the migrants, then, is that they will be able to secure legal rights elsewhere.

That this hope too is uncertain can be witnessed in the confusion and ambivalence surrounding the categorization of petitioners at the U.S. borders. There appears to be little qualification and in practice no real cap on the number of *political* refugees allowed under U.S. immigration policy. *Economic* migrants, on the other hand, must meet specific criteria to be admitted and their numbers are carefully controlled. U.S. courts, as a consequence, are filled with cases of persons classified as economic migrants ineligible for legal entrance, who seek reclassification as eligible political refugees. And American academics have taken up the cause of those excluded by reintroducing arguments, once heard in debates about the causes of poverty, concerning the differential influence of individual and extra-individual societal factors on human behavior. For these scholars to resort to semantics is appropriate: the ostensible "economic migrants" are, in reality, "economic refugees"; since purported societal and especially political conditions created the migrants' economic misery, migrants, like refugees, are also victims and should be treated in the same way.

But even for those for whom the distinctions appear to be conceptually clear (a refugee flees persecution, a migrant poverty[7]), the way the distinctions are linked to U.S. policy generates confusion. The United States has allowed liberal migration in the form of political asylum from "totalitarian" communist regimes (such as Vietnam and Cuba), but not necessarily from regimes, "authoritarian" or otherwise, that are not communist. That such a policy is subject to political manipulation, for reasons quite apart from the migrants and their particular circumstances, can be seen in the creation during the Carter administration of the "Haitian/Cuban entrant" status, a kind of nether-status that effectively put the migrant in limbo.[8] The same thing can be seen in the speculation, amid the Reagan administration's conservative budget-cutting, that many Vietnamese and Cuban migrants might be economically rather than politically motivated after all.[9] These distinctions, like all policy distinctions, are subject to the vagaries of fluctuations in the political climate.[10]

Nor is it implausible to believe that the present link between diplomatic goals and migration policy might someday be reversed. In friendly Third World countries both metropole-emulating middle classes and metropole-aspiring working classes can be thought of as creations clearly beneficial to metropolitan powers and therefore legitimate goals of metropolitan foreign policy. Thus, one possible alternative for U.S. policy might be to reward America's friends rather than its enemies with migration categories that allow developmental escape valves. Such was the case with the United States and Puerto Rico, as well as with the European nations and their former colonies.

Unintentionally the "escape valve" policy has also become the policy *de facto* each time Cuba, not exactly a friend of the United States, has opened its borders to tempt its disaffected to leave. But when Mexico has attempted to export its share of development problems to the United States, it has had to see its population cross the border as illegal aliens.[11] A new policy might want to reward the Mexican government by awarding it, instead of the Cuban government, the capacity for legal migration. Should such a shift in U.S. policy come about—rewarding our friends rather than our "adversaries" with migration escape valves—both the purposes and the goals of U.S. foreign policy and U.S. immigration law would have changed, and proving "persecution" would have become either more difficult or less relevant.

According to estimates, there are between 4 and 12 million undocumented aliens in the United States, people who have either entered illegally or have over-stayed their visas. The U.S. Immigration and Naturalization Service (INS) stops about one million persons trying to enter illegally each year; they estimate however that for every person they catch, two others have been missed. These undocumented aliens have evidently learned how to beat the complicated bureaucracy of the U.S. immigration law, but their vulnerable political status has set them up for a whole range of problems.

Because of the so-called "Texas proviso," the United States has created the anomalous distinction making it illegal to be an undocumented alien, while not making it illegal to be the employer of one. This has created the closest thing in the United States to what Barrington Moore Jr. termed a "labor-repressive mechanism."[12] Such a mechanism, in distinction to the labor market, refers to a mechanism for controlling workers by political as opposed to economic means. The Texas proviso ensured that wages would be kept below the market value, as workers fear their employer might reveal their illegal status to INS officials. Essentially, what has been created is a new underclass of migrant farmworkers and urban sweatshop laborers, workers with no legal rights.

When Jimmy Carter became president of the United States he announced that one of the reforms that he intended to achieve was an overhaul of U.S. immigration law. Even given the impetus of the Cuban/Haitian onslaught, he was unable to achieve his goal during his term in office. Ronald Reagan's election also brought forth an announced commitment to immigration reform, in order to "regain control of our own borders." During 1983–1984, immigration reform was nearly achieved with passage of the Simpson/Mazzoli bill. That bill attempted to eliminate the Texas proviso and sought to impose fines on employers who hired illegal aliens. The thought was that employers facing sanctions for hiring illegals would refrain from doing so; since the job market for illegals would be diminished, illegal migration to the United States would be less attractive. Although the bill also offered amnesty for illegal aliens who had entered the United States before a specified date, it met strong objections from the Hispanic community, which expressed fears that all Latinos would be discriminated against.

Simpson/Mazzoli would have both eliminated the Texas proviso and offered amnesty as a two-pronged attack against the political vulnerability of aliens, but it did not become law.[13] In late 1985 Senator Simpson guided another bill through the Senate, pending action in spring 1986 by the House. By the end of 1985 no provision had been made for amnesty for longtime illegals and in exchange for the elimination of the Texas proviso and the penalizing of employers who hire undocumented workers, a deal was struck with fruit and vegetable growers to implement a guestworker program for 350,000 laborers.[14] Many questions concerning potentially negative consequences of the guestworker program will be raised—especially since it is slated to be administered by those close to the very agricultural interests who have a history of shamelessly mistreating their migrant workers.[15]

But it is not clear whether Simpson's or any other bill will pass Congress and garner the president's signature to become law. Should U.S. immigration law be reformed, however, the goal must be not simply control of U.S. borders but also protection for the vulnerable within these borders as well. The most pressing of the many problems relating to the Caribbean exodus thus concerns the clarification and consolidation of the legal rights of the migrants.[16] It is only this that will ensure that the migrants will not be exploited by labor repressive mechanisms in the workplace, nor be made superfluous in the society at large.

Cultural marginality in American society not only can be tolerated but should even be encouraged; such marginality is often both stimulating and productive for human interactions. But political marginality must be limited and minimized. Too often, when it is not, the results are injustice for those not protected and insensitivity by those not bothering to care.

NOTES

1. The "reconquest" is worrisome to many. Colorado Governor Richard Lamm, arguing against liberal migration policies, anxiously pointed out that "the nation's largest number of immigrants came not in 1911 or 1893 but in 1980" ("America needs fewer immigrants," New York *Times,* July 12, 1981). However, as Silvia Pedraza-Bailey points out, "Contrary to Lamm's assertions, the decades of highest immigration remain those around the turn of the century. In the decade 1890–1900, immigration constituted 0.6 percent of the population, in the decade 1900–1910, that of the highest admissions, 1.2 percent. By contrast, in the decade 1970–1979, immigration comprised only 0.2 percent of the total population" (*Political and Economic Migrants in America; Cubans and Mexicans.* Austin, TX: Univ. Texas Press, 1985, p. 166).

Alejandro Portes ("Notes on the reconquest; The Latin Americanization of the United States?" *Caribbean Review,* 12, no. 3 (Summer 1983):23) argues:

"the current wave of immigration to the United States must be placed in historical context. The present period is definitely one of high immigration. However,
the overall significance of immigration, both in demographic and economic
terms, is but a fraction of what it was in the beginning of the century. . . . immigrant flows have a significant economic and cultural impact in the areas where
they settle. . . . [but] each foreign minority, no matter how large, has been absorbed into the United States without altering the fundamental economic and
political structures of the country."

2. See Levine, "Puerto Rican Exodus," for an elaboration of this point.

3. Cited in "Closing the Golden Door," *Time,* May 18, 1981.

4. See Michael S. Teitelbaum, "Forced migration: The tragedy of mass
expulsions" in Nathan Glazer, ed., *Clamor at the Gates* (San Francisco: Institute
for Contemporary Studies, 1985).

5. Richard Rubenstein, *The Cunning of History* (New York: Harper &
Row, 1978).

6. José Antonio Burciaga, "Children of Sanchez remember," Kansas
City *Times,* Jan. 15, 1981.

7. See W.R. Smyser ("Refugees: A never-ending story," *Foreign Affairs,*
64, no. 1 (Fall 1985):164):"Unlike migrants, however, refugees leave their
homes because of fear, not because of opportunity. Whereas migrants travel to
escape stagnation and poverty, refugees travel to escape persecution, conflict,
and perhaps death. Migrants seek opportunity. Refugees seek haven. A migrant
does not *wish* to return home, a refugee does not *dare*."

8. Mario Rivera ("Refugee chess; policy by default," *Caribbean Review,*
13, no. 4 (Fall 1984) explicates the politics of that policy. As of mid 1986, the
Cubans but not the Haitians had been allowed to pursue residency. Regarding
the Cubans, see George Volsky ("U.S. life improves for many Cuban refugees 5
years after exodus by sea," New York *Times,* Sept. 29, 1985).

9. Should immigration from Cuba be normalized, the rules for future
Cuban migrations surely will be changed. See Karen Payne and Ellen Hampton,
"Reagan will seek repeal of Cuban immigration act," Miami *News,* February 8,
1985.

10. The most dramatic policy shifts concern sudden, often forceful,
changes in attitudes regarding the tolerance of illegal aliens. When a group is
tolerated but not given legal status "mass expulsion without benefit of formal
deportation proceedings is an available legal option" (Teitelbaum, "Forced
migration" p. 274). Dramatic cases of this occurring have taken place in Uganda
and Nigeria in Africa as well as the Bahamas and Venezuela in the Caribbean.
Concerning the Venezuelan policy shift, see Andrés Serbin, "The Venezuelan
reception; Human resources and development," *Caribbean Review,* 11, no. 1
(Winter 1982).

11. During summer 1984, when the Simpson/Mazzoli bill to reform U.S.
immigration rules almost became law, Mexican newspapers were filled with discussions about both the possible effects of the law and the causes of the illegal
migration. Blame was imputed to factors as diverse as U.S. colonialism, the lack
of land reform and jobs in Mexico, and even the lack of nationalistic sentiments
on the part of the emigrants. Mexican soul-searching was complicated by the fact

that at the same time they were trying to understand U.S. attempts at immigration reform, they were being forced to come to terms with hundreds of undocumented Guatemalans settling in southern Mexico. Behind most of the arguments was an awareness of the need for the migration outlet. *Excelsior,* June 19, 1985, editorialized: "the establishment of laws designed to result in massive expulsions of Hispanic Americans . . . closes another safety valve for the developing nations."

12. Barrington Moore Jr., *Social Origins of Dictatorship and Democracy: Lord and Peasant in the Making of the Modern World* (Boston: Beacon Press, 1966).

13. Wayne Cornelius does not believe that employer sanctions will prevent exploitation: ". . . employer sanctions legislation does not reduce the employment of undocumented workers. Such actions only drive the hiring underground. They intensify the immigrants' fear and increase the employer's power to manipulate this fear through threats to call immigration authorities when workers complain about wages or working conditions." See "Simpson-Mazzoli vs. the realities of Mexican immigration" in Wayne A. Cornelius and Ricardo Anzaldua Montoya, eds., *America's New Immigration Law: Origins, Rationales, and Potential Consequences* (La Jolla, CA: Center for U.S.-Mexican Studies, 1983), p. 146.

14. Robert Pear, "Institutionalization of the illegal alien—Growers persuade the Senate to approve a program admitting 350,000 foreign workers," New York *Times,* Sept. 29, 1985.

15. It is not clear whether guestworker programs offer workers better protection than illegal migrants are offered. Sidney Weintraub and Stanley R. Ross (*"Temporary" Alien Workers in the United States—Designing Policy from Fact and Opinion,* Boulder, CO: Westview, 1982, p. 105) suggest that it does: "A legal program would afford the workers some protection under the law from mistreatment by employers, or from others preying on their illegality. The workers would have some right of appeal to the consular authorities of their home countries." The contrary argument is articulated by Philip Martin and Richard Mines: "Guestworkers enter the United States with restricted economic rights and no rights whatsoever to participate in our political system. Decisions are made for guestworkers, not by them. Guestworkers cannot bring their families, cannot normally quit or change their status from worker to worker-citizen. This second-class status is unavoidable, because to extend the basic right of permanent residence would negate the guestworker concept . . . a class of temporary helots is morally offensive in a democracy, even if individual aliens and their U.S. employers benefit" ("Debate on guestworkers to continue," *J. Inst. Socioeconomic Studies,* 8, no. 2 (Summer 1983):98–99). For a negative statement concerning a guestworker program in Puerto Rico see Barry B. Levine, "Modern Irizarrismo—A return to labor repression in the sugar fields?" in Basil A. Ince, ed., *Essays on Race, Economics and Politics in the Caribbean* (Mayaguez: Cuadernos de Artes y Ciencias, 1973), pp. 163–79. Pro and con positions appeared in *Caribbean Review,* 11, no. 1 (Winter 1982): see Franklin W. Knight, "Who needs a guest worker program? They do; we do" and Mark J. Miller and William W. Boyer, "Foreign workers in the USVI; History of a dilemma."

16. One new and positive step has been taken by the Dutch parliament which has awarded voting rights in municipal elections to 350,000 foreign settlers, "the right to participate if not to belong" ("Taxation without representation," *Economist*, May 11, 1985). The Scandinavian countries initiated this move in the late 1970s.

A History of West Indian Migrations: Overseas Opportunities and "Safety-Valve" Policies

Dawn Marshall

The history of the Caribbean can be seen as a succession of waves of migration. The populations of the countries of the Caribbean are almost wholly the result of migration: from initial settlement after discovery, forced immigration during slavery and indentured immigration during the nineteenth century, to the present outward movement to the metropolitan core countries. Nevertheless, observers tend to see the present outward movements as a recent phenomenon and are not generally aware that, certainly from the Commonwealth Caribbean, people have been moving out of their islands almost continuously for 150 years. This chapter presents a brief historical review of emigration from the Caribbean since Emancipation, for Emancipation granted to the ex-slaves freedom of mobility, a freedom which they have exercised at every opportunity.

While this chapter does not cover all Caribbean migrations, for example those from the non-English speaking countries, most of these islands have had similar experiences of emigration. Because of the need for labor in Trinidad and British Guiana, movement from the Eastern Caribbean islands probably began about 30 years earlier than that from any other country. But Puerto Ricans began to emigrate to Santo Domingo in the early 1870s and continued to emigrate, not only to Santo Domingo but to Cuba, Venezuela, and Guatemala.[1] Since the late nineteenth century Haitians have been emigrating to the Dominican Republic, usually under poor, and sometimes atrocious, conditions. They also sought work in Cuba after 1900 when the investment of American capital led to an expansion of sugar production.[2] Certainly since World War II migrants have left all of the Caribbean islands for the metropolitan countries of the North Atlantic, in particular the U.S. Thus the claim that has been made for Barbados, that emigration is an integral part of the social environment,[3] can also be made for the Caribbean Basin as a whole.

The Commonwealth Caribbean countries are small, even minuscule, by global standards. Guyana, the mainland country, is largest with an area of 83,000 square miles. Next in size are Jamaica (4,411 square miles) and the Bahamas, whose area of 5,400 square miles is made up of a sprawling archipelago. Except for Trinidad and Tobago which together make up 1,980 square miles, the other islands range in size from 33 square miles (Montserrat) to 305 square miles (Dominica). This small size means that the populations are also small. According to the 1980 census results, these populations range from 11,519 in Montserrat to 2,004,051 in Jamaica and total about 5.4 million in all. Resources and opportunities are also extremely limited, and it should be remembered that while the volume of migration may be small when measured in global terms, the impact on these small territories can be relatively large.

The population of the Caribbean is to a large extent the result of migration—from initial settlement, forced immigration during slavery, indentured immigration, to the present outward movement to metropolitan countries. The period since Emancipation can be divided into four phases of migration in the Commonwealth Caribbean: the first, 1835–1885, is dominated by inter-territorial movement while the second, 1885–1920, is dominated by the movement to Panama. During the period 1920–1940, there was little out-migration from the islands although there was some forced repatriation as well as some voluntary return migration. The present phase, begun in 1940, is dominated by movement to the metropolitan countries of the United Kingdom and North America.

INTER-TERRITORIAL MIGRATION (1835–1885)

Historically, this phase is of particular interest since it is the first movement out of the islands after Emancipation, and the origin of the almost continuous migration that followed. This first movement has to be placed in the context of general mobility after Emancipation: movement to small-holdings, movement to different occupations (often in the towns), and movement to different islands—all essentially movement away from the plantation. Statistics are available for most of the islands that show decreases in the sizes of estate labor forces, as well as increases in the number of small-holdings, in the years immediately following Emancipation.

In 1835 opportunities for migration existed mainly in the territories of Trinidad and Tobago and British Guiana. Trinidad and Tobago was newly acquired by Britain from Spain, and British Guiana from the Netherlands. Planters in these territories tried to retain their labor forces, but with little success. For example, in Trinidad, of the 22,359 slaves living and working on estates, only 8,000 remained after Emancipation.[4] In addition, thousands of laborers were needed for the opening up of virgin lands to meet the demand for sugar.

Both Trinidadian and Guianese planters sponsored active recruiting programs in the other islands. Their wage rates were double those in the other islands, and emigration agents were sent out to attract workers. Trinidadian planters adopted a bounty system in which captains of sailing vessels were paid for each laborer they imported; and in addition fringe benefits such as free passages and land for cultivation were also offered. Guianese planters must have focused their attentions on Barbados because, for the most part, the terms "Barbadian" and "West Indian" were interchangeable in the context of this phase of immigration into British Guiana.[5] Planters in the sending islands reacted mainly by enacting legislation to restrict out-migration. For example, as early as 1839 the Barbadian legislature had passed two acts explicitly designed to restrict emigration. The British government also objected to the inter-territorial migration at first because of the inexperience of the ex-slaves, which placed them at a disadvantage in their dealings with the fraudulent practices of emigration agents. But most of these efforts to restrict the migration were in vain.

Conditions in most of the islands encouraged migration. In some of the islands like Barbados and Carriacou, most of the cultivable land was already being utilized by the plantations. Movement away from the plantations therefore meant movement away from the islands. Moreover, the period after Emancipation was a period of increasing population due mainly to high fertility rates, on the order of 40 per thousand.[6] In Barbados the rates of growth during the early part of this period were some of the highest ever experienced, despite a cholera epidemic in 1854 that claimed 20,000 lives.[7] This situation of increasing population was exacerbated by two other events during the period. The Sugar Duties Act of 1846, which removed the protection that West Indian sugar had been receiving in the English market, resulted in low prices in sugar, which in turn resulted in low wages for work on the estates. In addition, prolonged droughts throughout the Eastern Caribbean in the 1860s caused widespread distress in most of the islands. These conditions forced a change of planters' attitudes toward emigration.

Whereas in 1840 the workers in Barbados found it necessary to protest against the legislative restrictions deterring their migration, by 1871 the Barbadian governor saw migration as the only alternative to starvation and pestilence; and by 1873 the Barbadian legislature passed an act that actually made provision for assisting certain poor classes to migrate. By the end of the period, then, a new policy toward emigration had evolved in Barbados—from a policy of active discouragement to one of active encouragement. This seemed to be true in most of the other islands, and the policy of active encouragement has remained ever since.

The movements began even before Apprenticeship ended. (Although slavery legally ended in 1834, it was followed by four years of "apprenticeship": a transition period during which the slaves, still bound to the plantations, were supposed to acquire the skills that would equip them for earning a living as free men and women.) These migrations seem to have had their origin in the practice by planters, after the abolition of the slave trade (1807), of selling slaves between islands—a movement in which some freed slaves also took part before Emancipation. Inter-territorial movement took place in waves depending not so much on conditions in the receiving territories or in the sending countries, but on external conditions affecting the sugar market. For example, the movement to British Guiana took place in three main phases: 1835–1846, ending when Indian indentured labor seemed sufficient and when the Sugar Duties Act of 1846 caused a drop in prices; the second phase from 1863–1886 coincided with the droughts and was used by Guianese planters mainly to supplement Indian labor; and the third phase from 1920–1928, which actually falls outside the period under review, was an attempt by Guianese planters to find replacements when Indian indenture came to an end.[8]

Regarding the movements to Trinidad and British Guiana two things seem clear: that all of the Eastern Caribbean islands took part in the movements, with the possible exception of Dominica (where movement seems to have focused on the gold fields of Venezuela) and that Barbados, with its larger population, dominated the movements. (In the Northern Caribbean, there was also movement away from the plantations, but distance prevented Jamaicans and Bahamians from taking part in these movements.) Between 1835 and 1846, 19,000 persons from the Eastern Caribbean islands entered British Guiana and Trinidad and Tobago; while between 1850 and 1921 Barbados alone contributed 50,000 persons to the populations of British Guiana and Trinidad and Tobago.

These migrants were mainly young adult males who worked on the sugar estates. Strenuous efforts were made by the planters in both receiving territories to get the imported workers to sign, and abide by, contracts that would ensure a labor force throughout the year. Despite this the movements were essentially seasonal, with workers arriving in the territories after June when work became scarce in their own islands, and then returning to spend Christmas and crop time in their own islands. Nevertheless, the recorded number of West Indians resident in Trinidad almost doubled from 12,106 in 1844 to 24,047 in 1881.[9]

Several characteristics of this early inter-territorial movement should be noted, since they tend to be true of the movements in other phases of Caribbean migration. First, the movements began and mainly continued as solicited contract movements—although individuals did move without the benefit of contracts and in some cases actually resisted efforts to make them sign contracts. Second, although quite a substantial number of workers remained in the receiving territories, the movements were seen as essentially temporary in nature. And finally, the impact of external global conditions was extremely important, affecting both the magnitude and timing of the movements.

Other movements from the sending islands also took place during this first phase: for instance in 1894 a "massive" movement of at least 7,000 poverty-stricken Dominicans from Dominica to the gold fields of Venezuela[10] and movements from Barbados to Surinam (1,495 between 1863 and 1870) and to St. Croix (3,500 in 1863).[11] But the movements to British Guiana and Trinidad dominated the period. Further, both these movements continued long after 1885; the movement into British Guiana until 1928, while the movement from St. Vincent and Grenada to Trinidad still continues today. But in 1880 a movement began to "foreign" territories, especially to Panama, which overshadowed all others.

INTER-CARIBBEAN MIGRATION (1885–1920)

During the first phase of emigration, movements from Caribbean islands were directed mainly toward other British colonies in the Caribbean. In contrast, movements during the second phase were directed toward "foreign" territories, though still mainly within the Caribbean basin. These included movements to Cuba and the Dominican Republic to work in the expanded sugar plantations there; movements to banana plantations and railroads in Central America; movements to work on a dry dock in Bermuda; and movements to the United States. These movements were the result of a demand for labor created by the expansion of a specific economic sector or venture, and in almost every case this expansion was the result of U.S. investments. Thus, although only a small proportion of the actual movements were to the United States itself, they were certainly movements in search of the "Yankee dollar."

Conditions in the Caribbean at the beginning of this second phase certainly were conducive to emigration. During the 1880–1890s Europe entered the world sugar market with beet sugar, which received substantial government subsidies. In 1884, for example, enormous quantities of cheap German beet sugar were sent to Britain and the price of muscovado sugar fell from 20 to 13 shillings per 100 pounds. For a brief period between 1891 and 1895 the United States accepted sugar from the British West Indian colonies, but this ended when the U.S. gave preferential sugar duties to Brazil, Cuba, the Dominican Republic, and Puerto Rico. This unfortunate position for sugar was compounded by serious outbreaks of cane disease in the British West Indies. Thus this was one of the most critical periods for West Indian sugar; there were widespread bankruptcies of estate proprietors and even the abandonment of sugar on some estates. Workers were laid off and wages lowered. Nature further compounded the problem: Barbados and the Leeward Islands were hit by a hurricane in 1898, Montserrat and Nevis in 1899, while Jamaica was hit by four hurricanes between 1911 and 1921. Then there was the volcanic eruption of Soufrière in St. Vincent in 1902, which claimed 2,000 lives. For the majority of the populations, labor emigration must have seemed the only practical alternative to poverty and distress.

Migration to Panama can be divided into three phases: that of railroad construction across the Isthmus between 1850 and 1855; the period of work on the canal between 1880 and 1914; and the period of railroad relocation between 1906 and 1914. Only Jamaicans took part in the first phase of railroad construction when 2–3,000 of them traveled to Panama. Recruitment of labor from the rest of the English-speaking Caribbean had to await the beginning of the excavation of the canal in 1880 under the French company, Universal Inter-Oceanic Company. When the French company failed in 1889, migration ceased. Between 1894, when the new Panama Canal Company was incorporated, and 1904 when the American government purchased the canal and railroad properties, labor was recruited mainly from those who had remained behind in Panama. With the American purchase in 1904 another, larger wave of emigration began and continued even after the canal was opened to traffic in 1914.

The nature of the movement was very much one of ebb and flow. This was not only a result of the stages of construction going on in Panama itself, but also as a result of other activities, mainly in banana cultivation, which at this time were taking place in other Central American republics such as Mexico, Colombia, Nicaragua, Honduras, Guatemala, and Costa Rica. Workers moved among these countries depending on conditions. There was considerable movement of West Indians between the United States and these republics as well as the islands themselves. Patterns of recruitment also varied, so that movement from Jamaica was mainly individual, whereas from the Eastern Caribbean movement very much depended on recruitment or emigration agents. Workers returned to their homes at the end of their contracts, or when they felt that they had earned sufficient "Panama money" to live off it for a while. As a result, there was a considerable turnover of workers and the opportunities to work abroad were open to a much larger number of persons than would have been the case otherwise.

Nevertheless, the movement out of the Caribbean during this 1885–1920 period was considerable. It is estimated that there was a net population loss to the English-speaking Caribbean of 130,000 during this period, the majority being from Jamaica and Barbados.[12] As a result, with the exception of Jamaica and Trinidad, all of the islands experienced not only declines in the number of males of working age, but actual declines in total population as well. The following statistics give an idea of the size of the movements. Between 1902 and 1932, 121,000 Jamaicans traveled to Cuba to work in the cane fields.[13] This movement ended in the 1930s with violence and forced repatriation. Between 1900 and 1920 there was a movement of 10,000 to 12,000 Bahamians to Miami to participate in the building boom then taking place there.[14] Between 1904 and 1914 about 60,000 Barbadians left their island for Panama.[15] Estimates of the numbers of West Indians who migrated to the United States during this period vary, but none are less than 46,000; one estimate for the number of Jamaicans alone who migrated to the United States during this time reaches 44,000.[16]

But conditions in the receiving countries were not always favorable. The majority of the West Indian migrants in Panama were employed in manual labor, in the actual excavation of the canal, working as "pick and shovel" men. There is a strong suggestion that the Isthmian Canal Commission discriminated against British West Indians not only by paying them lower wage rates but also by classifying the majority of them as laborers, no matter how skilled they might have been. Moreover between 1906 and 1923 more than 20,000 British West Indians died in Panama. In addition there was a racial bias against the black West Indians in most of the Central American republics, some of which enacted restrictive immigration legislation with a definite racial bias to halt the movements.[17]

The completion of the Panama Canal in 1914, the crash in sugar prices in 1921, the enactment of restrictive immigration legislation, and finally the Great Depression brought this period of considerable mobility to an end. Not only did opportunities for emigration no longer exist, but large numbers of West Indians were forced by circumstances to return home. This return movement and the lack of migration opportunities were perceived as trends against the tradition of migration that had evolved in the Caribbean. The relief of adverse economic conditions at home caused by problems with the sugar crop and the remittance of money earned abroad to enable the purchase of homes and land as well as the sustenance of those left behind had by now become an expected part of life. But the experience of work in menial jobs, the discriminatory practice of lower wage rates, and the closure of opportunities by racially discriminatory immigration legislation also became a part of the tradition of West Indian migration at this time.

A PERIOD OF CRISIS (1920–1940)

During the Panama phase, fertility rates in the Caribbean declined to a low of 34 per thousand, probably as a result of the massive male migration to the Canal Zone; and they remained more or less steady until the 1960s. But this decline in fertility was followed by dramatic declines in mortality. To use the example of Barbados, rates dropped from 33 per thousand in 1921–25, to 14 per thousand by 1951–1953.[18] This reduction, which took place over a period of thirty years in Barbados and the rest of the Caribbean, had taken place over a period of 170 years in Britain. It was due to a number of reasons including very large declines in infant and child mortality; the introduction from overseas of health measures such as DDT insecticide control; and improvement in general of socioeconomic conditions. The resultant natural increase caused concern from early in the 20th century. The Moyne Commission in its report after the 1930s disturbances, had no doubt that "absolute over-population" existed in some of the West Indies islands, to an acute degree.[19] Since population control via a further reduction in fertility rates was a long-term measure, emigration was the only perceived solution.

But the only outlets for emigration that developed during this period were those to the oil fields in Venezuela and to the oil refinery that had been established in Curaçao. Between 1916 and 1929 about 10,000 West Indians, mainly from Curaçao, Trinidad, and Barbados, found work in Venezuela in the developing oil fields. But in 1929, the Venezuelan authorities restricted the entry of foreign-born black people. An oil refinery was established in Curaçao in 1915, and these facilities were expanded in 1923. Thus, after 20 years as a sending country itself, Curaçao began receiving migrants. By 1945 one-fifth of the population of Curaçao was foreign-born. This foreign-born population was drawn from a number of sources including the parent country, Holland, the Dutch Windward Islands, Venezuela, and, of course, the British West Indies. Migration was again in a series of waves, the first one taking place between 1925 and 1930. By 1930 almost 3,000 of the 8,500 employees of the Shell Oil Company were British West Indians. However, as a result of the Great Depression migration ceased, and by the end of 1931, 70 percent of Shell's unskilled workers, including, of course, many West Indians, had been dismissed and repatriated. It was not until 1942 that Shell again turned to the West Indies as a source of labor, and 2,250 workers from the Eastern Caribbean entered Curaçao. But from about 1950, Shell began to introduce more automation, and by 1953 the entry of foreigners to Curaçao was narrowly restricted.[20]

This movement to Curaçao assumed greater importance than it would otherwise have done because of the lack of other outlets for migration. The numbers involved were small compared with the great mobility in the period before. Furthermore, West Indians were being repatriated from places like the United States and Cuba. These returning migrants had become accustomed to the high wages and higher standards of living of these receiving countries. Both their aspirations and their expectations had been raised by their sojourns abroad. It is to be expected, therefore, that there would have been discontent with the conditions in the Caribbean, even during normal times.

A series of disturbances—which began in St. Kitts in January 1935 and ended in Jamaica in 1938 and occurred throughout the West Indies—signaled a crisis in West Indian history. The period was one of especially bad economic conditions caused by the persistence of adverse market trends for export crops, the closure of emigration outlets, and the rapid increase of population.[21] More than one contemporary observer commented on the need for emigration opportunities at this time while the commission that investigated the disturbances stated in its report that this lack was an important element in the disturbances: "this extreme difficulty of movement . . . creates a sense of being shut in, of being denied opportunity and choice, and of subsequent frustration in the minds of many young men . . . it may be a more important element than appears at first in the psychology of discontent."[22] But the Moyne Commission did not see a possible solution within the West Indies. According to the commission, the solutions lay not within the island systems, but outside: in capital supplied from without, in a reduction of the birth-rates, and in securing, somehow, new outlets for emigration.

MOVEMENT TO THE METROPOLES (1940 to Present)

With World War II, American workers were absorbed by the armed forces and other war efforts. Agriculture, the railroads, the lumber industry, and factories suffered from shortages of labor. Migrant workers were therefore imported to alleviate these shortages. The majority of these were Mexicans under the Bracero Program, but

Newfoundlanders and French Canadians, as well as British West Indians from British Honduras, Jamaica, the Bahamas, and Barbados were also imported.

For the Commonwealth Caribbean, recruitment began with the Northern Caribbean, in the Bahamas and Jamaica. American employers were reluctant to recruit Barbadians because of the distance, and therefore the costs of transportation involved. But the Barbadian governor pressed for their inclusion and by 1944 Barbadians were numbered among those included. The numbers involved were substantial. Between 1942 and 1945 a total of just over 400,000 workers were imported. Almost three-quarters of these were Mexicans, but British West Indians made up 17 percent while the Canadians made up 10 percent.[23] This importation of British West Indians did not end when the Bracero Program ended, but in fact still continues, and has been extended to some of the other Eastern Caribbean islands such as St. Vincent and St. Lucia. But Jamaicans still make up the majority of the workers imported. Nor is the impact of the compulsory savings of the workers insignificant in the islands. In St. Vincent, for example, the contribution of compulsory savings to remittances has been increasing. In 1965 compulsory savings were just over three percent of total remittances. But by 1979 they represented almost 16 percent of total remittances. And this contribution in 1979 was from only 452 workers: 386 in the United States, and 66 in Canada.[24]

The Bahamians, however, no longer participate in the scheme. What is interesting about the Bahamian situation is that as tourism grew and employment opportunities grew with it, the recruitment of Bahamian workers gradually declined until it came to an end in 1966. Instead, the Bahamas became a receiving country: between 1901 and 1943, the proportion of the total population made up by the foreign-born varied between two and four percent. But by 1970, the foreign-born population enumerated by the census made up 18 percent of the total population—and this did not include the relatively large numbers of undocumented Haitians and Jamaicans in the country who were estimated to be anywhere between 10,000 and 40,000 at this time. (No data on the foreign-born population are included in the *Preliminary Review*, which is the only publication so far available on the 1980 Bahamas Census of Population and Housing.)

If the recruited contract labor scheme is excluded from consideration, three landmarks can be identified in U.S. immigration legislation as it has affected British West Indians. First was the

Immigration Act of 1924, which was the result of a fairly long public campaign for restricted immigration that had its first legal expression in the Chinese Exclusion Act of 1882. The act expressed a definite racial bias and devised complicated formulas to restrict immigrants from certain countries in order to retain the racial and ethnic composition of the U.S. population.[25] Unfortunately for the Commonwealth Caribbean, this act came at a time when, as we have seen, most other migration outlets for Caribbean peoples had also been closed. The next landmark was the Immigration Act of 1952, usually known as the Walter/McCarran Act, which is believed to have reduced the flow of West Indians (which had renewed after the Second World War) to a mere trickle. Then the third landmark was the Immigration and Nationality Act of 1965. Because of their new status as independent countries, Jamaica, Trinidad and, after 1966, Barbados were able to benefit from this act. As a result West Indian immigration to the United States for the decade 1961–1970 reached almost 500,000, more than three times that of the period 1951–1960.

Immigration to the United States from the Commonwealth Caribbean has continued during the 1970s, except that in the last few years much tighter controls have been put on the movement. As a result only 316,149 immigrated from Caricom countries during the 1970s. The total for the English-speaking Caribbean was 337,487. American immigration policies, like those of most other countries, tend to correspond closely with the economic fortunes of the host country. During the world-wide recession of the early 1980s, the United States again considered restrictive policies reminiscent of the 1920s. Debate on U.S. immigration policy during the late 1970s culminated in the Simpson/Mazolli bill, which by the end of 1984 had yet to be enacted. In the context of Caribbean migration, Simpson/Mazolli implies stricter enforcement of current laws and an attempt to control illegal immigration.

Like the movement to the United States, the West Indian movement to the United Kingdom also had its origins in the Second World War, when West Indians who went to Britain to support the war effort of the mother country were exposed to British conditions and opportunities. However, not until the 1950s did the stream become significant and it is generally accepted that the 1952 Walter/McCarran Act was partly responsible for this deflection to the United Kingdom. Although the movement was not massive, ranging between 20,000 and 33,000 per year during 1955 to 1959, citizens of the

United Kingdom reacted strongly to this black invasion and their government moved to halt the movement by hasty legislation. It was in the two-year period before the Commonwealth Immigration Act of 1962 that 55 percent of the West Indian immigrants entered the United Kingdom, anxious to be admitted before "the door slammed." Between 1960 and 1962, 168,000 West Indians entered the United Kingdom. The 1962 Act controlled immigration to the United Kingdom while the 1965 White Paper on Immigration from the Commonwealth established the principle on which all future legislation was to be based. The principle was quite simple: that black people were, in themselves, a problem and that the fewer of them in the United Kingdom, the better it would be. The immigration to the United Kingdom has more or less ceased but the "problems" created by their presence in that receiving country persist.

The movement to the British metropole is important for a number of reasons. It was the first movement to a totally white host society (since the acculturated Afro-Americans in the United States formed a buffer for white American society, a foil against which the black immigrant/white host interaction could be played, as well as a section of American society into which the black West Indians could be absorbed). It is also important to note that the movement to the United Kingdom occurred at more or less the same time that large numbers of "guestworkers" began entering other Western European countries in response to the labor shortages there. But the United Kingdom, on which "the sun never set," had its own "reserve" of guestworkers who had been brought up to consider themselves citizens of the United Kingdom and therefore entitled to the same treatment as native-born British. In this respect the movement can be compared with the movement of Puerto Ricans into the United States. But if there were still any doubts about the status of West Indians in Britain, the 1981 Nationality Act, which came into effect in January 1983, should have removed them all; henceforth the immigrants were aliens—black colonial subjects who are not wanted in the "Mother Country."

Movement from the Commonwealth Caribbean to Canada has been relatively small. It is also a relatively recent movement, beginning in 1955 with an experimental contract migration of 100 domestic workers from the Caribbean. Up until 1962, the discriminatory bias of Canadian immigration laws was quite explicit. As early as 1815 the immigration of blacks was disallowed because they were thought to be unfit by nature to the climate, and to association with the rest of the colonists. Even postwar immigration policy, which recognized the need for a population increase to enable Canada to achieve its economic potential, did not remove the racial bias against blacks and Chinese. Thus it was not until 1962 that the racially discriminatory provisions of the Immigration Act of Canada were largely removed and entry was based on education, skill, and training. As a result, 75 percent of the immigrants admitted to Canada directly from the West Indies entered after 1962: 149,741 between 1962 and 1976. Moreover, except for those entering Canada under the Domestic Scheme, the movement has been highly selective for professional, white collar, and skilled workers.[26]

In April 1978, a new immigration act came into force in Canada: the 1976 Immigration Act. It was the product of more than four years of intensive study and cooperative effort at all levels of government. It embodied four key elements: nondiscrimination, family reunification, an active refugee policy and programs, and careful selection of immigrants for the labor force.[27] This act has coincided with a slow rate of economic growth in Canada during the late 1970s, followed by the recession of the early 1980s. The result has been a decline of total immigrants to Canada from a peak of 218,465 in 1974 to 88,846 in 1983. Caricom immigration to Canada has likewise declined: 22,468 in 1974 to 6,616 in 1983.[28]

Because of its size, Jamaica has dominated all of these movements to the metropoles, although the old receiving countries of Trinidad and Guyana are also important contributors, as is Barbados. Traditionally, movement out of Caribbean territories has been dominated by young males, mainly because of the types of jobs available at the destinations. But since 1960 and the movement to the metropoles, the movements seem to have been dominated by females. This present phase of migration to the metropoles has resulted in a much larger distinction being made, at least in the receiving countries, between recruited contract labor and permanent immigration. The restrictive policies of the receiving countries directed toward landed immigrants or permanent residents have been accompanied by bilateral agreements between governments for the seasonal recruitment of farm and factory workers. In a very real sense, these provide the only opportunities for the unskilled, low-income and unemployed workers of the Caribbean to enter the metropolitan countries at the present time.

THE FUTURE

Emigration has always been an important aspect of life in the English-speaking Caribbean, especially since Emancipation when all inhabitants became, theoretically, free to move. "Escape" or "safety valve" perceptions of, and policies on, emigration have evolved in most Caribbean countries. The basic, underlying need for employment opportunities abroad seems to have persisted, and emigration has come to be perceived as necessary by Caribbean peoples and the need to move still exists. The response to a pilot scheme for 26 female farm workers to Canada from Barbados indicated this demand— 385 women applied for the scheme! A 1980 Institute of Social and Economic Research survey of four of the Eastern Caribbean countries indicates that this demand for opportunities to migrate is general, and not likely to diminish in the near future. The survey showed that the proportion of respondents who preferred to live overseas ranged from 19 percent in Barbados to 40 percent in St. Kitts, while the proportion planning to go overseas in the next five years ranged from 39 percent in Barbados to 52 percent in St. Kitts. The United States is by far the preferred choice of these potential migrants although the popularity of Canada seems to be increasing.[29]

Conditions in the receiving countries have been the main controls of the magnitude, characteristics, and directions of the movement by Caribbean peoples. Mainly economic in nature, sometimes political, these conditions have reflected global trends in trade and economic prosperity and have resulted in fluctuations in the movements that do not necessarily reflect conditions in the Caribbean sending countries. These global conditions at present are not conducive to Caribbean migration. It remains to be seen whether the necessity of carrying their populations within their stagnant economies will result in that psychology of discontent observed by the Moyne Commission under similar conditions in the 1930s.

NOTES

1. History Task Force, *Labor Migration Under Capitalism: The Puerto Rican Experience* (New York: Monthly Review Press, 1979), pp. 84–85.

2. Dawn I. Marshall, *The Haitian Problem: Illegal Migration to the Bahamas* (Kingston, Jamaica: Institute of Social and Economic Research, 1979), pp. 11–13.

3. Dawn I Marshall, "Emigration as an aspect of the Barbadian social environment," *Migration Today* 9 (1980):6–14.

4. C.R. Ottley, *East and West Rescue Trinidad* (Port of Spain: Crusoe, 1975), p. 6.

5. Walter Rodney, "Barbadian immigration into British Guiana 1863–1924" (Paper presented at the Ninth Conference of Caribbean Historians, University of the West Indies, Bridgetown, Barbados, 1977), 1.

6. Joycelin Massiah, "Population policies in Barbados," in *Population Policies and Programs in the Caribbean* (Santo Domingo).

7. Governor R. W. Rawson, *Report on the Population of Barbados 1851–1871* (Bridgetown, Barbados: Barbados Government, 1871).

8. Rodney, "Barbadian Immigration," p. 3.

9. Mariande Ramesar, "The role of the British West Indian immigrants in Trinidad 1870–1921" (Paper presented at the Ninth Conference of Caribbean Historians, University of the West Indies, Bridgetown, Barbados, 1977).

10. Robert Amory Myers, "I Love My Home Bad, but . . . ": The Historical and Contemporary Contexts of Migration on Dominica, West Indies (Ph.D. diss., University of North Carolina, 1976), 75.

11. Rawson, *Population of Barbados*, p. 2.

12. Velma Newton, "Aspects of British West Indian Emigration to the Isthmus of Panama, 1850–1914" (Paper presented at the Ninth Conference of Caribbean Historians, University of the West Indies, Bridgetown, Barbados, 1977), 22.

13. George W. Roberts, *The Population of Jamaica* (Cambridge, U.K.: Cambridge Univ. Press, 1957), p. 140.

14. Paul Albury, *The Story of the Bahamas* (London: MacMillan Caribbean, 1975), pp. 168–69.

15. Newton, "Emigration to Panama."

16. Ira De Augustine Reid, *The Negro Immigrant: His Background, Characteristics and Social Adjustment* (New York: Abrahams Magazine Service Press, 1939, reprinted 1979), pp. 239–40.

17. Newton, "Emigration to Panama."

18. Joycelin Massiah, "Population Trends in Barbados" (Institute of Social and Economic Research Lectures on Development Problems in Barbados, Bridgetown, 1974).

19. Lord Moyne, Chair., *Report of the West Indian Royal Commission, 1938–1939* (London: HMSO, 1945).

20. Jan van Soest, "The World on an Island: The International Labour Force of Shell in Curacao, 1915–1960" (Paper presented at the Ninth Conference of Caribbean Historians, University of the West Indies, Bridgetown, Barbados, 1977).

21. Moyne, *Royal Commission Report;* W. Arthur Lewis, *Labour in the West Indies* (London: New Beacon Books, 1938, reprinted 1977); W. M. MacMillan, *Warning from the West Indies* (London: Penguin Books, 1938).

22. Moyne, *Royal Commission Report*, p. 11.

23. Julie J. Henderson, *Foreign Labor in the United States, 1942–1945* (Ph.D. diss., University of Minnesota, 1945), 23–26.

24. Dawn I. Marshall, "Vincentian Contract Labour Migration to Barbados: The Satisfaction of Mutual Needs?" *Social and Economic Studies* 33 (1984): pp. 63–92.

25. Thomas U. Curran, *Xenophobia and Immigration, 1820–1930* (Boston: Twayne, 1975).

26. George W. Roberts, "A note on recent migration from the West Indies to Canada," in *West Indian-Canada Economic Relations* (Kingston, Jamaica: Institute of Social and Economic Relations, 1967).

27. Government of Canada, *New Directions: A Look at Canada's Immigration Act and Regulations* (Quebec: Employment and Immigration, 1978).

28. Government of Canada, *Immigration Statistics Canada Annual Reports for 1970–1983* (Quebec: Employment and Immigration, 1984).

29. Institute of Social and Economic Research, *Preliminary Report: Four Country Questionnaire Survey, 1980* (Bridgetown, Barbados, 1981, mimeographed).

A Social Psychology of Caribbean Migrations: Strategic Flexibility in the West Indies

Charles V. Carnegie

A basic assumption in the study of international migration is that the movement of people from one region to another, and more so from one country to the next, is unusual. Conversely, those who are raised, have their children, and grow old on the same piece of ground we regard matter of factly, and find nothing of inherent interest in their sedentariness. To make the point by using a simple binary distinction: migration is regarded as the "marked" phenomenon, and staying put as "unmarked." Yet it is just as persuasive, logically, to assume the reverse. Or again, we might regard them both as being equally worthy, or equally undeserving of scholarly attention. My point here, however, is that at least with respect to particular peoples at particular times, to move is as ordinary and expected a thing to do as to remain sedentary. People from the Caribbean routinely use cultural ideas that emphasize flexibility and the building of multiple options. "Strategic flexibility" expresses these cultural patterns that people value and talk about in a great many contexts of Caribbean life. These ideas do not become any less salient when West Indians cross national frontiers; indeed migration itself is a preferred means of acting them out.

TWO VARIANTS OF STRATEGIC FLEXIBILITY

Being flexible has at least two dimensions: adjusting rapidly to whatever comes along; and the actual building of multiple options,

32

potential capital as it were, to hedge against future insecurity. A person must be ready and willing to use whatever comes along rather than cling doggedly to a single path that might prove fruitless. This idea is aptly expressed in the St. Lucian saying: *"mantche shien, pwen shat,"* or, "if you lose the dog, grab the cat." To illustrate: an inter-island trader (known in St. Lucia as a speculator) goes to the countryside intent on buying an item, say mangoes, for shipment to Barbados. She has made arrangements in advance to buy from a particular person. For some reason, however, this quest proves unsuccessful. If she is lucky enough to come across another item that she had not figured on, then, other things being equal, she will quickly grasp this new opportunity. But this new opportunity might be as opaque in its immediate significance as the making of a new acquaintance who will prove helpful in the future. Here too she will be quick to counter her gains.

This readiness to take hold of opportunities is voiced by informants when they share their plans, or express the wish, to emigrate. They are very likely to have a definite goal in view. But should the possibility of going someplace else present itself, it will be taken up readily. An instance of this is the case of a young man who recently migrated from St. Lucia to French Guiana. A fisherman in St. Lucia, he had long wanted to go to the United States. An aunt of his who lives in French Guiana came to St. Lucia on a visit. It was arranged that he would go to French Guiana and get help from her, during which time he would work and continue efforts to get a U.S. visa. Before leaving he sold his boat and fishing gear to get enough money for the trip. In the year prior to his leaving for French Guiana, he visited Barbados for a few weeks and stayed with a cousin of his mother. This too, seems to have been a trip designed to explore options. In a conversation with his mother in the months after he had left for French Guiana, she said she had not yet heard from him, but that she would not be surprised if he had gone from there to Venezuela to work, and continue trying to find a way of getting to the United States. Not knowing Spanish, she said, would not be a problem; he would make it somehow. Certainly it seemed that this was not perceived as a deterrent to his going to Venezuela.

Another instance, this one planned but not yet acted upon, is of an unemployed teenage youth living in the coastal town of Soufrière, in St. Lucia. He expressed a desire to go to the United States, and hopes to do this by getting a job on a yacht or larger vessel, then having the owner sponsor his visa application. He has had experience sailing to other Caribbean islands by using just this method. He spends a lot of time hanging out at the town's jetty, a good place for meeting strangers who are just passing through town. He associates with Rastafarian youth and dons many of their symbolic marks of style and dress. Yet his "locks" were not very evident, and he seemed willing to give up Rastafarian symbols should any opportunity come up for him to work his way to North America.

Market vendors in St. Lucia often express another aspect of the notion that you should take what comes when they say that if something is meant for you, you will get it. If you are meant to have the patronage of this or that person then you will. On the other hand, if business is bad one day then it's just bad, and there is nothing you can do about it. It is clear from the same people's resourcefulness in most things that this is not a simple attitude of fatalism. The view underlies what may seem to be an attitude of truculence on the part of St. Lucian vendors: "either you take it or leave it," they seem to say. A corollary of this idea as they see it is that if you are especially looking out for something—the money owed to you, or the particular item you have to get sold—then it will never come through when you want it to. This contrasts in my personal experience with the attitude of the Jamaican "higgler", who is always ready to "sweet mouth" and bargain with her customer.

Of related interest is the way in which people speak about their special skill or occupation. There is the feeling that somehow one is born with certain technical aptitudes. When one has such innate talents, it is not necessary to be specially trained; one knows what to do and may develop and refine this knowledge over time. The reverse of this is also said to hold: if one does not have the aptitude to begin with, then no amount of training in the field can properly develop one's skills. Thus it is considered quite acceptable for a youth to give up an apprenticeship after only a few weeks, on the grounds that he simply does not like the trade or "doesn't have the mind for it." Since he is not cut out for it, it would be pointless for him to continue. While they feel strongly that perseverance is important in most instances, there are times when West Indians negate this with ideas that are held with equal firmness. It is permissible to be in flux for a long time before discovering the special talents you are endowed with and which you must then develop relentlessly.

Some support for the argument being put forward can be found in Frank Manning's study, *Black Clubs in Bermuda.*[1] Bermuda differs from other territories of the region in several respects, yet here there seems to be much similarity as well. Manning develops the idea that people at any point in time may be expressly marking time, awaiting the right opportunity, the appropriate set of circumstances that will then make them able to develop their schemes for achieving fortune. This is the less active aspect of the strategy of flexibility. Equally important, and occurring simultaneously, is the other component: the building of multiple options.

Here again statements about migration must figure large, as this is the sphere in which options are ideally realized for many. An elderly man, recently returned to St. Lucia having lived abroad since the age of sixteen, made the following point; "A man must always be ready to move . . . if he sees there is no opportunity where he is, then he must move on to somewhere else." He had done just that, having lived in Cuba, Venezuela, Brazil, the United States, and traveled as a seaman to various other countries in the course of his long life. He developed his options not only by moving, but by carefully planning ahead—taking a correspondence course while still a sailor, buying properties in New York City well before leaving a secure job on the high seas, and moving his family to the United States before making the decision to do so himself.

It is quite common to hear such strategies being discussed in open conversation. One day, traveling in a transport van, two young women were talking about the necessity for going abroad. They spoke of the way in which relatives who have gone before can facilitate migration by sponsoring others. Then, one of the two spoke of going to another island as a tourist and finding someone there to get married to, so as to be able to stay permanently. It was a public conversation in which other passengers on the van were free to join, and it was clear that the strategies being outlined were not idiosyncratic. There was a shared sense of appropriateness, and the conversation was a light exchange to pass the time of day.

Very striking and explicitly articulated is the code of behavior that West Indians extend to strangers. The stranger coming into town attracts great attention; people greet him and are eager to find out where he is from. They show extreme willingness to render some service or to provide him with hospitality. The host will often make statements to the effect that if he or she were in a strange place, he too would appreciate others looking out for him. A speculator whom I had just met once offered me fruit as a gift on our parting. When I protested her generosity the woman who was with her told me it was all right: "What you give with the right hand you get back with the left."

The West Indian world is viewed as a system of potential relationships. It is possible that a stranger to whom one extends hospitality may be in a position in the near or distant future to reciprocate, and in view of this you are making an investment in redeemable resources. But the reciprocity will not necessarily come from the guest in question. It may be from the most unlikely source and come when you least expect it. Acts of generosity and hospitality create resources in a generalized pool from which one periodically also receives.

This is not meant to suggest that St. Lucians or West Indians are merely instrumental in their relationships; that there is no genuine or altruistic sentiment to their warm hospitality. Far from it. What is more likely is that their long awareness of, and integration into, wider social and political systems, and a tradition of the circulation of population—people coming in as strangers or returning home from residence overseas, or natives leaving to visit or work in other countries—have led to the gradual emergence of codes of hospitality and interpersonal relations that cater to this smooth integration of the wider system with the local community. The way in which deeply felt sentiments are most genuinely expressed just happens, then, to favor reciprocity within what is regarded as a potentially limitless social field.

The building of options is inculcated into children in a number of ways. Any child from the collective group of children in a village or neighborhood can be called on by any adult in the community to do simple errands. This well-recognized practice means that the child who just happens to be around is readily marshaled to escort the stranger to someone's home, or to help in some other way with the provision of the required hospitality. The child invariable complies enthusiastically. In the more tangible domain of learning skills, of saving, and of investment, training also begins at an early age. From as early as the age of five or six, children routinely help to take care of domestic animals, help with household chores, and assist in doing odd jobs related to their parents' or guardians' occupations. One lady who was raising several nieces and a nephew explained to me her own system. The children, the youngest being about eleven, are each given a small outlay of working capital. They use this to buy ingredients that go into the making of small delicacies like tamarind balls or coconut cakes. The lady, Miss Evadne, might then help them to make the sweetmeats, which the children in turn are responsible for selling, both at school and from the home. Some of the proceeds must be put aside for re-investment, while the balance goes toward buying essential school supplies or personal items for the child. Miss Evadne was quite explicit in telling me that this is all intended to develop in the children a keen knowledge of buying and selling, and of how to handle their resources carefully. In this way they will be able to manage on their own in later life, or in the event that she should be incapacitated. It must be noted further that these are optional skills, quite apart from the career(s) that each child is expected to, and will, pursue on his or her own.

The development of alternative options is more clearly evident as a strategy in the stages of the life cycle between adolescence and middle age. The case of one St. Lucian youth may illustrate this. Hubert is nineteen. He left school at the age of fifteen. Between that time and the present he has worked in at least seven different jobs and learned, at least to some degree, three different skills. His employment history is all the more remarkable in a country with an unemployment rate estimated at over 20 percent. Hubert has probably not achieved proficiency in any one of his trades. He has, however, accumulated some amount of "skill capital", which may serve him in good stead in lean times. Other youths pursue the same strategy even when not being able to do so through paid employment. They might work with a friend who is a carpenter or auto mechanic to be able at least to work for themselves and their families later on, even if they have not yet become proficient enough to make the skill marketable.

Hubert held a number of jobs and developed several skills, but sequentially. For others the development is pursued simultaneously. Even people with very secure jobs often have part-time occupations or get training in other trades to develop other marketable skills. One friend in St. Lucia who has been with a particular public service department for about 14 years, holding a middle level position in the department, also had a steady extra income from furniture upholstering. During the time that I knew him he was also taking an accredited course in welding, and wanted to learn refrigerator repairs as well. He was also looking for opportunities to go abroad to study agronomy.

The speculators with whom I worked most closely exemplified the ideal of spreading one's risks, of not putting all one's eggs in the same basket. It is commonplace to have several sources of income and systematically to maintain each one, even if some may bring in very little cash. Together they allow the household to meet its many obligations and to meet sudden and unexpected changes in economic conditions. In addition, people are always looking ahead to see what other occupational possibilities they can develop; to predict changes in consumer demand for new products and services; and to explore new training opportunities. There is behind all this a striving for individual autonomy; and this is qualitatively different from the North American who gets a second job to increase his or her income or who goes back to college in middle life to enter a new profession. These ideas are for the West Indian far more pervasive and institutionalized. They filter through all sections of Caribbean society. Those who enjoy secure salaried jobs, and members of the professions, may show less interest in developing multiple sources of income. On the other hand they still subscribe to ideals of flexibility in personal relations, acquiring skills and so on; many will buy property and farmland with no immediate aim of putting it to productive use. The high level of emigration among this class also bears out their commitment to these life strategies.

The ethnographic evidence provided here suggests that the concept of "occupational multiplicity," first introduced by Lambros Comitas in 1963, does not simply describe a tendency to hold several occupations simultaneously.[2] The same strategy leads people to be constantly generating new sources of income and to be acquiring new skills to cater to the needs of their own households and possibly to allow for future new avenues of employment. It is not only that people hold many occupations. The fact that serial multiplicity of occupation is also common, that people tend to gain competence in many different skills, that they actively seek out new economic opportunities, that children are raised with these goals in mind—all point to related patterns of behavior informed by common ideas about flexibility, ideas which people of the Caribbean express constantly.

FLEXIBILITY IN INTER-ISLAND TRADE

St. Lucian speculators have done business throughout the island chain since Emancipation and possibly even before then.[3]

They trade in locally grown agricultural products (grapefruit, mangoes, plantains, and the like), in locally made items such as brooms and charcoal, and increasingly in manufactured items bought in other territories and shipped back to St. Lucia for sale. The pattern is similar in other Caribbean countries and a dense, if mostly unnoticed, network of trade exists along the island chain and beyond. Even places like Jamaica, which seem not to have developed such international small trading before, now boast cosmopolitan higglering ties.

One set of activities in which the speculator is always involved, and where the building of options is clearly played out, is in the rounding up of supplies for trading. Speculators in agricultural produce, for instance, usually seek out numerous sources of possible supplies for any one shipping day. Several months before the peak of the mango season a speculator might purchase a few mango trees laden with green fruit, which then entitles her to harvest the entire crop for that season, when the fruit matures. As soon as the sailing schedule of the freighters becomes known from week to week, she will seek to make definite verbal agreements to buy one or another product from neighbors or distant farmers. To help ensure their sources of supply, speculators have a widely flung network of contacts on whom they rely as customers, or simply as people who will look out for supplies for them. These contacts are especially valued in times of scarcity when they are competing with each other, with local vendors, and with the government's Marketing Board, for supplies.

I gained insight into this pattern when I accompanied a speculator on a buying trip to the country. During the journey she asked the passengers and the driver of the van, an acquaintance of hers, whether they knew of anyone who had mangoes that she could buy for shipment. After collecting the pineapples she had arranged for beforehand, she then visited an older cousin who worked nearby to ask if people in her village some two miles away would have any fruit for sale. The cousin then promised to seek out a supply for her that evening, and to pass on the information by phone. The following morning, even after having put out all these feelers, she went early to the market in town with her nephew, each searching on different sides of the market for fruits being sold wholesale by farmers arriving on trucks and vans from the country.

Several of the speculators with whom I worked have done business in a number of different territories. One such example is a woman who currently travels to Barbados, Puerto Rico, and the Virgin Islands, and in the past has traveled also to Martinique. These women trade goods back and forth along a circuit which does not necessarily terminate in their home island; that is, they may in some instances even trade between points other than their island of residence. Their trading horizons are limited by markets, government regulations, the cost of transportation, and the like. But, conceptually at least, they would be prepared to go almost anywhere.

Most speculators, and many who consider going into the business, have a wide breadth of market knowledge. Even a speculator who currently trades with only one other island will readily tell you about market conditions and other requirements for trading with a number of other places. She will have information about what goods are available and at what prices; she knows the immigration requirements of several different countries (that, for instance, she must deposit a refundable F 2,500.00 on entering Martinique, Guadeloupe, or French Guiana); she will have an idea of relatives or other contacts with whom she will be able to stay while visiting in these other countries, and so on. The information that allows her to build this up-to-date "market knowledge" (in reality, as one can see, it is much more than this), is gathered by various means in the course of the working day. Conversations with friends and acquaintances who have traveled recently will point to current prices being paid and asked in other islands; will reveal difficulties with scheduled transportation services; or might pass on information about the new tax imposed by the Barbados government on vendors and other self-employed persons, including the traders from overseas doing business there temporarily. Information from one source is checked and verified against that from others. Even though she may have had a letter or phone call from Barbados telling her what condition her fruit arrived in and the prices being paid, she will ask people who traveled that week to verify the information. It is not merely that the trader has a fixed network of persons on whom she regularly draws for help and information; in effect she routinely "looks lines all about." People who had not traveled for a while will ask what prices were like, or try to corroborate information: "I hear the market is dirty" or, "They tell me the fruit traveled badly last week." The speculator's knowledge then is likely to exceed greatly the span of her trading activities. The capital stock she requires for trading is relatively inexpensive, and the outlay of funds for any one trip sufficiently reasonable, so that she enjoys tremendous versatility in deciding where she will travel to and what goods she will carry.

Flexibility has clearly been such a productive idea for Caribbean people for it facilitates integration into a social field that extends well beyond the local community and nation-state, and allows greater room for maneuver in a social system long characterized by uncertainty in its political and economic institutions.

MIGRANTS AND SPECULATORS

The assumption that migration is "marked," and staying put "unmarked," is questionable both on logical and empirical grounds. The speculator who spends a third of the year outside of her native island may or may not be classified as a "migrant" by the social scientist. She has not after all changed her legal resident status, or uprooted her hearth. Yet, even if the skeptic is reluctant to classify her as such, I argue that the same ideas which so powerfully inform the speculators' transient mode of adaptation also inform that of the migrants who leave St. Lucia and other Caribbean territories and move among the countries of the world. We do know that they have been leaving for some considerable time; that many end up having lived in several host societies; and that they return to the West Indies in large numbers. It would seem that from the emic point of view these are not distinct conditions; "speculating" and "migrating" are not, for West Indians, qualitatively very different. The intuitive insights of Caribbean writers and the persistent theme of movement that we find in their works, as well as the scholarly literature on the history of Caribbean migration, all tend to support this claim.

But how has the assumption of migration as "marked" activity affected the questions posed by scholars? The model has, for one, allowed us to find out what factors influence population movement: those that make for "push" and those that "pull." Striving for more finely textured insights, some scholars have probed the varied personal motivations that lie behind the decisions that people make to move or not to do so. A great deal of attention has also been paid to the adjustments that individuals and migrant communities must make to their new environment.

This assumption, then, has allowed us to pose useful questions, and significant issues have been illuminated by its use. But for some time now there has been a sterility to much of the migration debate. We are being offered more and more particularistic studies that tread the same conceptual ground season in, season out.

Migration studies have relied heavily on the presentation of statistics, staccato fashion, that mask the nature of social reality as much as they illuminate it. Today's migrant, for instance, may have been yesterday's returnee, and may have lived in two or three places before making his way back; yet even the most sophisticated presentation of statistics will not show this. It is not even just a question of finding out the motivations of particular migrants; it is being able to find out the emic ideas of a cultural system: whether those who come from it are in fact "migrants" at all, in their perception of the situation.[4]

In popular usage and as conceptual tools, "migration," and "migrant" sometimes have distinctly pejorative connotations. Folks remain "migrants" even after a second and third generation. In the case of the Caribbean, the implicit (and erroneous) assumption that moving is an unusual thing to do has led some scholars to assert that West Indians as a people are lacking in self-confidence, and, as one scholar has argued, "subservient to metropolitan norms."[5] Such claims are usually poorly substantiated; indeed that particular author then went to great lengths to demonstrate the resourcefulness and achievements of West Indian migrants abroad. This alone suggests that cultural subservience is little more than an artifact of the perspective that argues that migration, rather than staying put, is the unusual phenomenon. Discussions of social disorganization and anomie said to be consequent to migration must also, at least in part, be regarded as induced by the same blinders.

Anthropologists have for some time come to recognize the limitations of studying social life with the assumption that people live in discretely bounded social and cultural units. Yet these lessons seem not to have transferred to the study of migration, where the typical model suggests that as people move from one discrete social unit to another, they lose one culture and gradually acquire another. It is clear that Caribbean societies are as much African and Old World as they are Western and New World, that a pristine and autonomous West Indian culture can exist only in the analyst's mind. The migrant from the Caribbean is not acting out an aberration but is doing something for which his culture has prepared him, just as it has prepared him for making tools and raising children.

By putting aside some of these assumptions we can focus less on the migrant and more on the nation-state itself. Migration and the circulation of population, "speculating," and other such activities, suggest that people by their actions are implicitly questioning some of the notions of the bounded nation-state as it operates in the modern world. Scholars too must begin to examine critically these same notions and begin to question ideas about the indispensability of the nation-state and the regulations that go with it: the exclusivity and the inflated pride, the mirage of self-sufficiency, and the threat of interdependence. By putting less emphasis on the migrant and his maladjustment, and more on the recipient societies and the restrictiveness of their conceptual framework and institutional structures, we will at the very least recognize more openly our prejudices and the limitations of our analytic frameworks.

NOTES

1. Frank E. Manning, *Black Clubs in Bermuda: Ethnography of a Play World* (Ithaca: Cornell Univ. Press, 1973).

2. Lambros Comitas, "Occupational multiplicity in rural Jamaica," in Lambros Comitas and David Lowenthal, eds., *Work and Family Life: West Indian Perspectives* (New York: Anchor Books, 1973).

3. Interterritorial movement and trading is poorly documented and has received little scholarly attention. Some clues as to the importance of this traffic for the peoples of the region are provided by the Blue Books of British colonial administration and occasional newspaper reports, which bear witness in spite of themselves. See also Charles V. Carnegie, *Human Maneuver. Option-Building and Trade: An Essay on Caribbean Social Organization* (Ph.D. diss., Johns Hopkins Univ., 1981); Bonham C. Richardson, *Caribbean Migrants: Environment and Human Survival on St. Kitts and Nevis* (Knoxville: Univ. Tennessee Press, 1983).

4. These strictures apply less forcibly to more recent scholarship, which examines migration in relation to changes in the structure of the world economy. See, for example, Michael Piore, *Birds of Passage: Migrant Labor and Industrial Societies* (New York: Cambridge Univ. Press, 1979); Alejandro Portes and John Walton, *Labor, Class, and the International System* (New York: Academic Press, 1981). It should be noted, however, that even these recent contributions tend implicitly to regard migration as unusual; one gets the impression that, were it not for the invisible hand of international economic forces, people would stay home. This essay is intent on pointing out, however, that cultural ideas also help inform the actions of those moving about in the nascent world society.

5. See David Lowenthal, *West Indian Societies* (London: Oxford Univ. Press, 1972), for scholarship that examines migration in relation to changes in the structure of world society.

The Caribbean Exodus in a Global Context: Comparative Migration Experiences

Aaron Segal

The Caribbean has been more deeply and continuously affected by international migration than any other region of the world. Its experience since 1500 is extraordinary and has no parallel elsewhere. Ten characteristics serve to differentiate the Caribbean migration experience from that of other regions. The Caribbean is defined here as the archipelago stretching 2,500 miles from the Bahama Islands and Cuba in the north to Guyana, Suriname and French Guiana in northern South America, and also including Belize on the Caribbean coast of Central America. These 22 islands and four mainland political entities share geographic proximity and related cultural and historical experiences. Their total population is estimated at slightly over 30 million in 1984, or 0.006 percent of the world population.

DISTINGUISHING CHARACTERISTICS

1. The Caribbean has borne the deepest and most continuous impact from international migration of any region in the world. From 1500 to 1900 the Atlantic slave trade and the subsequent post-emancipation import of indentured laborers constituted the basic peopling of the Caribbean. Although extracontinental migration was an important factor in the peopling of North America, Brazil, Argentina, Australia, New Zealand and other societies, its extent and duration were more limited. Since 1950, 5-18 percent of the total population of nearly every Caribbean society has permanently emigrated.[1] Thus the Caribbean diaspora represents a higher proportion of the region's population than any other area of the world.

2. Caribbean net migration since 1959 constitutes approximately 29 percent of all voluntary international migration—legal and illegal. The United Nations Demographic Divsiion estimated in 1974 that there were nearly ten million persons from developing countries working in developed countries; about 20 percent came from the Caribbean.[2] Thus the absolute size and relative proportions of Caribbean emigration place it ahead of all other sending regions including North Africa, the Mediterranean, India, the Philippines and China.

3. The Caribbean is the only region to export people to three continents: North America, South America, and Western Europe. The major receiving countries worldwide for voluntary migration since 1950 have been Canada, the United States, Australia, New Zealand, the United Kingdom, France, West Germany, Switzerland, the Netherlands, Belgium, and in recent years Saudi Arabia, Kuwait, and the Persian Gulf States, and to a lesser extent Argentina, Brazil, and Venezuela. The Caribbean, through its political ties to metropolitan countries, has participated in all the major international migratory movements except those to the Arabian Peninsula, Australia, and New Zealand. No other exporting region has had this access.

4. More than any other region, the Caribbean consists of countries experiencing simultaneously emigration and immigration. The emergence of economic "growth poles" has for more than a century provoked intra-Caribbean migration in search of employment and cash incomes. Large differences in wages and opportunities for employment have combined with low-cost transportation to generate intra-Caribbean movements.[3] Thus Dominicans emigrate to the United States while Haitians enter the Dominican Republic; Trinidadians emigrate to Canada and the United States while Grenadians and other Windward Islanders emigrate to Trinidad; St. Lucians come to Barbados for agricultural work while Barbadians emigrate for factory and service jobs. Although this phenomenon is known elsewhere, more Caribbean countries are both senders and receivers of migrants than in any other area of the world.

5. The Caribbean exodus consists of a broader cross section of home societies than among other sending societies. While the Caribbean experiences an acute "brain drain" with the emigration of professionals and technicians, it also exports unskilled labor, legally and

illegally. Although the immigration policies of receiving societies tend to skew the demographic characteristics of those entering, Caribbean emigrants are less characterized by adult males aged 20–35 than most other sending societies. This is not to deny that Caribbean emigrants represent disproportionately the better educated, urban, younger elements of their societies. However, compared with Turkish emigrants to West Germany, South Koreans to Saudi Arabia, Algerians to France, or other major flows, the Caribbean shows a much more even age, sex, and skills distribution. Caribbean emigrants are also drawn from all ethnic and racial groups, including East Indians from Guyana, Trinidad, and Suriname.

6. The economic and demographic impact of emigration is deeper in the Caribbean than elsewhere. Although exact data are lacking, several smaller Caribbean islands such as St. Kitts and Saba have become remittance societies in which money sent from abroad is the largest single source of income.[4] It has been estimated that remittances sent by one Haitian employed abroad support four Haitians at home.[5] Although remittances are important in Mexico, Turkey, South Korea, and elsewhere, their impact on the larger society is limited, constituting an additional source of foreign exchange rather than the principal one.[6]

If small island societies can become economically and psychologically dependent on remittances, so too could Cuba during the brief period (1977–1979) when exiles could freely send funds and visit. Emigration generates enormous expectations among those who remain behind, whether for education, employment, consumption, or lifestyles. Most people in the Caribbean have direct information through friends and relatives about living conditions abroad, information reinforced by return visits, retirees, and other sources.[7] This is simply not the case in the Philippines, South Korea, Turkey, or other sending societies where only a relative handful of persons emigrate and where knowledge of their experiences is confined.

Emigration has deep demographic effects in the Caribbean, as it does elsewhere. Because it removes young men and women in their most fertile years it has both exported births and changed the age distribution pyramid. In most Caribbean societies it has contributed to lowering annual net rates of population increase by one percent a year.[8] In some societies, like Puerto Rico, its demographic impact has been even greater. Except for Haiti and a few of the smaller islands, most Caribbean societies have partly completed the demographic transition from high fertility and mortality to low fertility and mortality. Three decades of selective emigration played an important role in reducing home society fertility and also changing expectations about numbers of children desired, child bearing, child raising, age when having first child and other variables. Here again the fertility-reducing values and practices of the diaspora have been transmitted through changed expectations at home.[9]

7. The Caribbean experience differs from the rest of the world in the incidence of migrant recycling and the retention of diaspora/ homeland ties. While strict immigration laws have effectively cut off traffic of West Indians into Britain, other diaspora communities have taken advantage of inexpensive air fares to frequently recycle. Studies of the Dominican Republic suggest that entire families go back and forth to the United States, legally and illegally.[10] While there is a high incidence of recycling among Mexican migrants in the United States, these are mostly young adult males returning to their families and villages.[11] The Caribbean is unique in developing migrant recycling as a way of life; the tiny island of Saba, for example, has 5,000 residents in New York City constantly coming and going. Recycling has produced its own new cultural folk heroes; the Dominican and Puerto Rican major league baseball players who winter in the islands and summer in the United States, and the West Indian cricketeers whose professional careers are in England, are examples of this phenomenon.

8. The Caribbean exodus is also distinct because its migrants have been quick to seek integration abroad, while yet rejecting assimilation. Whether or not in England and North America there has emerged a racial or "pan-Caribbean" ethnic consciousness, the Caribbean diaspora has nevertheless insisted on full civic, political, and economic rights and opportunities.[12] At the same time it has resisted assimilation and sought to retain homeland ties and cultural identities. The best examples of ethnic retention come from the French and Dutch Antilleans and Puerto Ricans who immigrate as metropolitan citizens with the political possibility of relatively easy assimilation.

The European Community, Saudi Arabia, Kuwait, and other labor-importing states have created the legal status of "guestworker" and the attendant economic and cultural ghettoes.[13] In this case, neither integration nor assimilation are available as options. And although invariably hundreds of "temporary migrant workers" in these countries come to acquire a de facto semi-permanent status, this has not prevented governments such as Nigeria, Ghana, and others from carrying out massive deportations of foreign workers in slack economic times.

The Caribbean diaspora is not immune to these conditions, especially in intra-Caribbean moves. However in the case of Caribbean movements there have been attempts to reunify families and to establish viable diaspora communities rather than ghettoes of young men. Ethnic pride has been an important feature of these diaspora communities, even where it may be transcended by second generation moves to the suburbs and further steps toward assimilation.[14]

9. Another feature of the Caribbean exodus is that in most instances it has been encouraged and even promoted by home governments. Barbados has trained young people in exportable skills. Caribbean governments have negotiated migrant labor agreements with the United States and Canada. Even the Cuban government has during several periods encouraged emigration by opponents of its regime. Governments have considered emigration as a means of removing surplus population, reducing the costs of social services, earning foreign exchange, and exporting discontent. Some have been more eager to encourage emigration than others and several, such as Puerto Rico and Trinidad, have sought to lure back the highly-skilled. Yet just as underpopulation was considered to be the problem of Caribbean sugar economies for four centuries, overpopulation has become the contemporary problem. It is lack of influence with receiving countries that constrains Caribbean governments from pushing emigration harder, although there is a definite desire to export somehow the unskilled while keeping the skilled.

Around the world, governments as different as the People's Republic of China, Egypt, and the Philippines negotiate agreements to export temporary migrant labor.[15] Most of these agreements involve a substantial return to the sending government in the form of a share of wages. In the Caribbean only the Haitian government operates such an agreement with the Dominican Republic to cover export of migrant labor for sugar harvesting. Most Caribbean migrants leave with their government's blessings but without any formal binational or multilateral agreement. Unlike South Africa with its mining companies recruiting labor in neighboring countries, most Caribbean emigrants make personal decisions to take their chances elsewhere, rather than being formally recruited. Temporary migrant labor schemes scoop up a few thousand West Indian farm laborers every year for seasonal work in Canada and the United States but not much more.

10. The last and most important characteristic that differentiates Caribbean emigration is that it is largely voluntary. This has been the century of involuntary migration resulting from two World Wars and hundreds of other conflicts; many millions more flee war and oppression than flee seeking better jobs. The Vietnam War alone resulted in more involuntary migrants than the Caribbean could voluntarily send forth in three decades. Most people do not voluntarily leave their home country for another. It generally takes a war, prolonged violence, or other acts to drive them out. One need only consider the estimated current five million refugees in Africa strewn across the continent and compare this with the much smaller voluntary migratory flows across boundaries.[16]

The Caribbean is unique and extraordinarily fortunate in that almost all of its emigration has been voluntary, in response to perceived opportunities and frustrations rather than war or violence. The Haitian boat people have fled from desperate economic conditions and political tyranny but from neither war nor attack by the Haitian military. Cuban exiles were allowed to leave by the Cuban government after some selection. They too were not fleeing a civil war or other violence although they were compelled to leave their possessions behind. During the 1930s Cuba and the Dominican Republic received small numbers of European refugees. Post-1960 Cuban refugees did not face comparable hardships in getting out.

It is this individualistic, pacific quality that differentiates Caribbean emigration. A Puerto Rican buys a plane ticket to New York City. A Jamaican decides to visit his brother in Boston, obtains a ticket and a tourist visa, and may or may not go back. A Guadeloupean wins a scholarship to study in Bordeaux. Compare this with the Turkish emigrant who must show a guaranteed job and temporary work permit, who will be sent back if he loses his job, and who probably cannot bring his family. Most Caribbean illegal emigrants to North America enter legally and then illegally find work and jump their visas. They are freer in some respects than legal temporary migrant workers, whether in Saudi Arabia or Belgium.

THE PAST AND THE PRESENT

If these ten characteristics have served to differentiate Caribbean from world migration for more than 30 years, there is no guarantee that they will continue to prevail. Receiving governments are constantly tightening immigration laws and their enforcement. The costs and knowledge involved in emigrating put a premium on its being used by those with more education, income, and skills. Changes in laws can make recycling easier or harder, as in the example of double taxation. Should there be civil war, the appearance of Caribbean refugees on a large scale might become a reality. The past is not a sure guide to the future; it is, however, a sure guide to the present.

The Caribbean has been important as a receiving region for involuntary migration from 1600 through the end of the 19th century. Archaeological evidence suggests the existence of domestic settlements in the region as early as 2,500 B.C. Yet the precolonial period was also one of extensive inter-island migration as successive waves of peoples moved northward up the archipelago from the river-flooded plains of northern South America. The Europeans brought forced labor and a fatal genetic disease pool that by 1550 had produced one of the greatest epidemiological and demographic disasters in human history.[17] While scholars continue to debate the estimated size of the precolonial populations on the island of Hispaniola and elsewhere, their dying out was the precursor to the Atlantic slave trade.

The consequences of 350 years of involuntary slave migration—followed by 80 years of indentured labor from India, China, and Java, and small streams of voluntary migration from the Portuguese Madeira and Azores Islands, Lebanon, Syria, and Spain—are the culturally and ethnically plural Caribbean societies of the present. Throughout this period inadequate nutrition, harsh labor conditions, disease, and other factors kept fertility barely above and sometimes below replacement levels.[18] Unlike North America and Brazil, the Caribbean lacked successful indigenous slave-breeding plantations, and the slave trade compensated for low fertility and high mortality. This continued reliance on imported slaves, and after emancipation on indentured labor, made these migratory societies par excellence. Continued slave imports also destroyed the economic, social, and political basis of free, non-slave-owning whites. Throughout the 17th and 18th centuries, free or formerly-indentured whites emigrated from the Caribbean, mostly to North America, including such distinguished figures as Alexander Hamilton and James Audubon.

Freed slaves and indentured laborers who had worked out their contracts also opted for emigration as soon as it became available. Ex-slaves were recruited from the Leeward and Windward Islands during the 1840s to work on newly opened sugar estates in Guyana and Trinidad.[19] By the 1880s an estimated 25,000 West Indians were working on the ill-fated French effort to dig a Panama canal. By 1914, 35,000 or more West Indians and others had been employed in the American canal dig, many to remain in the Canal Zone or Panama, or to re-emigrate to the United States.[20] Emigration, primarily of adult males, had already become a way of life for Barbados and a number of the smaller islands by the late 19th century and was quickly extended to include Aruba and Curaçao in the early 20th century with the availability of work in the new petroleum industry. Several hundred thousand Haitians and Jamaicans were recuited for Cuban sugar estates during the 1910–1930 boom. Intra-Caribbean migration during the postemancipation period was based on the desire for cash beyond subsistence incomes, availability of inexpensive transport, information networks, and the adaptation of households to absent males. These long-standing customs based on intra-Caribbean migration served to facilitate the long-distance emigration that swelled after World War II.

Throughout most of its colonial history the Caribbean problem was seen as a shortage of voluntary labor, complicated by appalling health conditions and low fertility. Between 1820 and 1924 an estimated 50–55 million persons left Europe, 70 percent for the United States and the rest to Canada, Argentina, Brazil, South Africa, Australia, and New Zealand.[21] Only a few hundred thousand Europeans went to the Caribbean during this period, mostly Portuguese and Spaniards, and many of those returned or re-emigrated. The Cuban and Dominican governments offered a number of incentives to white European immigrants with limited results. The Caribbean had neither the employment opportunities, agricultural land, nor physical climate suitable for European colonization. The Afro-American plantation societies had become the captives of their own history.

Nor was indentured labor successful. Large numbers left. Those who remained forsook plantation wage labor whenever possible for urban employment or independent small-scale farming. The Chinese brought to Cuba as estate workers in the 1880s had become by the 1960s an entirely urban small-business community that emigrated en masse after the Cuban Revolution.[22] Similarly Syrian, Lebanese, Sephardic Jew, and Chinese workers in Jamaica, Guyana, and elsewhere who came as voluntary migrants succeeded as retail and wholesale traders or else often re-emigrated. Only the East Indians and Javanese in Guyana, Trinidad, and Suriname stayed on the land.

The perceived problem of Caribbean overpopulation has occasional pre-20th century references but is primarily the product of recent improvements in health, sanitation, and education. Population growth through natural increase rather than migration became prevalent only after World War I with the introduction of measures to control yellow fever, malaria, and other tropical diseases.[23] Natural increases in population in many Caribbean societies combined with the massive unemployment and underemployment of the 1930s to produce for the first time a widespread perception that the region was "overpopulated." Immigration had virtually ended by the 1930s and the Depression greatly reduced intra-Caribbean migration, but infant mortality was gradually declining and the stage was set for the postwar exodus. Its roots lay in the postemancipation emigration but its potential numbers stemmed from profound demographic changes.

While a hundred or more developing countries are supplying labor to the developed world, the Caribbean has been in the forefront of this movement since 1950. What is so striking about the Caribbean exodus is its persistent flow, both legal and illegal, since 1950; the total by 1980 was about four million. Moreover the Caribbean exodus has been characterized by a permanent net outflow, unlike the temporary migrant workers that prevail in the European Community and the Middle East. Because they are worried about the growing numbers of dependents of Arabic-speaking migrant workers who are arriving, Saudi Arabia, Kuwait and the United Arab Emirates are increasingly turning to contract workers from India, Pakistan, South Korea, the Philippines, and elsewhere who are more likely to return home.[24]

The unique ability to send emigrants to both North America and Western Europe is a function of the persistence of metropolitan politican ties in the Caribbean. In spite of extensive and rapid decolonization since 1960, three million Puerto Ricans and nearly 100,000 Virgin Islanders are U.S. citizens; 80,000 Antilleans are French nationals and 200,000 are Dutch citizens. The loss of emigration outlets to the United Kingdom in 1962 prompted a remarkable switch of direction by West Indians to Canada and the United States, taking advantage of changing immigration laws and procedures as well as family ties. Yet even Cuba and Haiti, which have no formal political associations that facilitate emigration, have been able to find outlets. The Haitian diaspora has gone to the United States, Canada, the Bahamas, French Guiana, France, Africa, Venezuela, and elsewhere.[25] Caribbean peoples have become singularly adept at identifying emigration opportunities and responding to shifting policies of receiving governments.

These adaptive strategies help to explain the flows of intra-Caribbean migration. Still primarily determined by the existence of job-generating economic growth poles, as in the U.S. Virgin Islands or the petroleum-refining island economies, there is more and more "replacement" migration. Emigration and expanded employment opportunities at home have resulted in shortages of seasonal agricultural labor, especially for sugar. Barbados, the Dominican Republic, Guadeloupe and Martinique are currently importing temporary agricultural labor. Similarly, in the Middle East, Jordan with one-third of its adult males working abroad has imported Egyptian agricultural labor.[26] Some Caribbean societies are increasingly becoming senders and receivers of migrants. This is a global phenomenon, partly reflected in the proportion of foreign-born persons in various countries as reported in recent census data. Barbados, Bahamas, Trinidad and Tobago, Aruba, Curaçao, the Dominican Republic, and the U.S. Virgin Islands all have significant proportions of foreign-born although the presence of illegals results in underestimates. Replacement migration, whether of a temporary or a permanent character, is on the increase.

Caribbean emigration constitutes more of a cross section of the sending societies than does emigration in any other part of the world. In this respect it resembles more closely the great 19th century European emigration than other late 20th century flows. Legal migrant workers in the European Community are mostly unskilled and preponderantly adult males, due to the restrictions on family reunification. The Arab receiving states are drawing unskilled, semi-skilled, and highly skilled manpower but almost no employed women, and they also discourage family reunification. On the other hand, immigration into the United States, Canada, Australia, and elsewhere has consisted of the highly skilled and their dependents, from India, the Philippines, Argentina, Egypt, and other developing countries. It is only where immigration into the United States is largely illegal, from Mexico and El Salvador, that it consists of primarily single, unskilled adult males.

The adroit use of immigration laws that favor family reunification and chain migration, as family members leave one by one and finance the others, has produced this representative exodus. A study of Haitians in New York City estimates that 70 percent are in low-income occupations but that there are also substantial numbers of professionals, small businessmen, and skilled workers.[27] All but the poorest of the poor, the rural landless, are represented among the emigrants. Other studies indicate a preponderance of better educated persons emigrating from the smaller islands.[28] During the deep economic recession and political turmoil of 1972–1980, Jamaica experienced a pronounced exodus of professionals and managers—a small-scale voluntary version of the Cuban outflow of 1959–1962.[29] Emigration certainly favors those who have money, contacts, and education, but the Caribbean evidence is conclusive that others also manage to leave.

This large-scale, cross-sectional emigration over three decades has resulted in a more profound impact than in other sending areas. A few Middle Eastern states such as Yemen and Jordan have known comparable emigrations since the 1973 increase in oil prices. However these are to neighboring Arabic-speaking countries with similar cultural values, and dependents are often left behind. In spite of the large absolute numbers involved, emigration is of no demographic significance to Egypt, India, Pakistan, Mexico, Turkey, or other sending countries with large populations and high birth rates, and remittances are minor factors in total foreign exchange earnings. The contrast with the Caribbean is pronounced. Caribbean countries currently have between 5 and 30 percent of their total populations living abroad, figures comparable with Yemen, Oman, and the Cape Verde Islands. Estimates of remittances are extremely difficult to calculate since they may be received in so many different forms, but several smaller Caribbean islands may be receiving 5–15 percent of their gross domestic product from abroad.

Demographically, emigration has contributed to reducing population growth rates and fertility in the Caribbean while reshaping age distribution. The emigration of a high proportion of the active labor force, both female and male, has left the home societies both older and younger. This trend has been accentuated by some return migration of older persons and by diaspora children born abroad being sent home to relatives for rearing. Probably there has also been a substantial loss of potential political and business leadership and educated human capital. The skewed age distribution raises dependency ratios and the economic burden of social services on those employed. Remittances may or may not be partly captured by the tax system to offset these costs. These effects have occurred in other sending societies but generally to a much lesser extent.

The scattered evidence suggests that the Caribbean diaspora maintains continuing and extensive contact with its home societies. Frequent inexpensive flights, often charters organized by social clubs, make home visits possible although risky for those who are illegal immigrants. There are considerable economic and other advantages for working emigrant parents to send their children home, although there are no data on the incidence of this phenomenon. There are fragmentary reports from Puerto Rico, the Dominican Republic, Jamaica, Trinidad, Barbados, and elsewhere of return migration, often of individuals who return to invest their savings in small businesses.[30] Growing numbers of retirees are returning to live on savings and their U.S. social security payments. Return migration, though, may be the tip of the iceberg, since many more persons recycle—working overseas, returning for a visit or a stay, returning abroad, and so on. Recycling may be especially widespread among Puerto Ricans, U.S. Virgin Islanders, and French Antilleans, who experience no legal difficulties in going back and forth and who may have employment or income contacts in two societies.

Living and working abroad and maintaining contact with one's homeland is easier for Caribbean migrants than for anyone else, except perhaps Mexicans in the United States. The legal migrant worker in the European Community risks losing his job and his work permit if he returns home for an unauthorized visit. Persistent unemployment since 1973 has caused governments to seek to reduce the numbers of legal guestworkers by limiting permits. Migrant workers from outside the European Community are discouraged from acquiring permanent residence. Although there are some bilingual schools for Turkish immigrant children in West Germany and elsewhere, the prevailing emphasis is on return migration rather than recycling. Arab receiving governments have also come to prefer one-shot recruited workers living in isolated enclaves without dependents and returning home on completion of their contracts. Some Jordanians, Palestinians, Egyptians, Sudanese, Yemenis, and other Arabs employed in neighboring states take advantage of geographical proximity and open borders to recycle frequently. However there are significant barriers to their reunifying their families and changing nationalities.

Essentially Caribbean emigration operates on a highly individualistic, voluntary basis that makes integration, if not assimilation, possible. There are some exceptions including Cuban emigration, which is based on government selection or at least approval, and West Indians in Britain who since 1962 are legally restricted to reuniting closest kin. No exact numbers are available but thousands of Caribbean emigrants are becoming eligible for and acquiring new nationalities: British, Canadian, U.S., French, Dutch. Children born abroad are automatically citizens of that country unless they choose a Caribbean nationality; those born abroad since World War II may number 1.5 million or more.

Migrants in the European Community and the Middle East are legally confined to the status of "guestworkers." National laws make naturalization extremely difficult, sometimes even when marriage to a national has taken place. Kuwait and the United Arab Emirates actually have more non-nationals than nationals in their work forces, and they strictly reserve citizenship rights including voting, senior government employment, and other benefits. For them neither assimilation nor integration in the sense of the officially sanctioned Turkish-German communities are legally or politically accepted. Migrants are to remain foreigners no matter the length or nature of their residence.[31] While the treatment is quite different the concept is similar to that of South Africa, which extensively recruits temporary male migrant labor for the mines and other economic sectors from Lesotho, Botswana, Mozambique, and other neighboring countries. Migrant workers in South Africa are racially segregated, required to return home at the end of a 12- or 18-month contract, and forbidden to bring their families.[32]

Ironically, Caribbean emigrants in the European Community are mostly able to escape the guestworker designation. Persons from the French overseas *départements* are French citizens and may migrate freely within the European Community. Their legal, economic, and social status is significantly better than the hundreds of thousands of legal and illegal African, Algerian, Moroccan, Tunisian, and other migrants in France. Immigrants from the Netherlands Antilles are Dutch citizens as are Surinamese who emigrated within five years after independence in 1976 (as nearly one third of the Surinamese population did). No matter how difficult it is to be a black or brown person in the Netherlands, it is better to be a Dutch citizen than a Moroccan or Turkish guestworker. Most West Indians entered Britain before 1962 and have acquired British nationality. They may experience racial discrimination and other problems, but they are "Black Britons" rather than immigrants.

Since Caribbean emigrants are living in a dozen or more societies it is hazardous to generalize about their experiences. There is a growing literature on these diaspora communities although there are as of yet few studies that compare, for example, Haitians in New York City with Haitians in Montreal, or Jamaicans in London with Jamaicans in New York City.[33] Tracing migrants from the same areas to different destinations presents important opportunities for cross-cultural and longitudinal analysis. Since emigrants come from similar but different societies and cultures there are also opportunities for examining family and other adaptive strategies.

The overall impression is that the diaspora communities are achieving considerable integration in their new societies while rejecting assimilation or seeing it denied. There certainly is much exposure to racial prejudice and some response through racial and/or ethnic pride. Retained and even heightened ethnicity is often functional in terms of access to jobs, social networks, recreational facilities, and housing. Employment appears to be the single most critical integrative device, followed by education. Cubans and West Indians in the United States have displayed marked upward economic mobility, partly based on education. On the other hand West Indians in Britain and Surinamese in Holland experience high unemployment (especially among youth), low-income jobs, and poor educational performance. Educated Haitians are remarkably upwardly mobile in several countries; uneducated Haitians rely on sheer hard work to compensate for low-paying jobs and lack of skills. Dominicans and Puerto Ricans as emigrants are now widely stratified socially, with a growing middle class minority and a low-income, poorly educated majority. French Antilleans in metropolitan France, a highly selective group, have done well in both education and employment.

Constant feedback from emigrants drives the exodus, which thus acquires a momentum of its own. Driven by remittances and family-shared funding of chain migrations, it is slowed but not arrested by periodic economic recessions and job layoffs abroad. The total annual number of Caribbean emigrants may exceed 300,000 but its multiple sources and destinations give it a partial safeguard against recessions. What has become operative are new concepts of space and distance. New York City now is viewed as "close" to Port-au-Prince. It is where friends and relatives live and the source of remittances. The second city in population numbers for nearly every Caribbean country is now an overseas community; for example, Miami for Cuba; New York City for Haiti, Jamaica, and Barbados; Toronto for Trinidad; and so on.

The Cuban government is the only one in the region that controls its exodus. Cuba follows the practice of Eastern Europe and the Soviet Union, where there is neither a recognized right to emigrate nor legal temporary migrant labor on a large scale.[34] The suppressed desire to emigrate was revealed in the 1979 incidents that led to the permitted exodus of 125,000 Cubans from the port of Mariel. There is no reliable estimate of the number of Cubans who wish to emigrate, but there are hundreds of thousands with family abroad. The Grenadian government of Maurice Bishop (1979–1983) encouraged emigrants sharing its radical political views to return, but made no effort to deter the thousands who left for Trinidad and elsewhere.

Other Caribbean governrnments continue either to discreetly promote emigration or to confine their reservations about its detrimental impact. Emigration has become a way of life for too many people: an expression of expectations and a search for opportunities not available at home. A few governments advertise abroad for highly-skilled nationals to return but there is no talk of discouraging people from leaving. After all, politicians and civil servants also have their families and friends abroad, visit to and fro, and may themselves want to reserve emigration as a future option. The doubts about the value of large-scale emigration that have been expressed in the Sudan, Tunisia, Egypt, and elsewhere are still latent in the Caribbean. Too many people hope to catch their plane.

Three decades of voluntary emigration has reinforced this individualistic lifestyle and option. The sole exception has been Cuba and the Haitian boat people. It is arguable that many of those who have fled Haiti in boats did not have the money and skills to acquire a passport, exit visa, and U.S. entry visa. As for the Cubans, they were the hostages of one government willing to let them leave and another willing to permit their entry. It is not certain that this coincidence will again occur, in which case the only Cuban emigrants will be defectors or escapees. Can the Cuban government afford the onus of large numbers of people publicly expressing their desire to leave? Can the U.S. government risk public hostility to massive admissions? Time will tell.

The Caribbean diaspora communities have acquired the resources and the acumen to reunite their families and to assist the entry of others, legally and illegally. Incomes and opportunities are so much greater abroad than anywhere in the Caribbean that the perceived gaps will continue to attract many. Even with the diminution of the population increase in the Caribbean there is still a large absolute number of young men and women who are potential emigrants. No Caribbean economy, including Cuba with its military and make-work, can even approach generating full employment at present wage levels. Thus there is good reason to believe that voluntary emigration will continue.

THE EFFECTS OF MIGRATION

This argument has rested on the assumption of commonalities within the diverse Caribbean exodus experiences, experiences that mirror the other diversities of one of the most heterogeneous areas of the world. These need to be reemphasized. Puerto Ricans, French Antilleans, and Dutch Antilleans go to and fro if they have the money or join the military as citizens of a non-Caribbean state. Cubans have their movements controlled. Haitians and Dominicans, Jamaicans, Barbadians, Trinidadians, and others take their chances on legal and illegal emigration. The structural factors plus first and second languages, education, culture, race, kinship, religion, and other variables all accentuate the diversity. The richness of the experience needs to be articulated in all its diversity: Sabeans in Brooklyn, Anguillans in New Jersey, Martinicans in Bordeaux, and so on.

Finally, this diverse experience of 30 years, four million emigrants, and 30 million persons left behind, needs to be assessed. This means looking at the emigrants, their home societies, and the receiver countries. The pros and cons of international migration have been examined in a highly charged and controversial literature.[35] Some but not all of what applies to Italian emigrants in Australia, Yemeni workers in Saudi Arabia, or Turks in Sweden makes sense in the Caribbean. Some of the assessment requires specific empirical data not always available. Ultimately the assessment is moral.

Caribbean emigrants have clearly benefited individually in terms of employment, incomes, living standards, education, and, not the least, opportunities for their children. Many have suffered cultural and emotional alienation, racial discrimination, mental and physical stress, and other problems. Some have become trapped in dead-end jobs and poverty cycles. The price of adjustment has been high for many. Yet private individual gains are substantially greater than losses. There is much nostalgia for home amidst recognition that life is better if harder in New York, Miami, Toronto, London, or Amsterdam.

Receiving societies are also net beneficiaries. Caribbean emigrants represent productive human capital contributing to economic growth, reducing inflation, paying taxes, and adding cultural diversity. They contribute not only skills and entrepreneurship but also cultural forms such as reggae, salsa, calypso, steel bands, and carnivals. There is friction over low-income entry jobs with other minorities and some job displacement but much more job creation from savings, investments, and productivity. West Indian emigrants have contributed in disproportion to their numbers to black American and Canadian political and cultural leadership, and other Caribbean emigrant communities are also generating talent. Everywhere the number of emigrants is absolutely and relatively small, so that they are no threat to established social structures. Instead, as 1–2 percent of larger societies in Canada, Britain, France, the United States, or Holland, they make significant economic contributions and add welcome and needed cultural diversity.

Assessment at the level of the sending societies is another matter. Emigrants provide remittances that may be spent on consumer goods, saved, invested, or taxed. The data from the Caribbean are inadequate but suggest that much is spent on imported consumer goods, thus adding to inflation and skewing values.[36] Much is also spent in Haiti and some of the smaller islands on basic necessities where other sources of income are few. Negatively, emigration costs societies potential leadership, scarce skills, educational expenses, and may demoralize those who stay behind. Emigration is a disincentive to small-scale agriculture with its low rate of return. It also lowers productivity, especially where the skilled leave as in Jamaica during the 1970s. Emigration results in the elderly and the young staying behind with high social costs and an inadequate productive base. It can also distort local labor markets, causing costs to rise and a need for replacement workers.

The detrimental effects of mass emigration can be partly offset by the local investment of remittances, return migration, especially of the skilled, recycling, and lower fertility. The Egyptian, Sudanese, and other governments have offered tax incentives to induce emigrants to invest in bonds, banks, savings schemes, and certain imports such as agricultural equipment, although with limited results. There have been similar experiments in the Dominican Republic but much more needs to be done to channel remittances into productive local investments. Return migration and recycling need further study in the Caribbean. After remittances, the most important advantage to date has been reduced fertility. It is sobering to consider how Caribbean societies would have developed without emigration and the consequent lower fertility over the last 30 years.

The most important negative effect is the malaise that overcomes any society when its most ambitious young people leave. It is the sense of powerlessness and hopelessness, of living from remittances and the chance to emigrate. When emigration becomes the only outlet, a society loses its rationale. A few small Caribbean islands have reached this situation and others are on the way. The contrast is illustrated by Barbados, which has experienced massive emigration for a century but where invested remittances, return migration, and lowered fertility have helped to transform the island and the economy. Caribbean emigration benefits the emigrants, benefits the receiving countries, and has mixed effects on the sending societies. And no doubt it will continue, firmly based as it is in cultural, demographic, economic, and political realities.

NOTES

1. Aaron Lee Segal, ed., *Population Policies in the Caribbean* (Lexington, MA: D.C. Heath, 1975), Chapter 1. Similar high incidences of emigration are found in other island societies such as the Cape Verde Islands, Mauritius and Reunion in the Indian Ocean, and Cyprus and Malta in the Mediterranean.

2. United Nations Department of Social and Economic Affairs, *Trends and Characteristics of International Migration Since 1950* (New York: Demographic Studies 64, 1979), p. 44.

3. Rosemary Brana-Shute, ed., *A Bibliography of Caribbean Migration* (Gainesville: Univ. Florida, 1983). This contains comprehensive citations on intra-Caribbean migration. Among the most useful surveys is Mary Kritz, *Migraciones Internacionales en las Américas* (Caracas: Centro de Estudios de Pastoral y Asistencia Migratoria, 1980).

4. Rosemary and Gary Brana-Shute, "The magnitude and impact of remittances in the Eastern Caribbean: A research note," in William Stinner and Klaus de Albuquerque, eds., *Return Migration to the Caribbean* (Washington: Smithsonian, 1982); Stuart B. Philpott, "Remittance obligations, social networks and choice among Montserratian migrants in Britain," *MAN* 3 (1968):465–476; Julia Crane, *Educated to Emigrate. The Social Organization of Saba* (Assen: van Gorcum, 1971); Bonham L. Richardson, *Caribbean Migrants, Environment and Human Survival on St. Kitts and Nevis* (Knoxville: Univ. Tennessee, 1983).

5. Brian Weinstein and Aaron Segal, *Haiti, Political Failures, Cultural Successes* (New York: Praeger, 1984), pp. 136–37. The authors estimate annual remittances in the 1980s from Haitian emigrants at $100 million.

6. Gurushri Swamy, *International Migrant Workers Remittances, Issues and Prospects* (Washington: World Bank Working Paper 481, 1981).

7. Vera Green, "Racial vs. ethnic factors in Afro-American and Afro-Caribbean migration," in Helen Safa and Brian Dutoit, eds., *Migration and Development* (The Hague: Mouton, 1979); Michel S. Laguerre, *American Odyssey, Haitians in New York City* (Ithaca: Cornell Univ. Press, 1964), pp. 34–38.

8. Malcolm Cross, *Urbanization and Growth in the Caribbean* (London: Cambridge, 1979), pp. 67–69.

9. Aaron Segal, *The Politics of Population in the Caribbean* (Río Piedras: Institute of Caribbean Studies, 1969); J. M. Stycos and K. Back, *The Control of Human Fertility in Jamaica* (Ithaca: Cornell Univ. Press, 1964); Brana-Shute, *A Bibliography of Caribbean Migration* (op. cit.).

10. Glen Hendricks, *The Dominican Diaspora* (New York: Teachers' College Press, 1974).

11. Wayne A. Cornelius, *Mexico and Caribbean Migration to the United States: The State of Current Knowledge and Priorities for Future Research* (La Jolla, CA: Program in United States/Mexican Studies, 1981).

12. Constance R. Sutton and Susan R. Makiesky, "Migration and West Indian racial and ethnic consciousness," in *Migration and Development* (Safa and Duloit, op. cit.), pp. 113–45).

13. Janet Abu-Lughod, "Recent migrations in the Arab world," in William McNeil and Ruth S. Adams, eds., *Human Migration* (Bloomington; Indiana Univ. Press, 1978), pp. 225–41; and in the same volume, Hans-Joacim Hoffman-Novotny, "European migration after World War II," pp. 85–106. J.S. Birks and L.A. Sinclair, *International Migration and Development in the Arab Region* (Geneva: International Labor Office, 1980). The only official temporary migrant worker program in the Caribbean is operated in the U.S. Virgin Islands to import labor from the British Virgins and the Leeward Islands. Its pros and cons are discussed in Franklin W. Knight, "Who needs a guest worker program?" *Caribbean Review*, 11 (Winter 1982), pp. 46–47, 64, and Mark J. Miller and William W. Boyer, "Foreign workers in the USVI," *Caribbean Review*, 11 (Winter 1982), pp. 48–51. On a micro scale the U.S. Virgin Islands have encountered problems similar to the European community—of guest workers who seek to stay and reunite their families.

14. Useful surveys of Caribbean diaspora communities in the United States are contained in Stephan Thernstrom, ed., *Harvard Encyclopedia of American Ethnic Groups* (Cambridge, MA: Harvard Univ. Press, 1980). It includes Lisandro Pérez, "Cubans," pp. 256–60; Glen Hendricks, "Dominicans," pp. 282–64; Michel S. Laguerre, "Haitians," pp. 446–49; Joseph P. Fitzpatrick, "Puerto Ricans," pp. 858–67; and Reed Ueda, "West Indians," pp. 1020–27. Materials on other Caribbean diaspora communities can be found in Brana-Shute, *A Bibilography of Caribbean Migration* (op. cit.).

15. New York *Times*, June 3, 1984, cites 380,000 Filipino guestworkers in foreign countries, increasing by more than 1,000 per month. The same edition claims an estimated 40,000 Chinese workers employed on overseas projects, mainly in the Middle East and Africa.

16. A survey of voluntary migrations and refugee situations in Africa is

provided by Philip D. Curtin, "Postwar migrations in Subsaharan Africa," in Adams and McNeil, *Human Migration* (op. cit.), pp. 188–99.

17. William H. McNeil, "Human migration: A historical overview," in Adams and McNeil, *Human Migration* (op. cit.), pp. 3–20.

18. The historical demography of the Caribbean is discussed in Philip D. Curtin, *The Atlantic Slave Trade: A Census* (Madison: Univ. Wisconsin Press, 1969).

19. Richardson, *Caribbean Migrants*, pp. 79–108.

20. Ibid., pp. 20–21.

21. Brinley Thomas, *International Migration and Economic Development* (Paris: UNESCO, 1961), pp. 9–15.

22. Denise Heily, *Idéologie et Ethnicité, Les Chinois Macao à Cuba* (Montreal: Presses de l'Université de Montreal, 1979).

23. Sergio Díaz-Briquets, *The Health Revolution in Cuba* (Austin: Univ. Texas Press, 1983) contains a discussion of the 20th century mortality decline in Cuba that is applicable with qualifications to other Caribbean societies.

24. J. S. Birks and C.A. Sinclair, *International Migration and Development in the Arab Region* (Geneva: International Labor Office, 1980). Table 14, pp. 138–39, breaks down migrants by countries of residence and origin in 1975, offering a truly cosmopolitan panorama.

25. Weinstein and Segal, *Haiti*, pp. 123–27.

26. Birks and Sinclair, *International Migration*, pp. 86–89.

27. Laguerre, *American Odyssey*, pp. 68–107.

28. Richardson, *Caribbean Migrants*, pp. 133–34, 173.

29. Ransford W. Palmer, *Problems of Development in Beautiful Countries: Perspectives on the Caribbean* (Lanham, MD: North-South, 1984), pp. 31–38.

30. Stinner and Albuquerque, *Return Migration* (op. cit.); José Hernández Alvarez, *Return Migration to Puerto Rico* (Berkeley, CA: Institute of International Studies, 1967), Barry B. Levine, *Benjy Lopez: A Picaresque Tale of Emigration and Return* (New York: Basic Books, 1980), Hendricks, *Dominican Diaspora* (op. cit.).

31. Hoffman-Novotny, "European migration."

32. Jill Nattrass, *The South African Economy: Its Growth and Change* (Cape Town: Oxford Univ. Press, 1981), p. 46.

33. Nancy Foner, "West Indians in New York City and London: A comparative analysis," *International Migration Review*, 13 (1979), pp. 284–97. This is one of the few comparative studies. There are individual studies of Haitians in New York City, Quebec, France, the Bahamas, and Miami, but no comparative analysis. Laguerre (*American Odyssey*) and Nancie Solien González ("Multiple migratory experiences of Dominican women," *Anthropological Quarterly*, 49 (1976), pp. 36–44) have examined Haitian and Dominican working women in New York City, including discussion of changing gender relationships.

34. There is limited legal temporary work migration from Poland to East Germany and occasionally elsewhere in Eastern Europe. Migration within the Soviet Union is discussed in Edward Allworth, ed., *Soviet Nationality Problems* (New York: Columbia Univ. Press, 1971).

35. See Thomas, *International Migration* (op. cit.); Birks and Sinclair, *International Migration and Development* (op. cit.); Michael J. Piore, *Migrant*

Labor and Industrial Societies (New York: Cambridge Univ. Press, 1979); and R.S. Bryce Laporte and D. Mortimer, eds., *Caribbean Migration to the United States* (Washington: Smithsonian, 1976). Radical literature frequently denounces the conditions that prompt people to emigrate and the exploitation they encounter. Rarely does it propose that emigration should be forcibly terminated.

36. Studies of Caribbean remittances include: Rosemary and Gary Brana-Shute, "The magnitude and impact of remittances in the Eastern Caribbean: A research note," in *Return Migration* (op. cit); Richard Frucht, "Emigration, remittances and social change: Aspects of the social field of Nevis, West Indies," *Anthropologica N.S.*, 10 (1968), pp. 193–208; and "Migration and the receipt of remittances," in *Resource Development in the Caribbean* (Montreal: McGill Univ. Center for Developing Area Studies, 1972), pp. 275–81; Howard Green, "Basin emigration and dollar flows," *Caribbean Basic Economic Survey*, 5 (April–May 1979), pp. 12–15; Philpott, *West Indian Migration: The Montserrat Case* (New York: Humanities, 1973); and Richardson, *Caribbean Migrants* (op. cit.), pp. 154–56. There are many other scattered references in the migration literature.

Exodus to
the United States

The Mexican Exodus: Setting the Patterns

Aaron Segal

The language used to discuss Mexican emigration is riddled with controversy. The Mexican media and Mexican academics generally refer to "undocumented workers," while in the United States the prevalent term is "illegal aliens." This chapter refers to legal and illegal Mexican immigrants—a status entirely defined by the government of the host country.

Much basic and essential information concerning illegal Mexican immigrants is lacking at a macro level. In spite of more than 20 books and over a hundred articles on the subject, huge information gaps remain, sometimes filled by guesses not subject to verification. We do not know the number of Mexicans illegally in the United States, where they are living, what jobs they are holding, what are their earnings, what proportion of their earnings are remitted to Mexico, how long these persons remain in the United States, or how frequently they return to Mexico. Although there is much more that we do not know, it is lack of reliable information about these basics that has contributed to the distortion of the policy debate in Mexico and the U.S. The frequent substitution of guesses for factual information has permitted observers to support their prejudices with unsubstantiated estimates.

Five principal methods have been used to study Mexican emigration. Several studies have relied on data from Mexicans apprehended by the U.S. Immigration and Naturalization Services (INS).[1] Several Mexican studies have relied on data from Mexicans deported by the INS and interviewed on reentry into Mexico.[2] A few have interviewed small samples of Mexicans living illegally in the United States.[3] More frequent are studies that survey Mexican villages and towns in which there is a high incidence of persons who have at one time illegally emigrated to the United States.[4] And there have been macro demographic studies that used U.S. and/or Mexican population census data to estimate numbers of illegal immigrants.[5]

Each of these methodologies has serious problems. The micro studies of Mexican villages and deportees do not permit valid generalization or extrapolation, especially since they are usually conducted at a particular point in time and the migration process is subject to considerable change. The micro studies have not been replicated; the total universe is unknown (whether of sending villages in Mexico or receiving communities in the United States); and the handful of available studies is scattered in time and space. As interesting as it is to study a village in the Mexican state of Michoacan that has been continuously sending emigrants to the United States since 1911, it does not help us to know currently whether there are 1, 2, 3, 4, 5, 6 or even 12 million Mexicans in the United States, numbers that have been alleged by different parties to the debate.[6]

The data from persons apprehended and deported tell us little about those not apprehended. Since 90 percent of INS apprehensions are of emigrants who have been in the United States 72 hours or less, and are picked up near the border, the data set has an obvious distortion. Mexican studies of returned deportees are, by their own admission, subject to their fears of the Mexican authorities as manifested in attempts by those interviewed to bribe the interviewers.[7] How reliable are data obtained by government-sponsored interviewers from persons who are frequently shaken down by Mexican Customs and Immigrations personnel to whom the interviewers are reporting?

The macro studies based on census and related data acknowledge the problem of undercounting of illegals and seek to compensate in various ways. Although this is probably the most satisfactory data available it does not discuss earnings, jobs, remittances, return migration to Mexico, and other important matters. It simply provides a "guesstimate" at a given point in time of the total number of Mexicans then in the United States, relying on those who responded to the 1980 U.S. Census short form or other data.

The gap between the micro studies, with their rich detail about emigrants from a particular village or in a particular neighborhood in the United States, and a full-scale profile of Mexican emigrants persists. Most Mexican emigrants enter the United States illegally, unlike emigrants from the Caribbean and elsewhere who enter on tourist, student, or other legal visas and then "overstay." The prerequisites for obtaining a legal visa, even for a temporary visit, are beyond the reach of most illegal Mexican emigrants. Since their only access route is illegal their desire for confidentiality is strong, even with well-intentioned academic researchers.

Intense partisanship concerning the issues presents additional problems. Mexican government-funded studies generally conclude that the absolute number of Mexicans illegally in the United States is substantially below all U.S. estimates, that these emigrants are not taking jobs from Americans, that they mostly return to Mexico, and that they are often poorly paid and badly treated.[8] Some American researchers, often funded by U.S. government agencies, have concluded that the absolute number of illegal Mexican immigrants is several times greater than Mexican estimates, that a significant portion of these immigrants have become permanent U.S. residents, and that they are competing for jobs with low-income Americans in skilled and semiskilled positions. While not all studies or researchers are partisan, the extensive limitations on the studies themselves make it possible to line up data and studies to support opposing views.

Numerous efforts have been made to classify Mexican emigration to the United States (Mexican emigration to all other countries including students in France and Spain, and legal temporary migrant workers in Canada, is minuscule).[9] This chapter divides emigrants into those who have legally acquired the status of permanent resident aliens in the United States; those who live on the Mexican side of the border while legally or illegally being primarily employed in the United States (border crossers); and those who illegally enter the United States. Clearly there are crossovers among these categories, as there are Mexicans who enter legally on tourist, student, or other visas and then remain illegally. Similarly there is a distinction between those who enter illegally and return to Mexico after a limited period, the "sojourners," and those who enter and settle, sometimes bringing other family members.

The admittedly partial evidence suggests though that these three categories do represent important distinctions between types of emigrants. Legal immigrants have immediate kin legally resident in the United States willing to sponsor them. Compared with the other categories they are more likely to be urban, have some secondary education, are older, skilled or semiskilled, or else have an elderly or youthful dependent. Border crossers are generally resident in the 17 Mexican cities and towns along the U.S. border, young, single or leaving family behind, either sex, and connected to employers, friends, or relatives on the U.S. side of the border. Border crossers generally seek and find work on the U.S. side, returning daily or less often to Mexico, rather than venturing farther into the United States. Illegal immigrants are a much more diverse and heterogeneous group, but they are primarily rural, from the six states of the semi-arid central highlands of Mexico, have only a primary education, are predominantly single males, and are almost exclusively unskilled or semiskilled. Few are residents of the Mexican border cities; most need the paid help of a smuggler, known as a "coyote," to get across the border; and most are headed away from the border where wages are higher and job prospects better.

Estimating the number of persons involved in each category is an imprecise exercise. INS figures on apprehensions do not indicate how many times the same person has been deported, although multiple deportations, even on the same day, are common. There is no way of knowing how many persons escape apprehension nor how many fraudulent documents (a booming business on the Mexican side of the border) are available. The late 1982 devaluation of the Mexican peso brought severe cuts in the standard of living of millions of Mexicans, especially those who no longer had access to U.S. dollars. INS apprehensions reached record numbers, especially as the U.S. economy climbed out of the 1981/82 recession while Mexico's did not. There are problems, then, in citing data from any one particular year or in looking for "trends" in the face of a sharp break in the economic fortunes of either country.

Another approach is to estimate the actual and potential numbers of persons in each category. This provides both a sense of current and projected Mexican demand to emigrate and a breakdown by categories. Legal immigration into the United States has been subject, since 1976, to a 20,000 person-per-year nonrefugee quota and preference system, for all countries. One result of this quota is a backlog of approximately 380,000 Mexicans who have applied legally to emigrate to the United States yet face a wait of over 6 years to have their applications processed—the largest waiting list and longest wait of any country in the world. Most of these applicants seek to enter under the strict family reunification criteria, which require a parent, brother, or sister, spouse, or child over the age of 21 who is legally resident in the U.S. to act as sponsor. (Close relatives of U.S. citizens may enter outside the quota.)

Most U.S. immigration reform legislation since 1977 has included a proviso to give Mexico a temporary or permanent exception from the 20,000 annual quota. The bill introduced by Senator Alan Simpson (Rep./Wyoming) and Congressman Romano Mazzoli (Dem./Kentucky), which was narrowly defeated in 1984, would have given Canada and Mexico annual quotas of 40,000 nonrefugee immigrants a year and allowed unused portions of one country's quota to be shifted to the other. Less clear under this proposal was whether Mexican illegal migrants who obtained amnesty would be able to use this clause to reunite eventually their families. Probably a legal immigration quota of at least 50,000 persons a year for Mexico would be needed to reduce the backlog and stabilize the demand for qualified legal entry. As long as strict family reunification rules prevail, the demand for legal entry will continue to exceed the available quotas.

Economic conditions along the 2,000 mile U.S./Mexican border, with its 17 twin cities and towns, provide the major constraints on actual and potential border crossers.[10] The two million Americans living on the border in 1985 had the lowest per capita incomes and the highest rates of unemployment in the entire nation. The four million border Mexicans, whose numbers are growing at 5–6 percent a year compared with 1–2 percent on the U.S. side, have the highest per capita incomes in all of Mexico outside Mexico City. Low wages and lack of jobs limit the legal and illegal border crossers, although post-1982 Mexican devaluation and inflation has widened appreciably the wage differentials. The U.S. Border Patrol, whose force of nearly 1,000 in 1984 was less than that of the Philadelphia police department, is another constraint to border crossers. Most crossers are in Tijuana and Juarez with access to the labor markets of San Diego and El Paso, as well as the assistance of networks of friends, relatives, and employers on the U.S. side of the border.[11]

Approximately 50,000 Mexican border residents have legal "green cards" that permit them to seek work in the United States. Since the mid 1970s few new green cards have been issued. Another 100,000 or more border Mexicans have valid temporary visas that permit them to enter the United States for 72 hours and within 25 miles of the border (so-called shoppers' cards). There is a lively business in counterfeiting these and other documents.[12] A plausible estimate for the mid 1980s would be 100,000 regular border crossers, half of whom are illegal; 80 percent or more are employed in San Diego and El Paso.

The creation since 1970 of 150,000 factory-related jobs in assembly plants on the Mexican side of the border has probably reduced some of the pull of the United States.[13] However after the 1982 devaluation and inflation reduced effective earnings in the assembly plants, it again became attractive to seek unskilled work across the border. The INS rate of apprehensions rose dramatically and included, for the first time, substantial numbers of persons resident in the border. The precipitous drop in the value of the peso cut drastically the numbers of border Mexicans able to shop in the United States, at the same time increasing the demand to earn dollars.

The potential number of border crossers is basically a function of the nature and level of economic growth on the U.S. side of the border. San Diego is the only border city with a healthy, diversified economy, but its demands are increasingly for skilled labor. Elsewhere unemployment rates in excess of 10 percent, low wages, lack of new construction and investment, and the presence of the Border Patrol limit opportunities on the U.S. side of the border. Although demographic projections indicate that by the mid 1990s there will be four border Mexicans for every border American, a major increase in the number of border crossers is unlikely. The pull factors are too weak, while the Mexican border economies continue to generate jobs and investments.

Estimating actual and potential illegal migrants is a hazardous enterprise. The adjusted 1980 U.S. Census recorded 900,000 Mexicans illegally in the United States, an estimated 46 percent of all illegal migrants enumerated. These figures are subject to adjustment, undercounting and other challenges.[14] They are considerably higher than the estimates derived from Mexican surveys of INS deportees and considerably lower than estimates by proponents of immigration reform. The census data do not indicate length of residence or intention to return to Mexico.

A working estimate for the mid 1980s would be 1-1.5 million Mexicans illegally in the United States, concentrated in California and Texas, but also living in a dozen other states, with increasing numbers moving from unskilled agricultural labor to urban construction and service jobs. Economist Clark Reynolds, projecting American labor force needs, declining birth rates, and other factors, foresees a demand for several million Mexican workers by the mid 1990s. Several Mexican studies also project that U.S. demand for Mexican labor will grow rapidly although this view is controverted by other American studies.[15]

The push and pull factors that help to explain illegal Mexican migration are multiple and complex. Nor are the interrelationships well understood. The pull includes the availability of jobs in the United States, wage differentials on the order of 6–15 to 1, kinship networks that facilitate job hunting, transport and savings, and reduce risks, unemployment and underemployment in Mexico, landlessness and lack of arable land, traditions of emigration, growing economic interdependence, and other factors. Research suggests that Mexican emigration has been concentrated from six Central Highland states where agricultural development has lagged, and within certain villages in those states. An unknown but allegedly high number of migrants are soujourners who return to Mexico, and may or may not recycle to the United States.[16]

Also relevant is the fact that 45 percent of the Mexican population is under 15 years of age, creating a labor force that is growing by an estimated 900,000 new jobseekers every year, and the structural problem of the capital-intensive industrial sector in generating new jobs.[17] The growing gap between mechanized, irrigated, cash-crop agriculture and the low-productivity semisubsistence sector is another push factor. Just as millions of rural Mexicans have migrated to Mexico City and its environs over the last 40 years, it is probable that millions more will continue to migrate somewhere for at least another two decades. The reduction in fertility beginning in the mid 1970s is lowering birth rates, but the absolute numbers of young people, newlyweds and newborn continue to increase. Thus the number of Mexicans who constitute potential illegal migrants to the United States under various circumstances will continue to grow. There is little prospect of controlling or reducing the push factors, which are deeply embedded in the Mexican economy and society.[18] Approximately 5 percent of the total Mexican labor force is currently employed in the United States and it is reasonable to expect this figure to continue or increase unless drastic changes occur in both countries.

HISTORICAL CONTEXT

Mexican emigration was not subject to any legal restrictions until 1929. The 1850 U.S. Census recorded 13,000 Mexican nationals. Treaty settlements and land transfers ending the Mexican-American War in 1854 added another 80,000, mostly in New Mexico. Until the outbreak of the Mexican revolution in 1910, a steady stream of Mexican migrants continued, responding to employment opportunities in the ranges and mines of the American Southwest and on the new railroads. Migration routes closely followed railroad lines after 1880, when the first U.S.-Mexico connections were completed.[19]

The Mexican revolution (1910–1917) wreaked economic devastation on much of northern Mexico and prompted a flood of refugees to El Paso and other border towns. Most were farmers, mineworkers, shopkeepers and other ordinary people driven out of their homes by marauding armies and economic hardships. Refugee camps and emergency health facilities were provided as the 1920 U.S. Census reported 478,000 Mexicans, up from 220,000 in 1910. Most stayed, and many moved away from the border area in response to the improved U.S. economic conditions of the 1920s. Mexican muscle was instrumental in the construction, railroad, mining, agriculture, and livestock industries in the Southwest, and colonies of Mexican workers found employment in Chicago, Detroit, and other Midwestern industrial centers.

The Depression was a traumatic experience for Mexicans in the United States. Utilizing the 1929 immigration legislation, which was the first to put limits on Mexican immigration, and the U.S. Border Patrol, which had been established in 1924, the United States summarily deported an estimated 400,000 Mexicans, including some who had become U.S. citizens.[20] Competition for too few jobs fed anti-Mexican feelings, and the total number of Mexican-born persons in the United States had dropped to 377,000 by the 1940 census. Ironically, that massive repatriation of Mexicans meant that for the first time in 1940, persons born in the United States of Mexican origin outnumberd those here who were born in Mexico.

Mexican emigration to the United States historically has been extremely quick to respond to economic opportunities and wage differentials. World War II created a severe U.S. labor shortage in an overheated economy where food production was vital for domestic and global needs. Thousands of Mexican workers, often recruited by Southwestern farmers, had already found work prior to the establishment in 1942 of the U.S.-Mexican government *bracero* temporary agricultural labor program (which lasted until 1964). Some of these migrants were able to utilize village and kinship networks that went back to the 1920s or earlier. Since U.S. agricultural work was often seasonal, migrants were able to retain families and plots at home and travel back and forth. The scantily populated border and the undermanned Border Patrol represented minor obstacles in the face of the urgent U.S. wartime need for workers.

During the 22 years of the legal bracero program, the number of illegal migrants almost certainly exceeded the 650,000 braceros.[21] Networks and patterns of migration, which became firmly established, have persisted as jobs moved from seasonal agriculture to the cities. The braceros were recruited in Mexico, principally from the Central Highlands, and then assigned to a U.S. farm or ranch. Their working and living conditions were supposed to meet minimum standards agreed upon by both governments. They were in fact indentured laborers although a few were able to change employers or obtain permanent residence status and labor mobility. While there were many abuses by American employers and Mexican government recruiters, the braceros earned far more than they could in Mexico, remitted savings, and acquired some experience with mechanized agriculture that was applicable to Mexico. The bracero agreement was not renewed in 1964 due to extensive lobbying pressure from American trade unions and a diverse coalition of business interests.

The bracero program served to reinforce Mexican desire to seek work in the United States. Volunteers regularly exceeded numbers recruited, and it is alleged that kickbacks to recruiters were widespread. Nonbracero migrants relied on border smugglers, bracero friends and kin, and other contacts to cross the Rio Grande and find work. INS apprehensions grew steadily throughout the bracero program and reached one million in 1954, after a major crackdown at the border; this total was not reached again until the 1982 Mexican peso devaluation brought a flood of jobseekers. The legal bracero program, in effect, complemented illegal migration rather than providing an alternative.

The formal ending of the bracero program in 1964 prompted another increase in the number of apprehensions. Illegal migration has become increasingly responsive to both U.S. and Mexican business cycles, and to the existence of unskilled and semiskilled urban construction, service, and manufacturing work. Illegal immigrants continue to find work in seasonal harvests in the Southwest, but most observers agree that over the last two decades there has been a major shift toward urban work. Previous networks have been extended from farms to towns, and accommodation is often found at the low-income end of large urban Mexican-American neighborhoods.[22]

What is often overlooked is the striking increase in legal Mexican emigration since 1950. This has occurred in spite of the 1965 immigration law, which imposed a Western Hemisphere annual quota of 120,000 immigrants and the 1976 law, which reduced the Mexican quota to 20,000. Legal immigrants not subject to the quota include spouses, children, and parents of U.S. citizens; combined with those entering under the quota, they keep legal Mexican immigration at a level of about 60,000 a year. Since 1970 Mexico has accounted for 15 percent of total U.S. legal immigration with over 700,000 Mexicans acquiring legal residence in the United States; the rate of return to Mexico is unknown.

The demographic implications of these trends are worth noting. The 1980 U.S. Census recorded 2.2 million persons born in Mexico, and a follow-up study estimated that 900,000 were illegal. Mexicans constituted 16 percent of the total of 14 million foreign-born Americans, more than twice the number from any other country. Persons born in Mexico comprised 22 percent of all Mexican-Americans and 15 percent of all Hispanics in the United States in 1980. Even allowing for undercounting, the census data indicate that Mexicans who are legally in the United States outnumber the illegal ones. Mexican emigrants represented about 2 percent of the total population of Mexico in 1980, and 4–5 percent of the Mexican labor force, due to the high concentration of employed males. Emigration is having a minimal effect on Mexico's rate of unemployment. The striking increase in legal migrants may also repesent a small-scale brain-drain, although the criterion for departure is family reunification rather than skill level. Finally, the continued high fertility of the Mexican-American population means that generations born in the United States will substantially outnumber newcomers.[23]

CHARACTERISTICS OF IMMIGRANTS

A comparison of Mexican legal and illegal immigrants with those of other nationalities demonstrates that Mexicans comprise

16 percent of all foreign-born in the United States, and 45 percent of estimated illegal migrants. One third of Mexican census respondents had arrived in the United States between 1975 and 1980, a higher proportion than migrants from all European and most Latin American and Caribbean countries. The figure indicates though that a significant proportion, perhaps 10–15 percent, of illegal migrants had arrived prior to 1975. Mexicans, with 21.3 percent graduating from high school and 3 percent completing college, lag behind most other foreign-born nationalities, reflecting in part the low level of educational attainment of the illegal migrants. However, even assuming that all the high school and college graduates are legal migrants and that many of this group are elderly or young dependents, Mexicans in the United States lag educationally well behind other foreign-born, Mexican-Americans, and the U.S. population. The census figure of only 2.5 percent of those employed in professional specialty occupations is another indicator of educational lag and the absence of a significant brain-drain from Mexico.

The 1980 census reported the median household income of Mexican-born persons as $12,747 (1979 dollars) compared with a total foreign-born median of $14,588 and a U.S. median of $16,841. Earnings of those born in Mexico are near the bottom for all nationalities, pulled down by the low incomes of the illegal migrants and by the high dependency ratios of legal households. The 23.6 percent who have become naturalized U.S. citizens is slightly fewer than for other Caribbean and Latin American nationalities and is a reflection both of the continued ties to Mexico and the high number here illegally. The predominance of illegal males raises the overall Mexican-born sex ratio to 111.4 males per 100 females, the highest ratio for any group of immigrants born in the Western Hemisphere.[24] The census recorded 14.7 percent of those Mexican-born as under 15 years of age, 7.6 percent age 65 and over, with 82.7 percent of males and 43 percent of females in the civilian labor force. The dependency ratio (22.3 percent) is slightly higher than for other Latin American and Caribbean immigrants, and the rate of female participation in the labor force significantly lower.

This broad picture of Mexican migrants is somewhat altered by focusing on those who are permanent resident aliens or naturalized U.S. citizens, perhaps 50–55 percent of the total. Like all Mexicans in the United States, the legal migrants are concentrated in California (60 percent), Texas (23 percent), and Illinois (8 percent).[25] However they are more urban, better educated, and more likely to come from the cities and towns of northern Mexico. Almost all continue to speak Spanish at home, and only one fourth have become U.S. citizens, a factor which weakens Mexican-American participation in U.S. politics. Recent voter registration drives for Southwestern Hispanics have emphasized the need for citizenship first.

Mexican legal migrants enter at the low end of the Mexican-American socioeconomic scale, but often demonstrate strong achievement orientations for themselves and their children. Their continued entry strengthens the Mexican cultural presence in the United States and the demand for Mexican-oriented radio, television, films, and publications. The waiting list in Mexico in 1981 included 69,000 spouses and unmarried children of permanent resident aliens, 21,000 married children of U.S. citizens, and 44,000 siblings of adult U.S. citizens and their spouses or children.[26] Family reunification and chain or step migration are driving Mexican legal migration, and will continue to produce a steady stream of migrants.

Border crossers or commuters are a geographically and socially diverse group distributed over 17 cities and a few small towns along the border. Their characteristics have been the subject of only a few, now somewhat dated studies.[27] Many are permanent resident aliens who prefer to live in Mexico, and some are U.S. citizens. The overwhelming majority are born or resident on the border, where educational standards and income are higher than in rural Mexico. Most are unskilled, but some have construction or other skills. The motivation to cross the border is primarily the wage differential and to earn dollars: the post-1982 peso devaluation makes a day's work at minimum wage in San Diego or El Paso in the U.S. the equivalent of a week's work at minimum wage in Juarez or El Paso in Mexico. Border crossers rely on Mexican and American friends and relatives to evade the Border Patrol, find employment, and to cross and recross the border. Some become legal resident aliens through marriage to a U.S. citizen or sponsorship by an employer, but most remain commuters. A few border Americans also commute to work or school in Mexico, particularly those studying in medical schools on the Mexican side of the border. The Mexican government operates a strictly regulated system of work permits for foreigners that discourages legal work commuting from the United States.

Any composite profile of illegal immigrants must be subject to qualifications and reservations, given the many unknowns. Moreover this group is geographically diverse and in a constant state of flux and change.[28] The illegal migrants are preponderantly young males (ages 18–35) from small towns and villages in the semi-arid rural areas of Central Mexico. Many own or have access to small plots of land but have experienced seasonal employment, underemployment, and limited opportunities for agricultural wage labor or cash cropping. Most are unskilled but have 4–5 years of formal education, high for rural Mexicans of their age group. Many have parents or relatives who have worked in the United States, often in the bracero program. Certain communities have been sending emigrants to the United States for several generations and have legal and illegal colonies and kinship networks to assist migrants with the several hundred dollars needed to cover the costs of transportation to the border and the U.S. interior, hiring a border smuggler, false documents, or other needs. No doubt for each of these organized and relatively informed migrants there are others who risk apprehension with much less assistance. Spouse and children are usually left behind, and some studies indicate that one third to one half of the migrants are single males.

Although seasonal and some full-time agricultural labor is available in the Southwest, increasingly illegal immigrants seek better-paying work in the cities of Los Angeles, San Diego, San Francisco, Houston, Dallas, Chicago, Denver, and elsewhere. Kinship and village networks facilitate job-hunting in service, construction, unskilled manufacturing, and other occupations. Illegal immigrants share accommodations in low-income neighborhoods to reduce costs and the risk of being caught. Studies suggest that most illegal migrants are paid somewhat below or at the U.S. minimum wage which, in 1985, was four to ten times higher than the geographically varying minimum wages set in Mexico. Some illegal migrants manage to obtain better-paying semiskilled work, especially in construction, but this seems to be the exception. Female migrants are usually employed as domestics, in seasonal agriculture, or unskilled manufacturing. Their wages are lower than those of the men but still well above what is available to them in Mexico.[29]

The limited evidence indicates that illegal migrants, even with all their costs, are earning several times more than they could in Mexico and remitting to their families one third or more of their earnings.[30] It has been estimated that their total remittances are one billion dollars a year or more, although this figure is subject to many qualifications.

The illegal migrants are subject to INS arrest and deportation and to various forms of exploitation by employers. Attempts to organize them into unions in the garment industry and among farmworkers in California have had limited response. Their living and working conditions are often substandard, but their principal objective of earning and saving is realizable.

Much controversy has been generated over whether Mexican illegal immigrants are "settling" in the United States, or are going back and forth.[31] We do not know the numbers of those who come and go. However the 1980 census data and other studies suggest that some portion of the illegals have acquired permanent or semipermanent residence. This issue is also at the crux of the debate over whether or not amnesty should be offered to illegal immigrants and on what terms. We do not know how many Mexicans illegally in the United States would be interested in amnesty if it were available or on what terms.

We do know that many illegal immigrants return to their homes in Mexico, often bringing U.S.-made consumer goods and investing their savings in residential construction, land, livestock, or small businesses. For some Mexico has become a place of vacation or retirement and the United States the land of work.[32] As in many other emigration-oriented societies, work abroad is accepted as the responsibility of adult males until they reach a certain age and status.

Although illegal migrants are far from being the poorest people in Mexico, they are certainly driven by poverty and lack of opportunity at home. Many from the Central Highlands see the options as migration for work to Mexico City or to the United States and some have tried both and found higher wages in the United States. They are mainly from rural areas where commercial agriculture has failed, with or without land reform, and where available work is low paid and often seasonal. Yet the economic crisis of 1982 brought many new migrants and would-be migrants, some from the burgeoning border cities of Northern Mexico hit by large-scale unemployment. While there is little middle class illegal migration and few migrants come from Mexico City, poverty-stricken Southern Mexico, Guadalajara, or Monterrey, it is premature to assume that illegal migration has a stable, cyclical character, origin, or destination.

CONSEQUENCES OF EMIGRATION

What are the consequences of Mexican emigration for the individuals and families involved and their communities, for the United States, Mexico, Mexican-Americans, and for U.S.-Mexican relations? An examination of the consequences is a prelude to a discussion of policy options.

The perceived benefits to hundreds of thousands of migrants outweigh the risks of their being caught and deported, being abused by employers, smugglers or Mexican officials, or waiting years to enter legally. These benefits are primarily material but they also include social mobility, informal on-the-job learning experiences, and exposure to other societies. While some anthropologists lament the loss of leadership, high dependency ratios, and new forms of social stratification based on remittances in Mexican towns where emigration has become a way of life, the risks incurred by these same people through migration to Mexico City are, if anything, greater.

What are the consequences for those who reach the United States and become socially isolated, or for those who are deported and lose their savings to the smugglers and corrupt officials? The emotional and physical risks involved in illegal migration are real but apparently buffered by its being so widespread, with multiple opportunities to cross and find work. Being deported from the United States for illegal entry bears scant onus in Mexico.

The consequences for Mexico are also largely beneficial, although there is much official rhetoric about the abuses to which Mexican migrants are subject in the United States. Legal and illegal migration is an important source of foreign exchange, the largest net dollar earner after petroleum, manufacturing exports, and tourism. The Mexican fiscal system has only limited access to these transfers but remittances generate purchases of imported and domestic consumer goods, and at least some small-scale investments. Remittances from legal and illegal migrants account for perhaps 5 percent of Mexico's total foreign exchange earnings. More importantly they provide the principal monetary income in a number of rural communities that otherwise would be totally dependent on government services.

Migrants who return to work in Mexico also often bring useful job skills. Bracero workers helped to introduce agricultural mechanization in parts of northern Mexico, and current migrants have had some impact on rural small-scale industry in a few places.[33] Returning migrants are also important sources of new attitudes toward education and other values. Legal migrants who do not return may represent a loss of potential entrepreneurs, especially for self-employed small businesses. The net effect of emigration is to enhance Mexico's human resources even if migrant savings go primarily for consumption rather than investment.

Emigration is also a significant safety value for Mexico's structural problems of unemployment and underemployment. Former president José López Portillo (1976–1982) admitted in 1977 that Mexico could not provide jobs for all those seeking work.[34] Nor can it generate full-time work for the many employed part-time or in the informal sector. Legal and illegal migration probably represents no more than 5 percent of the Mexican labor force, but this is not an insignificant figure. The migrants are often found in the politically sensitive areas of central and northern Mexico. Their U.S. earnings and remittances support millions of people in Mexico, and their ability to find work serves to reduce open discontent and tension. Even though far more persons migrate to Mexico City than to the United States, emigration is one of several safety valves in a society characterized by severe maldistribution of income and opportunity.

What are the consequences for the United States? Legal migrants are hard working and law abiding, and achieve social mobility for their offspring. Their continued cultural attachments and proximity to Mexico limit the extent of their assimilation, but their children are entering the mainstream of the Mexican-American community and undergoing rapid Americanization.

The principal contribution of the border crossers and the illegal migrants is to lower prices, wages, and inflationary pressures, at least in certain areas of the United States and certain sectors of the economy. Their labor is important to seasonal agricultural harvests of several crops (chilis, tomatoes, and so on) that have yet to be mechanized. They also lower costs of urban services, construction, and labor-intensive manufacturing. Their willingness to work for low wages may prevent some businesses, such as garments, from relocating overseas and help other marginal businesses to remain viable. A particular contribution is made by domestics who free American mothers to remain in the labor force full-time.

Employed illegal immigrants almost certainly pay more in taxes than they receive in taxpayer services.[35] Few ever collect social security or are reimbursed for income taxes withheld. However they can constitute a major burden for local governments if they use hospital services or their children attend public schools. But illegal migrants are in the United States to work, usually without their families, and their illegal status makes them hesitate to use such services except in emergencies.

Do illegal migrants displace or take jobs away from Americans, especially low-income, unskilled workers? This issue has been debated with far more heat than light.[36] The answer is "Yes, but . . ." The "but" involves the wages and working conditions that would be needed to induce Americans to do similar work. Most illegal Mexicans, although not all, are employed in low-paid, socially marginal work that Americans will not take if they have other choices. If Mexicans were not available and employers had to pay higher wages or improve working conditions, would they stay in business? These questions cannot be answered due to the lack of data. Illegal Mexican migrants do take some jobs away from Americans, and they probably also save jobs that would not exist at higher wage levels.

The more valid objection to Mexican migration, legal and illegal, is political rather than economic. Mexicans legally enter and generally remain as permanent resident aliens, failing to become U.S. citizens. They speak Spanish and are reluctant to assimilate or even integrate, unlike many other current immigrants. Should we make it even easier for persons to enter the United States who do not wish to become Americans? Should family reunification be reduced in preference to other criteria for immigration such as professional skills?

The objection to illegal Mexican migrants is their very illegality. Having one million or more persons illegally working and living in the United States is an open invitation to exploitation. Living clandestinely and having minimal legal rights, illegal migrants encourage crime, fraud, and lawlessness. If their labor is needed, they should be admitted legally and treated like other workers. The consequences of encouraging massive illegal migration by underfunding the Border Patrol and the INS, and not imposing sanctions on employers, makes a travesty of American values and places an unfair burden on the innocent migrant who, after all, is only seeking work.

Another argument contends that the United States faces an endemic shortage of unskilled and semiskilled labor due to demographic and manpower changes.[37] While this argument may be valid for some regions, it confronts pockets of persistently high unemployment rates among black and Hispanic youth. Even if the United States needs to import unskilled labor, it need not rely on illegal immigrants.

Mexican immigrants have the most direct impact on Mexican-Americans among whom they live and work. Mexican-Americans are deeply ambivalent about immigration issues. Many fear that any laws imposing sanctions on U.S. employers will result in their experiencing discrimination. Yet illegal migrants often compete directly for jobs with low-income Mexican-Americans and their children attend the already overcrowded, inadequately funded, predominantly Mexican-American schools.[38] Most Mexican-American leaders opposed the employer sanctions of the Simpson/Mazzoli bill while proposing to increase funding and manpower for the Border Patrol, and supporting amnesty.

The regular inflow of legal Mexicans is both a burden on the strained educational and social services of Mexican-Americans and a renewal of cultural and personal ties to their homeland. The inflow of illegal Mexicans, mostly single men living in hiding, is only a burden adding to already overcrowded housing and using often low-quality health, public transport, and other services. The increasing employment of Mexican-Americans in the INS and Border Patrol adds to community tensions. Although Mexican-American political consensus is possible in opposition to employer sanctions, it is not on the issue of illegal immigration.

Emigration has become one of the permanent and intractable issues in U.S.-Mexican relations. Yet each government recognizes it as a sovereign domestic issue and denounces any overt interference in the other's affairs. Instead a pattern of off again, on again, formal and informal consultation has emerged between the two executive branches.[39]

The official Mexican view is that all Mexicans are constitutionally guaranteed freedom of movement, and therefore there should be no exit visas or other legal efforts to regulate the "undocumenteds." (Mexicans wishing to legally leave the country are required to obtain passports.) Instead the Mexican government emphasizes the obligation of the United States to protect the legal and human rights of the undocumented workers. Although an occasional Mexican politician has expressed support for a legal migrant worker scheme, the government has shown little or no interest and regards the bracero era as over.[40] The prospect of hundreds of thousands of Mexicans scrambling to enroll in an official scheme to work temporarily in the United States is not politically attractive.

The Mexican government is caught between a feeling of humiliation that so many Mexicans do work in the United States and recognition that this safety valve and the dollars it brings is needed. Hence it prefers not to comment publicly on proposed U.S. immigration legislation except to stress the need to protect the rights of the undocumenteds. It has eschewed lobbying members of the U.S. Congress and did not make its opposition to the Simpson/Mazzoli bill known until late in 1984 when its passage appeared possible. Mexican leaders are acutely aware of the possible damage to Mexico from changes in U.S. immigration laws but are reluctant to plead openly a case that is based on Mexican weakness and dependence on the United States.

The official U.S. view is also that immigration law is an entirely sovereign matter. In practice, though, several administrations have engaged in considerable discussion with interested foreign governments. But immigration issues have been deliberately kept separate from others that are explicitly bilateral, such as trade.

The Carter and Reagan administrations sought to devise immigration reforms that would be acceptable to "mainstream" American opinion, which dislikes illegal immigration, and to Mexican-Americans and other ethnic constituencies, while not antagonizing Mexico. This has not proved possible. Concern for Mexican sensibilities creates an overwhelming desire not to disrupt political or economic stability through abrupt change. This remains an important objective, but it is subordinate to finding a reform measure that will be politically acceptable in the United States. The U.S. government wants to avoid presenting Mexico with a fait accompli, and it recognizes legitimate Mexican concerns; but it does not consider U.S. immigration policy a matter for negotiation. Thus the Mexicans are left fearing a change that could hurt them but unable effectively to oppose it, while Americans anxious not to hurt Mexico press for a change that may do just that.

POLICY OPTIONS

The range of options runs the gamut from closing the border on the U.S. side to legalizing freedom of movement between the two countries. Freedom of movement is sometimes claimed as a human right and has been legalized within the European Community and the states of the Nordic Union. It has few advocates in Mexico or the United States due to the assumption that prevailing wage differentials and living standards would result in a massive Mexican exodus if the border were completely open. There has been little informed discussion of the implications of a large-scale influx of Mexicans, whether as refugees or as job seekers, although this occurred during the Mexican revolution and, in recent years, with the arrival of Guatemalan refugees in Mexico.

Nor is there significant support for sealing or rigorously controlling the border on the U.S. side, although this is occasionally proposed, and INS and Border Patrol budgets and staffs were increased in 1984. Mexico has become the third most important trading partner of the United States; millions of Americans and Mexicans cross the border annually as tourists and consumers; and tight controls over movement of persons would be a hostile act to Mexico and a threat to commerce.

Yet additional funding and staff will quickly increase the number of persons apprehended along the border, thus increasing the costs of risks of illegal migration. The advocates of employer sanctions argue that as long as jobs are available, migrants will accept multiple deportations as the price of finding work. Cooperation by Mexican law enforcement authorities in prosecuting smugglers, which would also raise costs and risks, has not been forthcoming; many Mexican customs and immigration border officials are themselves involved in the lucrative smuggling business.[41]

A different set of options has been proposed: to provide additional employment in Mexico, particularly in the areas where most of the migrants originate. The most imaginative proposal has been advanced by economist Sidney Weintraub, who advocates the creation of a gradual (20–25 years) free trade area between Mexico and the United States.[42] This phased-in free trade area would force protected Mexican industries to become competitive, generate trade and new jobs for Mexico in many sectors, and, over time, reduce wage differentials and the incentive to emigrate. In an earlier book co-authored with historian Stanley Ross, Weintraub supported employer sanctions, amnesty, increased border controls, and a transitional five-year legal Mexican guestworker scheme, to be phased out after sanctions are fully effective.[43]

While opposed to employer sanctions, Mexican sociologist Jorge Bustamente and American political scientist Wayne Cornelius have advanced proposals to accelerate rural development in Mexico directed at areas of traditional migration to the United States. These proposals involve rural small industries, guaranteed markets for certain crops, and subsidized credits and technical assistance.[44] The Mexican government has shown no interest in allocating priority resources to areas that have long benefited from remittances.

Structural change in the Mexican economy may be highly desirable but will not reduce wage differentials, Mexican expectations, or unemployment and underemployment for many years to come. The Mexican government has accepted U.S. financial and technical assistance for its narcotics control efforts, but the issue of U.S. aid to reduce illegal migration is politically supersensitive. Many illegal migrants do not come from rural areas. Moreover, successful rural development might even release or motivate labor to migrate. The highly skewed nature of income and services distribution in Mexico results in few alternatives to internal or U.S. migration for the ambitious rural poor. How else can persons having a few years of formal education and minimal assets sell their labor at a price that permits them to save?

Another set of policy options seeks to convert many of the illegal migrants into legal temporary workers. Several proposals have been advocated, including an expansion of the present U.S. Department of Labor H-2 scheme for legal migrant farmworkers to a scheme that would give Mexicans legal right to seek work in the United States with cards for specified periods of time but not designating employers. The shift in the United States to urban service employment makes tying recruited workers to employers difficult. The number of Mexicans seeking to enter under any guestworker scheme will likely be considerably greater than the places available. This potential surplus presents the risk of profiteering by recruiters as well as illegal migration by those not selected. The problems of guestworker schemes in Western Europe and the Middle East have been thoroughly studied and documented.[45]

Guestworker schemes in many countries have led to temporary workers attempting to reunite their families and to remain legally or illegally. A Mexican guestworker scheme that attempted to reduce illegal migration would have to enroll at least 500,000 persons. Even at that it might actually increase Mexicans' expectations and, hence, illegal migration. Enforcement of a guestworker scheme while safeguarding worker rights could become a sensitive political issue in U.S.-Mexican relations. There is some support for a small-scale experimental guestworker scheme, but it is difficult to see what this could accomplish. The conservative Census Bureau estimate of 900,000 illegal Mexican migrants in 1980 indicates that a guestworker program would have to be massive to have a significant impact.

Still another approach seeks to reduce illegal migration by strictly enforcing existing federal and state Fair Labor Standards laws and regulations.[46] Requiring employers to pay minimum wages, meet overtime and other wage and hour standards, and hygiene regulations would improve working conditions and thus make some jobs more attractive to Americans. However such enforcement would require more inspectors and court actions—low priorities for many years. If these laws are so poorly and unevenly enforced, it is hard to imagine their use in regulating illegal migration.

The Simpson/Mazzoli bill artfully stitched together employer sanctions and amnesty for illegal migrants who met certain conditions. It was opposed by Mexican-Americans and other groups who feared that employer sanctions could result in discrimination, and by conservative groups opposed to amnesty. Furthermore it was riddled with amendments sought by special interest groups such as California growers. However these two main components, together or separately, will likely dominate U.S. debate over immigration reform.

No one knows how many illegal Mexicans would or could take advantage of a generous one-time amnesty offer. Amnesty in Australia, Canada, Venezuela, and other countries has produced sign-ups of illegal migrants well below expectations.[47] Amnesty would be irrelevant to Mexican sojourners in the United States for brief stays, but of real value to settlers. Would pardoned persons be eligible for permanent resident alien status and to reunite their families? If so, where would they fit in the lengthy Mexican waiting lists? Would a one-time amnesty encourage more Mexicans to stay illegally in the hope of a renewed offer? Amnesty is essentially a humanitarian gesture recognizing that it is neither possible nor desirable to deport long-standing illegal migrants and that it is better to legalize their situation. It would be of greatest benefit to illegal migrants other than Mexicans, who come and go.

Sanctions on employers who knowingly employ illegal migrants have been tried in a number of countries and have worked badly.[48] Enforcement problems include the proliferation of small enterprises that hire illegals, the prevalence and ease of document fraud, the cost of enforcement, the delays involved in litigation, and the need for viable proof of nationality. The track record for such laws in U.S. states and cities reveals similar patterns of nonenforcement.[49] Some observers consider sanctions to be mostly symbolic and to have little impact on the actual number of illegal migrants.

Enforcement problems aside, sanctions do place responsibility where it belongs—on the employer—and not on the already harassed migrant. The nature and extent of fines, imprisonment, and prosecution would affect the deterrent potential of any sanctions. Elsewhere employers have repeatedly paid low fines rather than lose their workers. Those who believe that the United States faces a shortage of unskilled labor also see sanctions as a mistake.

The impact on Mexican illegals, and on Mexico, of any U.S. sanctions legislation is speculative. Strictly enforced it could reduce the number of illegals, but also the amount of remittances to Mexico, while adding to unemployment there. Loosely enforced by an understaffed INS, it would have little impact except to exacerbate Mexico-U.S. relations and frustrate its supporters.

The remaining policy option is the status quo, which tolerates extensive illegal migration without condoning it. The Mexican government and many Mexicans prefer the status quo, believing that reforms will be restrictive. The status quo has persisted since 1964, when the bracero program ended, and has historical roots. It is detrimental to some low-income Americans and to the majority of American businesses that do not employ illegal migrants. It also makes illegal migrants an easily exploited "sub-proletariat." It is a policy option that is defensible only when the alternatives are rigorously examined. The status quo may be the lesser evil in dealing with a problem for which there is no solution.

NOTES

1. Richard C. Jones, ed., *Patterns of Undocumented Migration: Mexico and the United States* (Totowa, NJ: Rowman and Allanheld, 1984).

2. Carlos H. Zazueta and César Zazueta, *En las puertas del paraíso* (Mexico

City: Editorial Popular de los Trabajadores, 1981).

3. Jorge Bustamente, "Migración interna e internacional y distribución de ingreso. La frontera norte de México," *Comercio Exterior* 34 (Septiembre de 1984):849–63.

4. Wayne Cornelius, *Mexican Migration to the United States: Causes, Consequences, and U.S. Responses* (Cambridge: MIT Center for International Studies, 1978).

5. Robert Warren and Jeffrey S. Passel, "Estimates of illegal aliens from Mexico counted in the 1980 United States census" (Paper presented at the Annual Meeting of the Population Association of America, Pittsburgh, PA, 14–16 April 1983).

6. Sidney Weintraub and Stanley R. Ross, *The Illegal Alien from Mexico* (Austin: Univ. Texas Press, 1980), pp. 8–21.

7. Zazueta, *En las puertas del paraiso*, pp. 31–43.

8. Alan Riding, *Distant Niighbors: Portrait of the Mexicans* (New York: Knopf, 1985), pp. 329–33.

9. Canada and Mexico have an agreement for the import of seasonal temporary agricultural workers. During recent summers Canada has recruited around 5,000 Mexicans for harvesting.

10. Niles Hansen, *The Border Economy* (Austin: Univ. Texas Press, 1981).

11. "Border town fears law may tear social fabric," New York *Times*, 17 July 1984. A discussion of border-crossing in Brownsville, Texas.

12. "False identity for aliens to buy," New York *Times*, 17 July 1984.

13. María Patricia Fernández-Kelly, *Women and Industry in Mexico's Frontier* (Albany: State Univ. New York Press, 1983), pp. 19–47.

14. Warren and Passel, "Estimates of illegal aliens counted."

15. Clark Reynolds, "Labor market projections for the United States and Mexico and their relevance to current migration controversies," Stanford University, Food Research Institute, 1979.

16. Jones, *Patterns of Undocumented Migration*, pp. 1–15.

17. Jorge Domínguez, ed., *Mexico's Political Economy: Challenges at Home and Abroad* (Los Angeles: Sage, 1982); Riding, *Distant Neighbors*, pp. 220–27.

18. Riding, *Distant Neighbors*, discusses Mexico's structural problems.

19. George C. Kiser and Martha Woody Kiser, eds., *Mexican Workers in the United States: Historical and Political Perspectives* (Albuquerque: Univ. New Mexico Press, 1979).

20. Abraham Hoffman, *Unwanted Mexican Americans in the Great Depression: Repatriation Pressures 1929-1939* (Tucson: Univ. Arizona Press, 1974); Riding, *Distant Neighbors*, p. 330.

21. Richard B. Craig, *The Bracero Program: Interest Groups and Foreign Policy* (Austin: Univ. Texas Press, 1971); Ellis W. Hanley, "The politics of the Mexican labor issue, 1950-1965," in Kiser and Kiser, *Mexican Workers*, pp. 97–119.

22. Jones, *Patterns of Undocumented Migration*, pp. 10–11.

23. A.J. Jaffe, Ruth M. Cullen, and Thomas D. Boswell, *The Changing Demography of Spanish Americans* (New York: Academic Press, 1979), pp. 140–55.

24. U.S. Department of Commerce, Bureau of the Census, "Socioeconomic characteristics of U.S. foreign-born population detailed in Census Bureau tabulations," *Department of Commerce News,* 17 October 1984, Table 2.

25. Ibid., Table 3.

26. Aaron Segal, "Mexican legal migration overlooked," *The Times of the Americas,* 7 July 1982.

27. Ellwyn R. Stoddard, "Illegal Mexican labor in the borderlands: Institutionalized support of an unlawful practice," *Pacific Sociological Review* 19 (April 1976):175–210.

28. Harry E. Cross and James A. Sandos, *Across the Border: Rural Development in Mexico and Recent Migration to the United States* (Berkeley: Institute of Governmental Studies, 1981).

29. Fernández-Kelly,*Women and Industry in Mexico's Frontier,* pp. 166–73.

30. Riding, *Distant Neighbors,* pp. 331–32.

31. Weintraub and Ross, *The Illegal Alien from Mexico,* pp. 8–21.

32. Jones, *Patterns of Undocumented Migration,* pp. 6–8.

33. Juan Diez-Canedo, "A new view of Mexican migration to the U.S." (Ph.D. diss., Massachusetts Institute of Technology, 1980).

34. Riding, *Distant Neighbors,* p. 333.

35. Vic Villapondo et al., *A Study of the Socioeconomic Impact of Illegal Aliens on the County of San Diego* (San Diego: Human Resources Agency, 1977).

36. Sidney Weintraub and Stanley R. Ross, *"Temporary" Alien Workers in the United States* (Boulder, CO: Westview, 1982), pp. 51–75.

37. Reynolds, "Labor market projections for the United States and Mexico."

38. The 1982 Supreme Court decision requiring public schools to educate children in the U.S. illegally has resulted in demands for federal subsidies for low-income school districts educating an estimated 29,000 illegal migrant children in Texas alone.

39. Robert A. Pastor, "U.S. immigration policy and Latin America: In search of the 'special relationship,' " *Latin American Research Review* 19 (1984):35–56.

40. Riding, *Distant Neighbors,* p. 329.

41. Zazueta, *En las puertas del paraíso,* pp. 75–91.

42. Sidney Weintraub, *Free Trade Between Mexico and the United States?* (Washington, D.C.: The Brookings Institution, 1984), pp. 172–187.

43. Weintraub and Ross, *The Illegal Alien from Mexico,* pp. 52–56.

44. Ibid. These and other proposals are discussed in pages 44–52.

45. Philip P. Martin and Marion F. Houstoun, "The future of international labor migration," *J. International Affairs* 33 (Fall/Winter 1979):311–33.

46. Carl Schwarz, "Employer sanctions laws: The state experience as compared with federal proposals," in Wayne A. Cornelius and Ricardo Anzuldúa Montoya, eds., *America's New Immigration Law: Origins, Rationales, and Potential Consequences* (La Jolla, CA: Center for U.S.-Mexican Studies, Monograph Series 11, 1983), pp. 83–102.

47. U.S. General Accounting Office, *Information on the Enforcement of Laws Regarding Employment of Aliens in Selected Countries* (Washington, D.C., 31 August 1982), pp. 6-7.

48. Ibid.

49. Kitty Calavita, "Employer sanctions legislation in the United States: Implications for immigration policy," in *America's New Immigration Law*, pp. 73-81.

The Puerto Rican Exodus: Development of the Puerto Rican Circuit

Barry B. Levine

The relationship between the United States and Puerto Rico can be characterized by the concept of imperial development. "Imperial development" describes a sociopolitical relationship where one nation controls the ultimate prerogatives of sovereignty of another, ethnically distinct nation, generally through some federal political mechanism, and is obliged to promote economic and social development in the dependent territory as a condition of that arrangement. Puerto Rico became dependent politically on the United States in 1898 when Spain ceded it to the latter at the conclusion of the Spanish-American War. Puerto Ricans were further incorporated in the political system of the United States in 1917 when they were given U.S. citizenship. In 1950, U.S. Public Law 600 gave Puerto Rico the right to draft its own constitution. The relationship took on its present juridical form in 1952 with the Puerto Rican constitution establishing the commonwealth status. Since then, Puerto Rico has been a "freely associated state" of the United States. This political relationship has been the basis for significant economic consequences for the island.[1]

The United States takeover of Puerto Rico in 1898 profoundly influenced the island's economy. Before then coffee had been the principal crop; soon thereafter sugar was raised to prominence. Whereas in the 19th century farmers in the hills had farmed for subsistence, or *haciendas* were run by individual families, U.S. businessmen rationalized the island's sugar cane production and organized it around large plantations for export production. As a result, the Puerto Rican rural worker became extremely vulnerable to fluctuations in the world economy.

At the beginning of the 1930s two hurricanes wreaked havoc on Puerto Rico's rural areas, and the world-wide economic depression equally devastated international trade. Agriculture organized for export production consequently floundered. A high birth rate made for a large population and further stagnated the economy. The living standard was low, and poverty abounded. Rural life offered little opportunity for economic achievement; and this agricultural listlessness had not been counteracted by a significant urban economy. Work in the needlepoint trades or employment as a domestic provided for not much more than a bare urban subsistence.

Since neither agriculture nor industry was responding to the economic needs of the Puerto Rican people, there was much unemployment. People either had no work or occupied themselves with work so inefficient that it was but a form of disguised unemployment. One commentator characterized the Puerto Rico of the 1930s as "an island of sick, starving, and superfluous people, without land, without work, without hope. . . ."[2]

Where, then, could individual Puerto Ricans look to find decent paying work, to find economic opportunities that would lift them out of economic stagnation? Federally sponsored emergency relief projects provided a stopgap solution for some people.[3] Industry initiated and owned by the Puerto Rican government helped others.[4] Still other persons in search of work enlisted in the federally funded National Guard, which upon being called into federal service for World War II became an active component of the United States Army. The latter's presence on the island was a consequence of the political arrangement that defines the relationship between the two societies.

While the army did not play a large part in any plans for solving Puerto Rico's economic woes, it nonetheless had an important, unintended economic impact. One author has argued that, in addition to actual service in the armed forces, dependents' benefits, GI benefits, and federal spending on the island for military expenditures, and so forth, were critical economic stimuli.[5] Most important, however, was that the United States Army became the institutional prototype par excellence of the United States employer. Some 76,000 Puerto

Ricans did military service during World War II.[6] And it was in the United States Army during the 1940s that many Puerto Ricans received their initial training in modern nontraditional urban skills. Others were able to get that kind of training working for Americans on the U.S. mainland, to which they would migrate, while still others were to get it working for American employers who later were invited to set up businesses on the island. The U.S. Army was thus the first example of this kind of "modernizing" experience.[7]

EMIGRATION TO THE U.S. MAINLAND

The Puerto Rican trek to the United States mainland in search of work began many years before World War II but did not gather speed until after the war. In 1910 some 1,500 Puerto Rican-born residents were living on the mainland.[8] By 1940 there were 70,000. The rate of migration kept climbing, and a great jump came in 1946 when 40,000 Puerto Ricans journeyed to the United States. At that time, approximately 135,000 Puerto Rican-born residents lived on the mainland, 85 percent of whom lived in New York City. During the first five years after the war, over 30,000 Puerto Ricans per year emigrated, and by 1950 the total number of Puerto Rican-born residents in the United States surpassed 225,000. The migration peaked during the 1950s at an average yearly rate of 40,000. In 1960 the Puerto Rican-born population on the mainland reached 615,000, and the total of all Puerto Ricans there approached 900,000.

In 1970, 810,000 Puerto Rican-born residents and 619,000 of their descendants were living on the mainland, representing 35 percent of the total population of Puerto Ricans on and off the island. By 1980 the total number of Puerto Rican-origin residents of the mainland reached 2,014,000, representing 40 percent of the total population of Puerto Ricans. In 1970, another one third of a million were return migrants living once again in Puerto Rico. If we assume, for the purpose of illustration, this figure to be constant until 1980, then nearly half of all Puerto Ricans have shared the mainland experience!

The Puerto Rican influx to the United States has been called "the first great airborne migration."[9] For Puerto Ricans, *embarcarse,* "to emigrate," has been relatively easier to engineer than for other immigrants. The former, as citizens of the United States, have had no political border to cross to get to the mainland: permission was needed neither from the sending country nor from the new host country; no passport, no visa. Moreover, air transportation after World War II became relatively inexpensive and rapid. Fares dropped below 75 dollars in some instances.[10] The planes reached New York from San Juan not in weeks or days but in a matter of hours. A "family intelligence service"[11] allowed easy communications with the island, making it less difficult for new immigrants to follow in the footsteps of their predecessors than had been the case among earlier waves of immigration. Furthermore, many Puerto Ricans had already been exposed to American society by virtue of having served in the U.S. Army.

These factors, however, were but the conditions for the possibility of a migration of such size. They do not, however, provide the subjective reasons that motivated each individual to emigrate. A pamphlet distributed to potential emigrants by the Division of Community Education of the Puerto Rican Government discusses several of the reasons frequently given by Puerto Ricans for undertaking the journey.[12] One goes north to escape the hard times of a depression or a labor market where there were more capable workers than there were jobs. Or, one leaves in order to get ahead on the assumption that one can live better elsewhere, or one leaves for adventure and to see the world or even to escape reality and one's problems. Or, one goes simply to imitate those who have already left.[13]

Economic reasons, however, have been the principal ones behind the Puerto Rican exodus: net emigration rates have dropped sharply during recession years in the United States;[14] years of net return flow to Puerto Rico have been years of high unemployment in the States;[15] there has been a high correlation between Puerto Rican migration and the U.S. business cycle.[16] Statistically, migrants moved in response to "significantly greater absolute and relative earning differentials from prospective jobs."[17] The typical Puerto Rican emigrant perceived migrating to be an economic opportunity, a chance to do better, a chance to make more money. Thus, Puerto Ricans often accepted jobs in the States that gave them more money, though less status, than they could expect on the island.[18]

Migration as an international social phenomenon has come to be recognized as one particularly effective means to escape from the accommodation to poverty.[19] It is the kind of opportunity that requires choice; moreover the person who chooses to emigrate must perceive its potential value and must have the capability to risk seeking that reward and the motivation to take that risk. Those who initially take such an opportunity can be expected to be either less insecure economically, having been able to take advantage of previous opportunities, or to be more adventuresome, or both.[20] Members of this nonaccommodating minority are the first to spot and take the opportunity. They demonstrate to others the feasibility and effectiveness of the adventure, and those others who so choose soon follow.

Indeed, the first Puerto Rican emigrants played such a role. A 1947 study reported that Puerto Ricans in New York City had higher incomes than Puerto Ricans on the island, that they were urban, more skilled, and more educated and had a more stable record of employment than those who had not emigrated.[21] It is important to note that although the Puerto Rican immigrants studied were characterized as more "urban/industrial" than those who stayed home, they were, of course, characterized as less so than the mainland work force. (Potential migrants themselves will make this comparison with the mainland work force as one way to test if migration is in fact an opportunity worth taking.)

Those who had come early were essentially urban dwellers: the rural proletariat had not yet begun to emigrate. Thus, emigration at first did not help those who needed it most (except possibly in some kind of trickle-down effect). It was the better prepared or the more adventuresome who went first. Once these forerunners were successful, and word of their success got back to Puerto Rico, others who were less prepared and less daring came to perceive the migration opportunity as less risky, and ventured forth to try to take advantage of it. Analyses of Puerto Rican immigrants during 1957–1961 demonstrate that about 35 percent of those people migrating who were in the labor force were farm laborers as compared with the few rural immigrants found by the 1947 study.[22] A comparison of the 1950 and the 1960 censuses with the 1947 study shows that an ever-increasing proportion of unskilled to skilled workers were emigrating[23]—until finally they came to form the bulk of the total emigrating population.

When compared with others in the States, the Puerto Rican immigrants have not done well economically. Even by 1981, analyses of family income data show the median Puerto Rican family to be substantially behind other groups (median income in 1981 of families headed by Puerto Ricans was $11,256—only slightly more than half the median for all U.S. families).[24] A study dealing with comparable figures for 1969[25] has suggested that the lag is largely traceable to less schooling, fewer wage earners, and the high percentage of Puerto Rican families headed by females. Areas of statistical parity between Puerto Ricans and non-Spanish whites, however, included the following: mainland-born Puerto Rican males had jobs similar to non-Spanish white males; mainland-born Puerto Rican males who had gone to college earned the same as non-Spanish white males who had gone to college; families headed by mainland-born Puerto Ricans who lived outside of New York had a mean family income close to the national average.

In 1976, the United States Commission on Civil Rights also articulated the economic difficulties Puerto Ricans face in the States.[26] The report warned, however, that the aggregate data disguised areas of economic success. Following the methodology of that report, figures for 1981[27] demonstrate that one quarter of all mainland Puerto Rican families earned over $20,000 (120,000 families) and 15 percent earned over $25,000 (74,000 families). In 1981, 309,000 mainland Puerto Ricans were high school graduates, 46,500 were college graduates, and 126,000 were enrolled in college. In 1981, over 64,500 mainland Puerto Ricans held professional, technical, or managerial jobs.

A balance sheet on the economic success of migration would have to compare Puerto Ricans who have migrated and their descendants with what their situation would have been had they not migrated. The preceding data, comparing Puerto Ricans in the United States with other groups in the United States, does not take into account Puerto Ricans who have struggled in New York only to make it back home.

RETURN MIGRATION TO PUERTO RICO

While the emigration was in process, the Puerto Rican economy was undergoing great changes. Not only were Puerto Rican workers traveling to the United States for jobs created by U.S. capital, but U.S. capital was invited to come to Puerto Rico where it created jobs for Puerto Ricans.[28] The Puerto Rican Government focused on the possibility that its political tie with the United States might provide the source for the development of its own economy.[29] In a sense it generalized from its experience with the United States Army and embarked upon an intense program to attract many United States institutions to the island, providing a variety of jobs. The plan, "Operation Bootstrap," offered tax exemptions, aid in the construction of manufacturing plants, inexpensive labor, inclusion within U.S. tariff walls, and many other incentives to entice the U.S. capitalist. As a result, massive amounts of money have been invested on the island, and a U.S.-style economy has been created there.

Puerto Rico went from a society that was largely underdeveloped and agricultural to one that was developing rapidly and has become urbanized and industry-oriented. In 1940, the gross national product (GNP) of Puerto Rico was $287 million. By 1965 its GNP had jumped to $2,748 million (in constant 1954 dollars economic production had multiplied four times). Per capita income, which was under $120 in 1940, had risen to $889 in 1965 and family income rose from $611 in 1940 to $4,292 in 1965 (in 1954 constant dollars family income multiplied 3.25-fold).

Agricultural employment declined from 45 to 16 percent of all employment on the island, losing some 100,000 jobs in the interim. Manufacturing, commerce, and the public sector, which had provided 24 percent of all jobs in 1940, increased to 51 percent in 1965—some 200,000 additional positions. During this period 1,000 factories opened, providing 70,000 jobs. Government bureaucracy emerged to become the principal employer on the island. The ratio of unskilled to skilled workers in the labor force was five to one in 1940 and two to one in 1965. In 1940 there were 500 medical doctors and 6,300 teachers; in 1965 there were 2,700 of the former and 18,600 of the latter. In these twenty-five years, registered motor vehicles climbed from 27,000 to 319,000; telephones from 17,000 to 195,000; annual electric energy production from 166,000 thousand kilowatts to 6,652,000 kilowatts. Urbanization increased from 30 percent of the population to over 50 percent.[30]

The growth has continued: in 1977, GNP was $7,900 million; per capita income was $2,472; family income was $9,838. Urbanization has continued climbing (over 58 percent of Puerto Rico's population lived in urban centers in 1970). Agriculture has continued declining: only 5 percent of the jobs were in agriculture in 1977. But growth had not been automatic; extremely serious problems exist in the Puerto Rican economy: the rate of growth fell to zero in 1974 and was a negative 2 percent for 1975.[31]

Also, in considering the so-called Puerto Rican miracle—that is, the rapid pace of economic growth on the island—one needs to remember that it was not simply a result of the industrialization of the economy; rather, it required both industrialization and heavy emigration.[32] Moreover, most of the recent gains in income are attributable not to increased production on the island but rather to the heavy influx of U.S. transfer programs, especially food stamps. And as long as caveats are in order, the reader should be aware that the great economic growth has not meant the elimination of poverty on the island. Poverty is a concept that measures relative economic rank. The growth of the Puerto Rican economy has meant the substitution of one system of inequality for another. Although at a much higher level of economic capacity, it has not eliminated poverty.[33]

Thus, the growth of the Puerto Rican urban economy increased the number and the quality of jobs available to Puerto Ricans whether they were living on the island or on the mainland. Consequently, for some who had migrated to the States return to the island became a practical economic alternative to remaining on the mainland. But returning to Puerto Rico was not like leaving it to look for work. As in the case of the original emigration, there were many reasons for a decision to return. Some returned to accept better work, some because of the "decreasing demand for blue collar workers performing repetitive and routine jobs"[34] on the U.S. mainland. Others returned to find jobs that, although possibly paying less than had their jobs in the States, would have more status.

Some returned for more existential reasons. Life in New York was unpleasant. The problems of living in the city were overwhelming: drugs, discrimination, language, the persistent hassle of everyday life—all made it difficult for one to create a meaningful life. For some Puerto Ricans it meant that they could rejoin family and friends; for others, that they could bring up their children properly; for still others, that they could satisfactorily deal with health problems. For many, return in fact meant that they could start to think in terms of building a better life in their own country.

Beginning around 1955 the phenomenon of the return migration began to gather momentum.[35] As in the case of the emigration from Puerto Rico, the first to return were both more skilled and better educated than those who stayed on the mainland.[36] As one commentator has written, "Return migration is selective of the occupational elite of the Puerto Rican migration population."[37] It is also apparent that the return migrants were better educated and more skilled than those who had not emigrated and against whom they would compete for opportunities back home.[38] Similarly, they were both more urban[39] and had higher incomes[40] than the nonmigrants. Furthermore, those who were returning were better skilled than those who were leaving the island for the mainland during the same period.[41] The net result during at least the initial stages of the return migration was thus to make the island labor force look more like the labor force of the mainland. As the return migration grew, however, the characteristics of the returnees became less selective; educational and skill levels of later returnees are notably lower than those of returnees who came back before 1960.[42]

During the time the Puerto Ricans on the mainland had been pressured to "Americanize," the Puerto Rican economy also was responding to similar "Americanization." Thus, when "America-smart" migrants returned to an "Americanized" Puerto Rico, they brought a whole host of skills and tastes that they had acquired in New York and that they were able to put to their own use back home on the island. In this sense, the mainland economy has served as a vast training ground where returnees learned both formal and informal skills relevant to the urban environment that had developed in Puerto Rico. Many returned not only with specific skills and new ways to do things, but also with knowledge of how to capitalize on these new ways. Thus, for example, Puerto Ricans who were employees of manufacturing concerns in the States might well, on returning to the island, work in or even start their own retail businesses.[43]

Among those who have returned, many have been relatively successful, while others have not. Comparing these two groups, a 1964 study drew the following differences. The successful returnees ". . . represent a middle-class element, bordering on the island's educational, occupational, and financial elite. Many have taken advantage of opportunities becoming available as a result of modernization, resuming life in Puerto Rico under favorable circumstances—as professionals, white-collar workers, and highly skilled technicians . . . that many started life in rural areas and ultimately settled in San Juan suggests a fair degree of social mobility."[44] Given their economic self-assurance, the subjective reasons they offered to explain their return most frequently had less to do with earning a decent living than with the social conditions that could allow them to live such a style of life.[45]

On the other hand, those who were unsuccessful on the mainland felt an economic compulsion to return. Having lost a job or having had a job "only once in a while" or not having ever had a job, such a Puerto Rican returned to the island for sustenance and maintenance by family and friends until he or she could find employment. And such a person was most likely to return to his or her birthplace, frequently a rural area or a small town—neither one a strong base for social mobility.[46]

THE MIGRATION EQUILIBRIUM

The exodus to the mainland and the modernization of the island have created a kind of migration equilibrium—or circuit—for Puerto Ricans, in that many individuals now have the option of going from one place to the other in search of economic and social opportunities.

The result is that today Puerto Ricans who want to work in industry, for example, can do so on the mainland or on the island, and those who want to lead a particular style of life can choose to do so in San Juan or in New York. Some Puerto Ricans will alternate, "migrating and returning at various intervals and for various lengths of time."[47] The more successful may "alternate periods of work in the United States with their main occupations on the Island . . . [and even] become scheduled commuters . . . [while the less successful may] drift from having no fixed employment to having no fixed residence in a pattern of almost aimless search for small job advantages."[48]

For some observers the development of the two centers of Puerto Rican life may seem to create an irreparable fissure in the Puerto Rican community, so that island Puerto Rican and mainland Puerto Rican share no common purpose. But for others the Puerto Rican circuit is but an expanded field for those potential voyagers who think in terms of ever greater, often varied, economic and social opportunities not hemmed in by mere geography and habit.

NOTES

1. For an elaboration of these ideas, see Barry B. Levine and Ralph S. Clem, "Imperial Development: The Cases of American Puerto Rico and Soviet Georgia," *Comparative Studies in Sociology*, I (1978): 319-36.

2. David F. Ross, *The Long Uphill Path: A Historical Study of Puerto Rico's Program of Economic Development* (San Juan: Editorial Edil, 1969), p. 1.

3. For a history of the Federal relief projects, see Thomas Mathews, *Puerto Rican Politics and the New Deal* (Gainesville: Univ. Florida Press, 1960).

4. For a history of the Puerto Rican government's industrial enterprises, see Ross, *The Long Uphill Path*, chap. 4.

5. A. J. Jaffe, *People, Jobs and Economic Development: A Case History of Puerto Rico Supplemented by Recent Mexican Experience* (Glencoe, IL: The Free Press, 1959), pp. 39–42.

6. History Task Force/Centro de Estudios Puertorriqueños, *Labor Migration under Capitalism: The Puerto Rican Experience* (New York: Monthly Review Press, 1979), p. 124.

7. History Task Force, *Labor Migration under Capitalism*, pp. 129–33, has argued that, for Puerto Rico, emigration and industrialization have been two sides of the same coin: that of the integration of the Puerto Rican worker into both the U.S. controlled economy and the U.S. controlled labor force. In any case, Puerto Ricans have thereby historically been faced with both options described by Galbraith for leaving poverty: "escape from" via emigration and "escape within" via urban employment. See John Kenneth Galbraith, *The Nature of Mass Poverty* (Cambridge: Harvard Univ. Press, 1979).

8. Migration statistics computed from sources cited in Clarence Senior and Donald O. Watkins, "Toward a balance sheet of Puerto Rican migration," in United States-Puerto Rico Commission on the Status of Puerto Rico, *Status of Puerto Rico: Selected Background Studies* (Washington D.C.: United States Government Printing Office, 1966), p. 703; Kal Wagenheim, *A Survey of Puerto Ricans on the U.S. Mainland in the 1970s* (New York: Praeger Special Studies, 1975), p. 71; History Task Force, *Labor Migration under Capitalism*, pp. 186–87; and Rita M. Maldonado, "Why Puerto Ricans migrated to the United States in 1947–73," *Monthly Labor Review* 99(9) (September 1976):13. Data compiled by the United States Bureau of the Census, the United States Immigration and Naturalization Service, and the Puerto Rican Planning Board.

9. Joseph P. Fitzpatrick, *Puerto Rican Americans: The Meaning of Migration to the Mainland* (Englewood Cliffs, NJ: Prentice Hall, 1971), p. 2.

10. José Hernández Alvarez, *Return Migration to Puerto Rico* (Berkeley: Institute of International Studies, Univ. California, 1967), p. 3. Also C. Wright Mills, Clarence Senior, and Rose Kohn Goldsen, *The Puerto Rican Journey: New York's Newest Migrants* (New York: Russell and Russell, 1950), p. 44.

11. Senior and Watkins, "Toward a balance sheet of Puerto Rican migration," p. 706.

12. René Marqués, ed., *Emigración* (San Juan: Division de Educación de la Comunidad, 2nd ed., 1966) pp. 20–21.

13. Marqués, "A donde va la gente, va Vicente" ("Wherever people go, so goes Joe"), *Emigración*, p. 21.

14. Lloyd G. Reynolds and Peter Gregory, *Wages, Productivity, and Industrialization in Puerto Rico* (Homewood, IL: Richard D. Irwin, 1965), p. 30.

15. Senior and Watkins, "Toward a balance sheet of Puerto Rican migration," p. 703.

16. Mills et al., *The Puerto Rican Journey*, p. 43.

17. Stanley L. Friedlander, *Labor Migration and Economic Growth: A Case Study of Puerto Rico* (Cambridge, MA: M.I.T. Press, 1965), p. 128. Reynolds and Gregory, *Wages, Productivity, and Industrialization*, pp. 246–47, argue similarly: they see migration as a "rational attempt to maximize income."

18. See Mills et al., *The Puerto Rican Journey*, chap. 4; and Senior and Watkins, "Toward a balance sheet of Puerto Rican migration," p. 736.

19. Galbraith, *The Nature of Mass Poverty*, chap. 8.

20. They are among "those best prepared for rescue" from poverty, in Galbraith's words (*The Nature of Mass Poverty*, p. 138).

21. Mills et al., *The Puerto Rican Journey*, chap. 2.

22. Friedlander, *Labor Migration*, p. 113. He hypothesizes that the beginning of the farm labor migration started with the decline of agricultural employment between 1950 and 1953 (ibid., p. 114, n.10).

23. Ibid., 112.

24. Data taken from *Persons of Spanish Origin in the United States: March 1982*, Series P20, No. 396 (January 1985). These surveys are based on samples one-fortieth the size of the decennial census and in contrast may prove somewhat exaggerated.

25. A. J. Jaffe, Ruth M. Cullen, and Thomas D. Boswell, *Spanish Americans in the United States–Changing Demographic Characteristics* (New York: Research Institute for the Study of Man, 1976), p. 238ff.

26. The United States Commission on Civil Rights, *Puerto Ricans in the Continental United States: An Uncertain Future* (Washington: Office of Management, Publications Management Division, 1976). Their data are taken from the current population surveys of the United States Bureau of the Census, published annually as *Persons of Spanish Origin in the United States.*

27. Data taken from *Persons of Spanish Origin in the United States: March 1982*, Series P20, No. 396 (January 1985).

28. Lloyd Best has aptly titled this style of economic development program "industrialization by invitation ("Black power and doctor politics," *Caribbean Review* 2(2) (Summer 1970):5.

29. See Levine and Clem, "Imperial development," pp. 322ff.

30. Sources for the statistics on development are drawn from Puerto Rico Planning Board, *Indices Seleccionados de Progreso Económico y Social* (San Juan: Commonwealth of Puerto Rico, 1970); Puerto Rico Planning Board, *Ingreso y Producto Puerto Rico 1970* (San Juan: Commonwealth of Puerto Rico, 1971); Puerto Rico Planning Board, *Informe Económico al Gobernador 1976-7* (San Juan: Commonwealth of Puerto Rico, 1978).

31. See Herman Nickel, "Puerto Rico's drift toward statehood—and dependence," *Fortune* (13 August, 1979), p. 165; and José A. Cabranes, "Puerto Rico; Out of the colonial closet," *Foreign Policy* 33 (Winter 1978–79):81: "the boom built on cheap labor may be over forever."

32. See Celia Fernández de Cintrón and Barry B. Levine, "Quienes son los pobres en Puerto Rico? " in Rafael Ramírez, Barry B. Levine, and Carlos Buitrago Ortiz, *Problems de Desigualdad Social en Puerto Rico* (Río Piedras; Ediciones Librería Internacional, 1972), p. 26.

33. Ibid., p. 15.

34. Hernández Alvarez, *Return Migration,* p. 7.

35. Ibid., p. 9.

36. Ibid., p. 48, analyzing 1960 census data.

37. Ibid., p. 91.

38. Ibid., p. 48; Friedlander, *Labor Migration,* pp. 90ff. The returnees also ranked higher occupationally when compared with all employed persons on the island in 1964 (Senior and Watkins, "Toward a balance sheet of Puerto Rican migration," pp. 755–56).

39. Hernández Alvarez, *Return Migration,* p. 29.

40. Ibid., p. 91.

41. Friedlander, *Labor Migration,* p. 102, analyzing 1957–61 ramp surveys taken at San Juan airport by the Puerto Rico Bureau of Labor Statistics, finds that those going to the island were very much more skilled than those leaving it; however, these data include, among those going to the island, not only returnees but also non-Puerto Ricans.

42. Steven Zell, Puerto Rico Planning Board, *A Comparative Study of the Labor Market Characteristics of Return Migrants and Non-Migrants in Puerto Rico* (San Juan: Commonwealth of Puerto Rico, 1973), pp. 74, 162.

43. Hernández Alvarez, *Return Migration,* p. 92.

44. Ibid., p. 104. A 1973 study similarly concluded that among return migrants there was a "group tendency toward upward mobility" (Celia Fernández de Cintrón and Pedro A. Vales, *Social Dynamics of Return Migration to Puerto Rico* [Río Piedras: Social Science Research Center, University of Puerto Rico, 1975], p. 54).

45. Hernández Alvarez, *Return Migration,* p. 110.

46. Ibid., p. 116.

47. Ibid., p. 2.

48. History Task Force, *Labor Migration,* p. 141.

The Cuban Exodus:
Political and Economic
Motivations

Robert L. Bach

Ever since the 1980 boatlift of over 125,000 Cubans from Mariel crashed ashore in South Florida, a controversy over their reception has raged. The word Mariel has come not only to symbolize the persistent problems with U.S. immigration policy but, in many ways, to highlight the weakened position of American influence and power in the hemisphere. Much about the incident has been inflated by stories of that very evident subgroup of criminals whom the Washington *Post* labeled the "Mariel toughs." Yet the dramatic character of this exodus cannot be minimized, nor can the problem it created be ignored, for there are many lessons to be gained. On the first anniversary of the Peruvian Embassy incident (in which 10,000 Cubans stormed the Peruvian Embassy in Havana seeking asylum), for example, the Miami *Herald* editorialized that the principal lesson was that immigration must be controlled in Washington, not in Cuba's Havana or Miami's Little Havana. Another was that an entire community suffers when its newcomers are denied adequate help in making the transition to a new life.

The motivations of Cuban refugees are hardly a new topic of policy or scholarly interest. Since 1959 Cubans leaving the island have been viewed either as "worms" or "heroes," largely depending on the evaluator's own ideological bias toward the nature of the exiles' political motivations.[1] A certain novelty, however, appears in the current discussion of the Mariel emigrants, for rather than debating political judgments, the issue is whether they even had such presumably exalted motives. Many have argued, including representatives of both the Carter and Reagan administrations, that these latest exiles more closely resemble economic migrants leaving in search of better jobs and consumption opportunities. Others declare the latest wave to be another group of anti-Castro, anti-totalitarian dissidents.[2] The novelty of the present debate lies both in the emotional intensity of the conflicting claims and the acceptance among a wide audience of the economic motives behind the Mariel emigrants. In part, the policy and analytical discussion took the form that it did due to the lack of control over the flow. The result was an absence of any clear, definitive judgment from the government as to how to view these newcomers.

POLITICAL OR ECONOMIC MIGRANTS?

The issue of political or economic motivations is not solely a problem arising from the Cuban experience, nor is it unique to the Caribbean. Continued emigration from South Vietnam poses a similar question, although it has not become quite so controversial since there the United States is not the country of first asylum.[3] Nor is the issue simply the Carter administration's problem. At least since World War II, the international community and specifically the United Nations has moved to develop a definition of a refugee founded on universally acceptable humanitarian principles.[4] At the same time, the United States has followed a practice of defining refugees according to its own national self-interest, explicitly meaning those who flee from communist governments. The tension between these two positions erupted soon after the UN definition was adopted as part of the Refugee Act of 1980. The juxtaposition of the Cuban and Haitian mass migrations brought the old and new commitments into stark contrast.

The political and economic distinction is also clearly an outcome of an intellectual tradition of viewing migrations as individually motivated events. Individuals make decisions to move, according to this view, based on their separate perceptions of its differential costs and benefits.[5] This tradition merges easily with the U.S. government's need to defend its differential policies toward various groups of migrants throughout the world, especially so within the Caribbean. The special "political" status of Cuban migrants is thus matched in U.S. policy terms with the historically favored "economic" status of Mexican immigrants.[6]

The overriding conceptual issue is whether individual motivations behind large-scale emigrations can actually be identifed and classified neatly into political or economic categories. Such an approach is particularly dubious when these individual characteristics are judged in comparison to the complex matters of international and domestic politics and world economic problems that underlie expulsion, reception, and resettlement. There is hardly ever a strong, direct connection between perceptions, motivations, and behavior.[7] A politically motivated person has many alternatives other than emigration, or as John Womack observed in introducing his book on the Mexican Revolution: "This is a book about country people who did not want to move and therefore got into a Revolution."[8] The traditional political/economic distinction holds that higher wages in the country of destination lure the economically motivated, while extreme social upheaval in the country of origin pushes out the politically sensitive. Given a choice, the political refugee would stay in his or her country of origin; the choice of the economic migrant is to leave. But it is also presumed that political refugees do not exercise much of a choice.[9] Their departure is either in immediate anticipation of or as a direct result of an emergency, or crisis; at the time of departure the political refugee seldom ever knows where is or her eventual place of resettlement will be.

U.S. economists are fond of using these divergent motivations to explain the characteristics of those who leave and the contrasting problems that political refugees and labor migrants encounter in the United States.[10] Economic migrants, who have the time and motivation to calculate the optimal strategy for obtaining higher wages, should include among their ranks only persons whose skills are directly transferable to the United States. Political refugees, on the other hand, because they have little time to calculate their move and their motivations are less narrowly focused, should have a wider distribution of skills. Lawyers, for instance, would be rarely found among economic migrants as they know beforehand that their country-specific skills are difficult to transfer abroad. Yet lawyers are frequently found within a pool of political refugees because, given their sensitivity to social justice, a threat to political freedom and security activates their desire to leave.

The dramatic conditions of refugee flight have also led some observers to attribute to them a special social-psychological behavior. Although different in social form than the criminal aggression of the Mariel toughs, analysts have observed among refugees an uncommon aggressiveness, a "burning desire to make a place for themselves and to prove their worth."[11] Statements about the special drive of refugees imply that economic migrants lack similar drive. Such conventional wisdom does not allow for enough heterogeneity between and within migration streams. There is little dispute with the observation that migrants and refugees have diverse experiences once they resettle in the United States. Yet it is a mistake to reduce this diversity to individual attributes.[12]

Individuals do perceive constraints and opportunities in their lives in different ways and are able to identify the pressures they believe that led to their emigration. Yet even these perceptions are often heterogeneous and ambiguous. For example, concerning a sample of Cuban exiles in 1973/74, A. Portes, J. Clark, and myself discovered that "when asked for major reasons for the decision to leave, respondents emphasized equally political concerns and social and economic aspirations.[13] Another scholarly practice toward Cuban exiles is to assume that pre-1959 Cuban exiles were economically motivated. Disregarded in this claim, however, are those who came to the United States in the 1950s as a result of the Batista coup. There is also an older group who came in response to the practices of General Machado in the early 1930s. A. Jorge and R. Moncarz have argued, in fact, that the entire history of the Cuban flow to the United States corresponds only to episodes of political upheaval and not to economic crises.[14]

IDEOLOGICAL TAINT

The obvious point here, but one persistently ignored by politicians and academics embracing the conventional wisdom, is that there is an ideological taint to the political/economic distinction. The foundations of the distinction lie with the administrative practices of the United States government. The actions of the U.S. government in treating the Cubans differently after 1959 lead social observers to presume differences in individual motivation. Consequently, "political" roots of migration flows have come to mean those from countries who oppose the United States. Similar political activities in Caribbean countries that support the United States are virtually ignored as producers of "political" refugees. Mariel emerges as a contradiction to this practice. Despite opposition of the United States to the Castro government, policy towards the latest emigrants has changed considerably.

No one has defined these political motivations—especially in comparison with economic migrants—except by simply asking the migrant or by accepting the legal definition and deducing personal differences. Problems are clearly evident when the attempt is made. For example, Jorge and Moncarz attribute the political basis of Cuban refugee's motivations to the failure of the redistributive policies of the Revoluionary government. Such policies and their failure have undoubtedly contributed to the outflow. Yet, if such failure is the basis of classification as political or economic, then how many other migration flows in the Caribbean Basin have been fundamentally political? For even in the presumably most economic case— Mexico—political problems and redistributive failures underlie the massive outflow. How many Mexicans have left the countryside for the United States because land reform policies have made it virtually impossible to remain? How many left, as have the Cubans, to rejoin family abroad and to regain security?

The critical difference, of course, is between the nature of the Cuban and Mexican governments and, especially, the differential way in which the United States relates to each. But that is precisely the point: the defining characteristics of migration flows are found at the level of social and economic organization and international politics, not among individual perceptions and motivations. One can find, for example, an extensive overlap of meaning in a Cuban exile's condemnation of the government's policies that result in economic hardship and the Mexican's perception of economic problems that manifest political failures. The difference lies in how similar problems of both an economic and political nature get interpreted by the two principal actors in any migration flow, the sending and receiving states. Before we move to condemn or embrace the motivations of individuals within any particular migration we must wonder why each state has labeled them labor migrants or refugees. This is hardly the kind of question government officials ask since it challenges precisely their own interests, but it should be the question that researchers, reporters, and social observers ask!

We must refer not only to the receiving state, but to the sending state as well. Whether it be Cuba, Mexico, Jamaica, or Haiti, they too are equally involved in determining not only how the migrants are to be labeled, but who among a potential pool of refugees and emigrants will be encouraged, allowed, or even required to leave. If the Mariel incident reveals nothing else, it is the importance of this labeling process. For during the episode the various labels promoted by both the Cuban and U.S. governments—either about the Cubans themselves or about other groups such as the Haitians—were so distant from the perceived reality of others that the legitimacy of both states was seriously shaken. This labeling process, however, is not simply engaged in freely by states at the time of each migration incident. Rather, the labels themselves are outcomes of complex political and economic relationships that constrain officials in responding to the flow. It is these relationships that account for the drama and ambiguity of refugee reception and resettlement.

WAVES OF CUBAN EMIGRATION

The social composition of the successive waves of Cuban refugees after 1959 can best be characterized in terms of their declining social status. As the Cuban revolution aged, both average educational backgrounds and the proportion of professionals and white-collar workers in each outflow decreased.[15] With time, the number of emigrants who held political motivations as the sole or overwhelming reason for leaving also declined. Part of these changing motivations was a result of the increasing importance of family reunion as the reason for emigration. As each wave separated larger numbers of family members, family reunification became intertwined with political disaffection. The differences between economic and political motivations also became virtually impossible to disentangle, if ever they could be, as the new government consolidated its control of all sectors of the society and economy.

Emigration was unrestricted during the first year of the Revolution. However, only those who had substantial wealth or had been members of the inner circle of the Batista government left during this time. This initial trickle of exiles resembled the historical pattern of political emigration, where it was common for groups who had lost power to leave the country temporarily. But this emigration soon took a dramatically different course when, instead of simply replacing one group of leaders for another, the revolution of 1959 targeted its efforts to a total transformation of the economy and society. The large-scale exodus began in 1960, following a series of urban land and legal reforms that initiated the redistribution of national wealth.

Although the earliest waves of emigrants defy any simplistic explanation of their reasons for emigration, especially those based solely on former class positions or overt political opposition, the social class origins of the earliest wave overwhelmingly mirrored the top layers of pre-revolutionary society. Fagen, Brody, and O'Leary[16] report that those who resettled in Miami between 1959 and 1962 overrepresented the professional, managerial, and middle classes of the Cuban population; 31 percent of the exiles were professional, technical, and managerial workers, compared with only 9.2 percent of the 1953 Cuban population. Similarly, 33.0 percent of the exiles were clerical and sales workers; 13.7 percent of the source population worked in these jobs. Only 8 percent of this early wave labored in semiskilled and unskilled sectors of the workforce, 7 percent were employed in service jobs, and 4 percent worked in agriculture and fishing. In each of these latter occupations, the refugees underrepresented the total Cuban population.

These early "golden exiles," as they would come to be known in the United States, also possessed a much higher level of education than the general Cuban population. Only 4 percent of the refugees had less than a fourth grade education, compared with 52 percent of the island's population. A large proportion of the refugees (36 percent) had completed either high school or some college. The comparable figure for the Cuban population was only 4 percent.

The first wave of exiles was certainly heterogeneous, but they constituted a group that vastly overrepresented the higher status, wealthier strata of pre-revolutionary society. Their departure clearly represented a severe loss of resources and talent to Cuban society. And, although there was significant heterogeneity, in general this same group came to the United States with its own resources and social connections and reestablished itself within a relatively short period.

The first wave was halted abruptly by the Missile Crisis of 1962 and the U.S. naval blockade. During the lapse in formal, regulated migration, perhaps as many as 50,000 made the trip to the United States. A fraction escaped in boats and a few in airplanes. One thousand political prisoners from the Bay of Pigs fiasco were exchanged for medical supplies, food and cash. Another 5,000 family members traveled with them. Others left through third countries.

The second major wave of emigration began in September 1965, when the Cuban government announced that those with families in the United States would be allowed to emigrate. Departures began in the port town of Camarioca, as hundreds of boatloads of Cuban-Americans from Florida arrived to pick up relatives. The two governments agreed on an orderly departure program involving an airlift between Varadero and Miami. These "freedom flights" were restricted primarily to the reunification of family members. When the airlift ended in 1973, 2,800 flights had carried more than a quarter of a million persons to Miami.[17]

A significant feature of this orderly departure program was that it allowed for controlled, prior screening of who would leave for the United States. The Cuban government restricted from departure young men of military age (15–26) and those whose talents and scarce skills might disrupt national production and service. For its part, the U.S. government was able to enforce the priorities of its own immigration law. Relatives of persons already living in the United States were given preference according to the following rankings: spouses, parents, then siblings. Throughout this period, the proportion of refugees who had relatives already living in the United States was consistently above 90 percent.

As a result of revolutionary reforms, reinforced by Cuban exit restrictions, the social class backgrounds of the exiles shifted dramatically. The proportion of professionals, managers, and technical workers among the refugees dropped from 31 percent in the 1959–1962 wave, to 18 percent in 1967. Skilled workers, however, increased their proportions. By the late 1960s, the revolutionary government moved to consolidate its control over the smaller sectors of the economy that, until this time, had remained fairly independent. The move to socialize these sectors raised the number of merchants, artisans, and small shopkeepers that joined the outflow.

Many Cubans who wanted to leave during this period of the "aerial bridge" were unable to gain passage. Registration to leave was a difficult step, frequently requiring periods of "voluntary labor." Many chose to leave Cuba to go to Spain, where they hoped to enter the United States later under normal visa eligibility requirements. In October 1973 they were allowed to enter the United States under a special parolee status. A study of this group conducted in 1973/74 showed yet another change in the occupational origins of Cuban refugees.[18] In contrast to the earlier waves, the proportion of men in this 1973/74 arrival group who worked in the service sector rose from 7 to 10 percent in the earlier years to 26 percent. The exile-generating capacity of the revolution had reached into the lower ranks of the social order.

A lull occurred in the Cuban flow between 1973 and 1979, a period when 38,000 Cubans arrived in the United States. Most of these arrived through third countries. Beginning with a change in relations with Cuba under the Carter administration, a new wave of emigration began. In October 1978 the Cuban government announced its intentions to release 3,000 political prisoners and 600 others who had been caught trying to escape the island. Although not all the prisoners would leave immediately for the United States, those that did were accompanied by their families. Together, they formed a small wave of between 10,000 and 14,000 exiles. In January 1979 another form of population exchange followed this prisoner release, when nearly 100,000 relatives from the United States were allowed to travel to Cuba for family visits. Both these visits and the release of political prisoners ended, however, in March 1980.

Soon after this abrupt halt, the next major wave of emigration occurred. During months of chaos and drama between April and September 1980, approximately 125,000 Cubans left Mariel. Unlike the earlier boatlift from Camarioca in 1965, no orderly departure agreement was reached by the two governments in 1980. As a result, neither the Cuban nor the United States governments had complete control over who emigrated or immigrated. And, as a tragic consequence, the social composition of those who left, and the character of the reception in the United States, became more a matter of highly charged political antagonisms than in any of the previous waves.

THE MARIEL "ENTRANTS"

No social or political label can stand the challenges of time and adversity if it is totally unconnected with empirical reality. Similarly, the controversial and pejorative nature of the Mariel reaction would not have survived if there was not sufficient evidence to maintain the labels attached to it. Such was the case, during the Mariel exodus with the all too familiar controversy over the social backgrounds of those placed on the boats by Cuban officials. The Cuban press, as it has for previous waves of refugees, labeled the exiles "social dregs" and "undesirables." The Cuban government even made some efforts to support the claim by not only releasing criminals and patients but by allowing others to leave who were willing to sign papers declaring themselves undesirable (*"un dross"*). Reports from the U.S. side echoed these labels, "anti-social" and "criminal." One immediate result was that within the first weeks the terms of the debate and the justification for the ambivalent reception had been set. Something about this group called for a very different program of resettlement.

Sufficient evidence existed at the time, however, to give a more accurate and balanced view. For instance, though it was hardly complete, the demographic profile developed from the files of the Immigration and Naturalization Service (INS) provided enough information to at least challenge the most extreme negative views. The U.S. Department of Labor actually prepared a press release using this information but the riots in Liberty City in Miami erupted and it became an issue of political impropriety to have a Federal office release positive information on newcomers while U.S. citizens released their frustrations over long-standing neglect. On several occasions U.S. government officials, especially those from the refugee offices of the Federal bureaucracy, used similar information from a variety of sources to counter the most negative reactions. This evidence, however, was not used sufficiently to seek a more accurate label of the type of flow and, thus, a more clearly perceived policy of resettlement.

Fortunately, we now have relatively complete social background profiles of the Mariel entrants to demonstrate the nature and size of the gap between the public labels and empirical reality. As anticipated, these data show that the group was very heterogeneous. More importantly, as a group, they had a much more positive social background profile than the initial or even continuing reports indicate. Overall, the entrants' education, job skills, job experience, and residential backgrounds were not only substantially higher than anyone claimed during the flow, but indicate a former role in the Cuban economy that was fairly typical of the source population. And compared to the Cubans who have come to the United States during the 1960s, Mariel exiles showed similarity in both their educational and occupational backgrounds. Major differences included the larger number of mulattoes and blacks among the Mariel group and a much younger average age.

The Mariel entrants' employment backgrounds are especially important considering that the specter of "social dreg" and *"lumpen"* was interpreted at the time largely as a fear of these individuals not being able to fit into the U.S. economy and being unable to become productive members of the new community. The concern was directed particularly at those who were initially placed in one of the four military camps. The large proportion of the total influx that was released directly into Miami has scarcely become a central feature of the public's knowledge of the characteristics of these entrants. Not unimportantly, this group also had a higher social status and more positive background profile, including a greater proportion of families, higher percentage married, more persons with relatives in the United States, and higher skilled job experiences. The camp population, however, received most of the attention, so it is the experiences of these people in Cuba that we must examine in detail.

Since most were from the largest cities in Cuba, including Havana, Cardenas, Cienfuegos, Holguin, Guantanamo, and Santiago, it is not surprising that few were farm laborers (2.0 percent) or farmers (1.4 percent). Instead, they worked in craft (25.3 percent), laboring (18.8 percent), machine operative (15.4 percent), and transport operative (11.0 percent) jobs. Many were skilled workers. The craftworkers, the single largest group, included mechanics that repaired factory equipment and automobiles, while others were brickmen and carpenters, roofers, painters, and electricians. The laborers worked most frequently in construction; others worked in factories or on the docks. Few gave evidence that these jobs were either temporary or self-contracted, although other sources have indicated a noticeable presence of day laborers among the camp population. Heavy equipment operators dominated the operative category, with welders appearing most frequently. Professional and technical workers, of whom we have heard so little, actually comprised nearly 8–9 percent of the group. They included teachers from all grade levels, accountants, entertainers, urban planners, and nurses, to name only a few.

Among the working age camp population, 74 percent reported they had held a job for most of their adult lives. Only 5 percent described themselves as unemployed. And, as one would expect, the great majority who said they had no job were housewives and students. This positive employment is hardly surprising given that one objective of the Cuban government's reforms has been to maintain virtual full employment. Indeed it would be more noticeable had these entrants shown evidence of high levels of unemployment.

Unquestionably, there was a subgroup in the camp population with prison records. Based on a subsample of the émigré group, it is possible to estimate that 16 percent of those in the camps fourteen years of age and over had been in prison during the last ten years. Their reason for imprisonment and length of time served varied from chicken-stealing to violent felonies and ranged from a month to over 20 years. There was also a significant group of young, historically violent youths who were processed at Fort McCoy and, from local studies, have been shown to have had serious social and psychological problems. It is on such evidence that the pejorative labels have been founded.

There is, however, a substantial number in this group that were imprisoned in Cuba for reasons that may not be considered a serious offense in the United States. They seem to fall into three categories. Those who were involved with economic problems predominate, especially in terms of participation in the black market as either buyer or seller. According to the INS biographical forms, many in this subgroup were arrested for buying basic consumption items: clothes and food were most frequent. Occasionally it was for selling jewelry or other such items for handsome profit. Second, there were those who had refused military service, deserted from the service, or refused to work for the state, particularly during the cane harvest. The passage of the law of *"peligrosidad"* was used to detain not only these persons, who had more or less directly challenged the state, but also the perpetrators of the former offenses involving the black market as well. Third, there was a small number of persons who had spent much of their adult life in jail, often with their prison terms beginning in the early 1960s. Although it is impossible to tell from these particular data, they compare favorably with a group that specifically claimed political (counter-revolutionary) activities as their reason for imprisonment, and who might have been eligible for the orderly departure program already established between the United States and Cuba.

Of course, these broad background profiles require much more in-depth study. In 1982, for example, Gastón Fernández, drawing on interviews at Ft. Chafee, Arkansas, reported that 81 percent of his sampled entrants admitted to having "outside" income in Cuba, with a full 14 percent admitting it was obtained through black market activities.[19] He also observed that a significant proportion, although they held jobs fully within the mainstream of the Cuban economy, may not have participated fully in the collectivization of social life on the island. These observations gain additional support from a series of interviews conducted at Ft. Indiantown Gap. Participation in black market activities was mentioned frequently and, important-ly, by people from a wide range of social backgrounds. But what is of additional interest here is that they show the complexity of personal motivations and circumstances and begin to identify the link be-tween the groups from which the individual migrants emerged and the organization of both the national economy and society. On the one hand, the collectivization of the Cuban economy and society has made virtually every point of dissatisfaction, frustration, and motiva-tion a political issue in the sense of having links to government ac-tivities. But, on the other hand, they also suggest that the political and economic are so intertwined as to make their separation mostly a matter of ideological judgment.

Since the following personal stories are only examples, I offer them without additional commentary to let the reader draw his or her own lessons: The first set refers specifically to the significance of "outside income" in their everyday lives. One person interviewed was jailed for selling 25 packs of cigars and a half pound of coffee in a private exchange; he was told it was a threat to the national economy. He came to the United States without his family because in addition to the nine months for selling cigars he received a special stamp that declared him a public danger and subject to four more years in prison. Another 29-year-old man from Marianco who was unem-ployed came to the United States "because there weren't many jobs in Cuba, wages were low, and working conditions unfavorable. The family income—his wife's wages as a taxi driver—was not enough to buy food. His house was old and falling to pieces, but he was doing some repairs. He was arrested and sent to jail for three months because he happened to be in a gambling house." A 37-year-old woman came to the United States because "everytime she had to go out and look for food for her five children she always had trouble with the police." She left Cuba with five other relatives but the government asked for more money than she could afford for permission for her sons to leave. She also had spent three months in jail for illegally buying food for her children. Another man, a welder in rural San Francisco de Paula, admitted to being engaged in counter-revolutionary activity. He was imprisoned once for sabotage; he also had bought food on the black market: one pound of rice for $2.00, one pound of meat for $6.00.

This next set of anecdotes gives meaning to Fernández's suggestion concerning the potential significance of the exiles' nonparticipation in the collective organization of Cuban society. In addition, they also reveal the importance of participation in selected social activities. One particularly bitter 32-year-old man said he was not allowed to attend the university because he was not a member of the Union of Young Communists. And he observed it would have been unbearable to join the Communist party in Cuba, despite the available benefits. However, he emphasized that membership in the party did not always result in these benefits: "We all know that there are three kinds of Communists: (1) The Communist who knows everything, who is clear on everything, who even knows he's working for the Soviet Union; he's boss, he gives orders, he's nothing but a member of the middle-class, things are taken to his home, good food—he is the materialist kind. (2) The Communist who believes that one day all men will be equal; he thinks that by fighting what they call imperialism everybody will become equal—these are men of good faith but they become slaves of Russian Imperialism—they are idealistic Communists. (3) The cardbearing Communist. He knows Communism is no good. The leaders are all living well; he gains membership because of his behavior and attitude towards work; this man is the one who takes avantage of his membership in the party."

These interviews also reveal two forms of social participation that lead to creating a pool of potential emigrants. Both involve activities that Americans would not consider damaging to their character. The first is related to refusal to serve in the military in Angola. The same 35-year-old mentioned above reported that many Cubans refused to go, including persons already in the military and members of the Communist party. A portion sought asylum in the Peruvian and Venezuelan embassies. The second activity involves marriage. The Ft. Indiantown Gap interviews suggest that marriage had much to do with underlying problems of consumption. One 33-year-old woman from Havana said she had always wanted to come to the United States; she observed that many couples live together instead of getting married because they cannot afford the cost of the civil ceremony. Others reported certain advantages to marriages of convenience in securing larger ration allocations.

The meaning of these social backgrounds will not be fully understood until we more fully appreciate the circumstances that led to the emigration. We need to direct our attention more to how these conditions of consumption shortages, widespread black market activities, and social repression developed. To do so we need to understand further the broader relationship among groups and nation-states: relationships that transcend the significance or capacity of the individual migrants who are controlled by them.

CRITICAL DIMENSIONS OF MARIEL

If individual characteristics or motivations are not the clues to the many lessons of Mariel, then what are the key dimensions? It is possible to propose a set of hypotheses about three broad relationships that not only apply to the Mariel exodus but are derived from the analyses of a wide range of migration streams. That they refer to a general context is important because the view that the Cuban flow is unique is too closely tied to U.S. policy interests to let it uncritically guide our observations. U.S. interests and historical actions are key determinants of the treatment and labeling of these emigrants and, therefore, must be the subject of as much study as the actions and interests of the Cuban government. The three relations include (a) the political and economic organization of Cuban society with special reference to its response to the then-current economic crisis; (b) the changes in U.S. refugee policy as influenced by internal economic and political realignments and shifting relations to Cuba; and (c) the relatively unregulated dynamic of social networks, particularly family reunion, as the activating mechanism of most migrations.

The first set of hypotheses concerns the severe shortages of consumption items in Cuba and the way in which this relates to both the black market activities so commonplace among many in this last wave and the labels of "scum" and "undesirable" that were attached to the entire outflow. Cuba shared with many states in the Caribbean the effects of the early economic crisis of the 1980s. Throughout the Caribbean deep-seated structural transformations have been underway, with specific problems formed in relation to the organizational capacity of each country to adjust to these changes. The nature of the crisis and the type of responses have substantial similarities among the countries, especially since the source of the general difficulty lies in the largely external conditions of world recession and inflation. Yet each state has adapted to the crisis within the limits of its previous strategies of national economic development and within its own historical alignment of class forces. Variations in response are also produced by the very different political relationships each state maintains with the United States.

Cuba has for some time now embarked on a strategy of national development that has placed great reliance on export activities. Dependence on sugar and tobacco production, in particular, has maintained a strong reliance on the world market. This orientation has also led to a substantial commitment to Soviet financing of local economic ventures. Both dependencies have made Cuba especially vulnerable to the economic downturn of the early 1980s. Cuba's economic problems, of course, have been no secret. For instance, the government admitted in December 1979, that the economy was "sailing in a sea of difficulties." Foreign trade imbalances had been exacerbated by serious blights in the tobacco and sugar cane crops. Already restricted supplies of consumption goods became even more scarce and created a general context of dissatisfaction. Within this context, the Cuban government warned repeatedly of another potential Camarioca, long before the Peruvian Embassy incident occurred.

Cuba's foreign policy, especially in relation to the United States, also provided an important dimension to the context of Mariel. The Carter administration had made overtures toward normalization of relations with Cuba, which if it had been accomplished would have involved a better opportunity, if not an actual expanded program, for organized emigration from Cuba on a family reunion and political prisoner basis. In fact, even at the time of Mariel there were discussions over how to enlarge the existing prisoner release program under the new provisions of the Refugee Act of 1980. The terms for normalization, however, clearly involved termination of Cuban activities in other areas of the world, particularly its active military role in Africa. Cuba's refusal to accept these terms virtually eliminated the possibilities for rapprochement when, during the months of the

Mariel boatlift, the Cuban government insisted that most of the elements of normalization of relations (for example, return of Guantanamo Naval Base) be part of the negitiations over the orderly regulation of the exodus. Indeed, it is this polarization of the negotiation stances before Mariel that helps explain why the Carter administration in 1980 could not obtain the same agreement from Cuba that the Johnson administration had been able to obtain in the contest of the month-long exodus from Camarioca in 1965.

Second, the progress of revolutionary reforms within Cuba had set overly rigid terms for the management of the consumption shortages and economic problems in general. As was very well known, long before Mariel the government had substituted a rationing program for a pricing mechanism as the principal means of regulating consumption and managing distribution. It had also embarked on a program of income redistribution and collectivization through a centralized, bureaucratic state apparatus. One consequence was the formation of a fundamental contradiction between, on the one hand, social ownership of the means of production and a political regime that represented the demands and needs of the peasantry and working class, and, on the other hand, a centralized, bureaucratic administration of both production and exchange activities. Excessive bureaucratic centralization meant that virtually the only way to enforce work discipline which for Cuba meant social discipline as well, was through repressive measures originating from the national government.

Faced with the general regional economic crisis, one that had forced not only many states in the Caribbean to submit to the relentless pressures of the marketplace but had even moved the United States to worry about productivity, the Cuban government moved with many other governments to expand its output and increase its market efficiency. In an important innovation, the government took steps to free the small but dynamic private farms from past constraints. These private farms, which still accounted for 80 percent of tobacco production, were permitted to sell directly to consumers (in *"mercados libres"*) anything produced over their quotas. They were also allowed to increase commodity prices.

Forced by economic pressures to reorganize part of its redistributive network (by late 1980, the Cuban leadership had reportedly advised the victorious *Sandinistas* on the benefits of a market-run as opposed to a state-regulated distribution system), Cuba also ran into problems on the production side. In the absence of decentralized workers' control and without the coercion of the marketplace as a disciplinary force for labor, efforts to enforce productive efficiency were imposed from above, including attempts to enforce the social discipline of collective participation around which the drive for national economic development had been premised.

The attempt ran afoul, however, of the very social and political distance between the government and the masses that centralization had helped create. It led to widespread "violations" of inflexible norms, including a surge in black market activities that, of course, had always been present. In response, control over the black market became one of the targets of efforts to reestablish social discipline and through it to promote production efficiency. Such an effort is not novel since, as we have seen in Vietnam, efforts to enforce economic efficiency through market mechanisms in socialist countries often lead to attempts to "clean up" the marketplace. To the Cuban government, then, those who could not or would not be disciplined became, by definition, "social dregs" and "scum." The Report of the Congress of the Communist Party in 1980, in identifying the need to strengthen its links with the masses, actually referred to this connection between the Mariel exodus and the need for general social discipline. The report explained the emigration by reference to the following: "socio-economic conditions which still produce some declassed, anti-social and lumpen elements that are receptive to imperialist sentiments and ideas. . . . The people's repudiation of the scum also meant that they repudiated undisciplined behavior, sponging, accommodation, negligence and other such negative attitudes."[20] In this sense, the Mariel exiles, and their labels, represented the political repudiation of economic and social inefficiency.

Nevertheless, the fact that Cuba's development, or underdevelopment, is public rather than private sector led does not mean the private path is any less political. Discipline from market pressure can be as harsh and arbitrary and involved in the unequal distribution of power and resources as much as direct government regulation. And, of course, unequal rewards controlled by a capitalist class are not any less unequal or political than when they are organized by a state bureaucracy. It does mean, however, that group responses to similar problems will take a very different form in relation to the public or private sectors and, therefore, will provide sufficient grounds for other groups outside the country to interpret or label that behavior according to their own interests. Consequently, in the United States the crisis in Cuba is called political, while that in Haiti is called economic.

It should not be surprising that the world economic crisis of the early 1980s also affected the U.S. economy and with it the ability of the government to move flexibly in political arenas. The fundamental point here is that long before Mariel, U.S. refugee policy had come into opposition with economic pressures that weighed heavily against granting the Mariel arrivals refugee status.

U.S. refugee policy throughout the late 1970s had to contend with the general national fight against inflation, fiscal conservatism, and a drift toward social disciplinary measures that have only become fully evident under the Reagan administration. This may seem contradictory to the clear generosity shown toward the Southeast Asian refugees since 1975 and legislated into the Refugee Act of 1980. Yet signs were developing even as these generous benefits were promoted that indicated the resettlement program was moving in a vastly different direction than fifteen or twenty years before when the earlier waves of Cubans arrived. For instance, the U.S. government's approach to the earliest waves of Southeast Asians was as quietly as possible to distribute them widely throughout the United States to prevent an anticipated negative reaction from the U.S. public. It was only after the number of arrivals grew and the refugees began clustering on their own that this policy was abandoned. Deeply rooted in both the language and intent of the Refugee Act of 1980 was also an expectation that refugees move quickly to adjust to the United States and to achieve social and economic self-sufficiency. To enforce this, the act set a timetable of three years for the cutoff of federally reimbursed costs for "unproductive" refugees. After that time, as the Reagan administration did with general assistance costs, the financial responsibility for refugees was thrust onto local areas.

Such an approach, developed long before the Reagan administration, was based on a view of social policy that desired to ensure the significance of the private sector. A White House memorandum of December 7, 1979, formulated the policy as follows: "the refugees are particularly well-suited for the Feds back-seat approach. It is a relatively limited and transient problem as compared say, to poverty, unemployment, inflation. Hence, relatively easier to handle, more suitable for voluntary private efforts."[21] Decisions concerning the reception of the Mariel exiles were made with these social policy and financial considerations well in mind. And when coupled with a presidential election campaign and a widespread anti-immigration public mood, the setting was ripe for the president to overrule many of his own refugee resettlement advisors and decide not to declare the arrivals refugees.

The label "entrant" was, in this sense, as much an economic symbol as a legal one. And as the Miami *Herald* recognized very early in the flow, and many Miamians continued to learn, the message was a harsh one. But the message was actually consistent with the generally conservative fiscal approach that many in South Florida, Washington, and throughout the nation had embraced. The reluctant economic side of the ambivalent "entrant" label merely indicated that refugee policy was as subordinate to the constraints of the national economy as were other affairs. And, as in the case of these other affairs as well, the result did not necessarily make particularly wise social sense. For if the suspicions from the negative images of the individual migrants were believed at all by those who promoted them, then the anticipated problems of resettlement should have argued for greater spending to prevent or at least control the impact.

Economics, however, were only part of the policy constraints that produced the "entrant" label. Economic conservatism had to be balanced against a contradictory tendency toward liberalism in foreign policy. And this meant confrontation with the implications of explicitly accepting the UN definition of a refugee. The response to the Mariel flow and the Haitian influx as well got caught up in a monumental clash between the United States reaching out to become involved in compelling international and humanitarian problems, while at home it withdrew from programs of domestic relief and assistance.

The acceptance of the UN definition of a refugee and the passage of the Refugee Act of 1980 had an important unintended consequence: it negated the Cuban exodus and the resettlement program, which had been the first such program that the government had taken an administrative role in, as the nation's unambiguous model of a refugee policy. It left little in its place as a positive statement of a new policy. It left, for instance, only the political and economic distinction among individual motivations as a means of defining a refugee and, consequently, led to the difficulties between the Haitian and Cuban flows. But in the absence of clear guidelines, the "entrant" label actually preserved the long-standing national bias in the practice of refugee policy. Despite the humanitarian gestures of the Refugee

Act, the "entrant" label allowed the special foreign policy status of Cuba to remain intact, while relieving the Administration of the need to confront and to justify its relations with the Duvalier government in Haiti.

The ambiguous treatment of the Mariel exiles, therefore, had at least as much to do with the real constraints of domestic and foreign policies as it did with the alleged questionable characteristics of the individual migrants. More importantly, the ambiguity is explained by the conjunction of two contradictory trends of which the Carter administration's treatment, had either appeared alone, would have been appropriate enough that it would not have been criticized by those who, ultimately, severely criticized the actual treatment of the overall Mariel incident. Given the constraints, the Carter administration made surprisingly clear and consistent policy choices that prevented a major international confrontation or domestic upheaval. Of course, thousands of people have become victims in one way or another of the harsh domestic resolution of the problem. But this has as much to do with the consequences of fiscal and social conservatism in general as it does with the specific decision over refugee resettlement.

One aspect of the episode which has so far not been discussed is why the boatlift was not simply stopped, by military force if necessary. Apparently the Reagan administration has plans to do so if another Mariel erupts. In a sense, that administration resolved the contradictory tendencies faced by the Carter government by simply abandoning the pretext of a humanitarian refugee policy and returning to a strict anti-communist practice. This kind of "control from Washington" seems to indicate that at least someone has learned from the Miami *Herald*'s lessons. But the simple clarity of this policy sacrifices other cherished aims. The Carter administration stopped short of pushing the confrontation with Cuba to the point of war. It also took reasonable measures to secure safe passage for those who ended up on the boats. At what point would the clear intentions of the Reagan administration stop?

Finally, what about the great importance of family ties in promoting and activating both migration and refugee flows. Comparatively few newcomers to the United States, including refugees, come without some family connections to the U.S. population. Family reunion is, of course, built into U.S. immigration law and heralded as the single most universal reason for allowing immigration. Because it is so basic, however, it has a dynamic of its own, a self-perpetuating mechanism, a virtual guarantee of future inflows or at least of demands for future entry. It also forms mechanisms that work through the law or, when necessary, around it to achieve the apparently unrelenting goal of families when their members are separated geographically. In the Mexican migratory flow, for example, families are perhaps the single most important mechanism for organizing the flow, determining who comes to the United States, how they get in, and, finally, what happens to them afterward.[22] This is especially the case when the persons who enter must do so without documents, that is, illegally.

The boatlift that emerged from South Florida during the Mariel episode was merely another, albeit dramatic, expression of this fundamental process. Indeed, it showed just as strongly as illegal Mexican migration the degree to which such actions are uncontrollable, in practice, if they are exalted in law and public policy. Like the Mexican flow, in the absence of clear, positive statements and actions, the self-generating activities of family reunion take precedence. However, since few seem ready to abandon the family reunion concept as the cornerstone of U.S. immigration policy, we must add another basic, irreconcilable contradiction to the context of administering this policy. The universal value attached to family reunion conflicts with the interests of individual nation-states who, like the United States, desire both to be guided by this principle and to reject it when the process takes a form that is either unpredicted or unacceptable at the time.

The role of family reunion in the Cuban exodus has, of course, been fundamental in shaping its volume and characteristics from even the earliest wave. However the Cuban community in South Florida has been criticized, indeed has chastised itself, for engaging in the evidently lawless rush to Mariel Harbor. Clearly they strengthened the Cuban government's hand through allowing it to prey upon the self-propulsion of family reunification to maintain the flow. But there is also reasonably good evidence that the Carter administration mistakenly read the potential reaction of the Cuban-American community and, therefore, did not close off the boat rescue sooner than it did. There is, in fact, a good case to be made that this was the principal policy mistake of the entire incident.

CONTINUING PROBLEMS

Many continuing problems face the Mariel entrants as they make their transitions to Cuban-American life. In many ways, the types of problems encountered perpetuate the earlier images of the questionable nature of the individuals' backgrounds. But to sort label from reality we must distinguish among at least three groups of entrants. First are the comparatively small number of criminals who roam the streets of Miami, Brooklyn, and a number of small communities. They clearly represent a tragic problem and require the appropriate response of law enforcement officials. Second, there is the other extreme, those who have all too silently slipped away into the Cuban-American communities and are progressing well. Much more about this group needs to be uncovered and made public. Third, there is an apparently significant number of entrants who have confronted or created problems in adapting to the United States that are not at all as serious as the criminals' behavior but that are serious enough to draw attention. Who are these people? Again we know very little about them. But there are a number of claims about the reasons for their problems. For example, Gastón Fernández hypothethized that these are people who have had experience in the black market in Cuba and have learned to manipulate and circumvent authority. This experience has transferred to the United States where they recreate similar circumstances and, therefore, similar problems. The degree of social nonparticipation suspected in Cuba could equally serve as an hypothesis for the cause of the social and psychological problems these exiles now encounter. This is especially plausible given that successful participation in the Cuban-American community represents a critical adaptive mechanism.

One could also propose other explanations based on the migrants' background characteristics. The problem, however, is that there is a danger of falling victim to a self-fulfilling prophecy. How many of the problems, for instance, are due to particular background experiences or to the inadequate, ambivalent reception and resettlement effort? The experience in the four military camps certainly frightened many and disoriented others. And there have been obvious tensions with the older Cuban-American community that makes full participation difficult even if the individual was among the most enthusiastic volunteers in Cuba. The danger of the self-fulfilling prophecy is that, in the past, labels have led us to believe there was something peculiar and difficult about this group, and because of this we have treated them differently; now we blame them when they turn out with special problems.

NOTES

1. Sergio Díaz-Briquets and Lisandro Pérez, "Cuba: The demography of revolution," *Population Bulletin* 36 (April 1981).

2. Juan M. Clark, José L. Lasaga, and Rose S. Reque, *The 1980 Mariel Exodus: An Assessment and Prospect* (Washington, D.C.: Council for Inter-American Security, 1981).

3. Astri Suhrke, "Global refugee movements and strategies of response," in Mary M. Kritz, ed., *U.S. Immigration and Refugee Policy, Global and Domestic Issues* (Lexington, MA: D.C. Heath, 1983), pp. 157–74.

4. See Charles B. Keely and Patricia J. Elwell, *Global Refugee Policy: The Case for a Development-Oriented Strategy* (New York: The Population Council, 1984).

5. See, among others, Barry Chiswick, *An Analysis of the Economic Progress and Impact of Immigrants* (Final report to the U.S. Department of Labor, Employment and Training Administration, 1980).

6. Silvia Pedraza-Bailey, "Cubans and Mexicans in the United States: The functions of political and economic migration," *Cuban Studies/Estudios Cubanos* 11 (July 1981): 79–97.

7. Richard R. Hagen, Richard A. Brody, and Thomas J. O'Leary, *Cubans in Exile: Disaffection and the Revolution* (Stanford: Stanford Univ. Press, 1968).

8. John Womack, Jr., *Zapata and the Mexican Revolution* (New York: Vintage Books, 1968).

9. E. P. Kunz, "The refugee in flight: Kinetic models and forms of displacement," *International Migration Review* 7 (Summer 1973): 125–46.

10. See Chiswick, *Economic Progress and Impact of Immigrants.*

11. S. Alexander Weinstock, "Role elements: A link between acculturation and occupational status," *British J. Sociology* 14 (1963): 111, as cited in Eleanor Rogg, *The Assimilation of Cuban Exiles: The Role of Community and Class* (New York: Aberdeen Press, 1974), p. 18.

12. For this argument, see Alejandro Portes and Robert L. Bach, *Latin Journey: Cuban and Mexican Immigrants in the United States* (Berkeley: Univ. California Press, 1984).

13. Alejandro Portes, Juan M. Clark, and Robert L. Bach, "The New Wave: A statistical profile of recent Cuban exiles in the United States," *Cuban Studies/Etudios Cubanos* 7 (January 1977): 1–32.

14. Antonio Jorge and Raúl Moncarz, "Cubans in South Florida: A social science approach," *Metas 1* (Fall 1980): 37–87.

15. Lourdes Casal and Andrés R. Hernández, "Cubans in the U.S.: A survey of the literature," *Cuban Studies/Estudios Cubanos* 9 (July 1979): 25–51.

16. Hagen, Brody, and O'Leary, *Cubans in Exile.*

17. Silvia Pedraza-Bailey, "Portrait of the Cuban exiles: Waves of migration" (Paper presented at the Tenth National Meeting of the Latin American Studies Association, Washington, D.C., March 4–6, 1982).

18. See Portes, Clark, and Bach, "A statistical profile of Cuban Exiles."

19. Gastón Fernández, "The flotilla entrants: Are they different?" *Cuban Studies/Etudios Cubanos* 11/12 (July 1981/January 1982):49–94.

20. Communist Party of Cuba, *Report of the Congress of the Communist Party* (Havana, 1980).

21. White House memorandum from Amitai Etzioni to Ellen Goldstein and Frank White, December 7, 1979.

22. Portes, Clark, and Bach, "A statistical profile of Cuban exiles."

The Haitian Exodus: Flight from Terror and Poverty

Alex Stepick

My name is Jean and I came to the United States in 1978 to find freedom and to work.

Well what happened to me was it was a Macoute that came to rent a bicycle from me for one dollar.

I didn't see him. I never saw him at all. I looked for him all over the place. Later on, I found him standing somewhere leaning on his bicycle. I went in and told him, "How come you didn't bring the bicycle back to me?"

He told me, "Don't you know that I bought it from you for a dollar?"

I thought he was kidding. I held the bicycle and took it away from him. Right away he hit me with a club.

Then, four more came and started beating on me. They break my head over here too.

I ran. I went. I ran and hid in the woods. One of my cousins who know where I was hiding came and told me they had taken one of my brothers. He said they were pressuring him to tell them where I was. When he couldn't tell them where I was, they took him to a public place in front of everybody and they killed him.

I went to the Northwest to find a boat to go to Miami. Finding a boat wasn't hard, but I did have to borrow the $1,500 for passage. I sold one of my small plots to a local *gros negre* who buys from anyone needing money to go to Miami. The price wasn't too good. We had the land in the family since the time of Dessalines, but I couldn't stay in the mountains forever. Anyway, I thought, once in Miami I could earn enough to buy it back and probably even some more.

131

Other families in the village received as much as $200 a month from their people in Miami. That's more than I could earn in three years in Haiti.

The boat left at the end of August in 1978. In the beginning there were 145 of us crammed into a twenty foot, leaky, wooden sailboat. Not everyone could even sit down at the same time. . . .

Their destination was 700 miles away, but Jean had little idea how long it would take to get there. The Captain said it would depend on the winds and luck. They apparently had little of either. They ran out of water first, and a few days later there was no more food. Many tried to drink the sea water, but it made Jean sick. He preferred to go thirsty. Some died, and after two weeks there were barely over 100. Although Jean didn't know it, they had gone about 600 miles and were still 120 miles south of Miami.

One evening a U.S. Coast Guard cutter approached them. Jean and the others leapt with joy and relief. "We're saved," he thought. Jean, along with everyone else, crowded the side of the boat closest to the cutter. Some began jumping into the water and swimming towards the cutter. The sailboat tilted and then capsized. Jean didn't know how to swim and he thrashed in a panic. Three others drowned before the U.S. Coast Goard saved the rest. Once in the cutter, they were given food and water. Jean ate so fast his stomach ached.

When they arrived in Miami they were greeted by Immigration and Naturalization Service (INS) authorities who transported them to an INS processing center filled with other Haitians all awaiting the U.S. government's decision either to allow them to stay in the United States or to deport them back to Haiti. Through an interpreter, Jean told an INS official his story of the bicycle, the *Macoute,* and why he left Haiti. The INS officer said that he didn't qualify for political asylum, that he was coming to the United States to work, that he left Haiti because of a personal dispute, and if he stayed in the United States he would remain in jail. If Jean wanted, the INS officer said he could fly back to Haiti for free, if he would just sign a piece of paper. Jean knew that others had signed the paper and disappeared, and he knew he didn't want to go back to Haiti where he believed he would meet certain death. Besides some of the others in the camp said there was still a chance they could be released.

THE HAITIAN PAST

Extensive migration has characterized Haiti for all of this century. But the peculiar form of the Haitian migration, the features distinguishing it from other Caribbean migrations, lie in Haiti's history: the pyrrhic victory of the Haitian Revolution and the "kleptocracy" of the Duvalier era.[1]

After 15 years of devastating struggle, on January 1, 1804, Jean Jacques Dessalines proclaimed the free republic of Haiti—the first black republic, the second free nation in the Western Hemisphere, and the world's first emancipation of the slaves. These tremendous political achievements unfortunately were at the expense of equally tremendous economic destruction. The large, white-run plantations based on black slave labor had made Haiti the "pearl of the Antilles," richer than the British colonies of North America or all the Spanish colonies in the Americas combined. After the revolution there were neither white plantation owners nor black slaves. Instead, to placate the soldiers, the newly formed Haitian government redistributed the land. Freed slaves squatted on the remainder.

Periodically, Haitian governments attempted to re-consolidate the large estates, but nothing could reproduce the former compliant labor force. The memories of slavery were too strong. The former slaves and their descendants preferred an increasingly marginal existence on plots continually subdivided by their heirs. The Haitian Revolution transformed America's most productive export colony into a nation of *minifundia* and subsistence peasants.

Following the land reform, the Haitian elite could no longer directly rely upon agricultural production to underwrite their status and ambitions. The only way of gaining an income from agriculture without being a peasant was to tax the goods produced and consumed in rural areas; and only the government could perform this function. Control of the state was not for the promotion of the common good, but to produce wealth for the controllers. Government came to serve the single purpose of providing those in power with a substitute for the income and wealth lost with the landed estates. Yet, virtually no effort was made to provide an infrastructure that might improve production and marketing. Roads fell into disrepair as did ports. Railroads came late and then there were only a few miles of track. There was never a cadastral survey or any effort to regulate land titles. While there were some notable exceptions to this dismal governmental neglect, it was unfortunately the norm.

With the common vision of a predatory state, two rival political elites emerged: the black, illiterate or semi-literate army officers epitomized by the leaders of the revolution, Toussaint and Dessalines; and the educated, French-oriented mulattoes. The elite, especially the French-oriented mulattoes, long had a tradition of migration. Many were schooled in France and spent a considerable portion of their lives on the continent. But the Haitian masses belonged to neither tradition. Their attention was instead focused on the far more fundamental issue of simple survival. The long period of slavery followed by attempts at serfdom inflicted by the black and mulatto autocrats only strengthened their desire for physical freedom, their desire to remain apart from politics and the central government.

The elites ignored the peasants, except to tax them. Instead they focused upon the continual battles for control of the treasury. Of the 22 presidents who served between 1843 and 1915, only one finished his term of office.[2] Successive governments ran up staggering debts, mainly with German and U.S. banks. To protect U.S. investments and to pre-empt any such move by the Germans, President Wilson sent in the U.S. Marines in July 1915. The U.S. occupation successfully effected a number of remunerative reforms, but the economic structure of Haiti changed little. The focus was administrative and political reform. Various elections and plebiscites were held from the beginning of the occupation until 1929, but all were rigged or controlled by the Marine Corps. The goal was not representative democracy, but the election of someone who would compliantly follow U.S. wishes, which were limited principally to the maintenance of public order, collection of tax receipts, and a few, isolated infrastructure projects, such as roads and a vocational high school.

An obvious racist disdain exhibited toward both mulattoes and blacks by the occupation forces vitiated any development efforts. After 15 years, the occupation remained an authoritarian monolith. The elimination of graft was a temporary phenomenon possible only because of the tight control exercised by the occupation forces over finances and government employment. The peasants remained as isolated as ever from political discussions and decisions. When the Marines were withdrawn in August 1934, the old problems of corruption and graft reemerged.

In contrast, the American occupation of Haiti's neighbors, Cuba and the Dominican Republic, produced significant economic changes important to future Haitian migration patterns. There large-scale agriculture, particularly sugar cane production, boomed under the tutelage and control of U.S. firms. In the beginning the plantations imported workers from numerous Caribbean islands. But the drop in world sugar prices in 1920 and the subsequent 1929 Depression encouraged a progressively greater reliance on the cheapest available labor, the Haitians. In 1920, there were nearly 30,000 Haitians in the Dominican Republic;[3] by 1935, the number exceeded 50,000.[4] Although their numbers were fewer in Cuba, they were still substantial.

In 1937, in the depths of the Depression, the Haitians suddenly became unwanted guests in both Cuba and the Dominican Republic. Batista expelled over 10,000 Haitians.[5] In the Dominican Republic, Trujillo massacred at least 12,000 in a three day orgy of rage.[6] But economic necessity dictated a quick return to the former status quo. The Cuban and Dominican economies needed sugar produced by cheap labor and the Haitians needed jobs. Despite unemployment in both Cuba and the Dominican Republic, the backbreaking job of cutting cane remained "Haitian work."

In 1939, only two years after the massacre, the Dominican Republic began regulating the importation of cane workers including military control of transportation. While the state regulation lapsed from 1940 to 1952, illegal Haitians remained the backbone of the sugar economy. Beginning in 1952, the contemporary period of Haitian labor in the Dominican Republic, a series of five year agreements between the Haitian and Dominican Republic governments had been enacted. These agreements have been characterized by the UN as a system of "slavery,"[7] While Haitians were no longer welcome in Cuba after the Castro Revolution, they continue to go the Dominican Republic. In 1980, it was conservatively estimated that there were 200,000 Haitians there.[8]

Immediately after World War II, Haitians were welcome in the Bahamas, even if most did arrive illegally. The economy was booming and native Bahamians were upwardly mobile. They wanted to leave the farm work and the lower levels of the service industry to the hardworking, low paid Haitians. In the 1960s, there were upwards of 40,000 Haitians in the Bahamas out of a total population of 240,000.[9] But with declines in the economy's growth, the welcome for the Haitians turned to resentment. Since 1957, Bahamian officials have engaged in periodic efforts to expel the Haitians: 1963 saw "operation clean-up" and 1967, "crackdown campaign."[10] In 1978, Bahamian immigration agents provoked a scandal by beating and raping many Haitian migrants.[11] In the fall of 1980, international attention briefly focused on one group of Haitians in the Bahamas. A boatload of Haitians on their way from Haiti to Miami became marooned on a small, uninhabited key, Cayo Lobos. Although the U.S. Coast Guard had apparently informed the Bahamas government of the Haitian landing, the Haitians went publicly unnoticed for nearly a month. They remained stranded on an island that had no food or water. Finally, the United States parachuted in supplies. The event attracted media attention and the Bahamas government responded. They landed a boat to pick up the Haitians to return them to Haiti. Armed with sticks and stones, shouting that they would rather die than return to Haiti, the boat people beat back the Bahamian officials into the sea. But the officials returned two days later. This time they were armed with pistols and rifles and they accomplished their mission.[12]

THE REFUGEES

When François (Papa Doc) Duvalier assumed power in 1958 Haitian emigration took an unprecedented turn. Political opponents of a new Haitian president have always seen the wisdom of leaving Haiti. All levels of Haitian society have successively felt the need to leave. The first to leave were the upper elite, who stood as a direct threat to Papa Doc's regime.[13] Then came the black middle class (around 1963) who found the brutality of the Duvalier regime and the lack of personal and economic security unacceptable.[14] Next many of the urban lower classes departed.[15] The primary U.S. destination of these groups has been New York City where by the 1970s there were between 200 and 300 thousand Haitians.[16] They form a most heterogeneous group reflecting all strata of Haitian society.

Haitians have long formed the core of sugar cane workers in the Dominican Republic, and have increasingly penetrated the urban labor market there. They have also formed an important component of the Bahamian labor market. And, there have grown up large concentrations of Haitians in Montreal, Paris, Boston, and Chicago.

But all these flows are different from that of the Haitian boat people; those individuals who crammed themselves 20–30 at a time into 25-foot, barely seaworthy boats for a perilous 700 mile trip to southern Florida. The first known boatload of Haitians landed on Florida's southeast coast in 1963.[17] They requested political asylum, were denied it by INS and returned to Haiti. In 1972, a virtually continuous flow of boats with refugees seeking political asylum began to land in Florida.[18] In contrast to the previous flows to the United States, the boat people are primarily poor, rural, and black. In the beginning the boat flow was largely unorganized. Peasants would get together, pool their money and labor, build a boat, and simply head out. Frequently, they made stops in Cuba and the Bahamas. But their goal was the United States.

As the flow persisted, as remittances and stories of success circulated in Haiti, entrepreneurs saw the opportunity for successful free enterprise. Captains began to solicit passengers and eventually a whole network developed fanning out from all the port cities, but especially those in the northwest. The trade increased and so did the level of organization. Freighters that could only produce a marginal profit with inanimate cargo could make a small fortune with refugees.[19]

In Port-au-Prince, an employment agency that apparently fronted for refugee smuggling advertised over the radio. It dispensed agents throughout the countryside who claimed to have many job offers in a country where most people are un- or underemployed. People poured into the agency camping on the floor inside and in the corridors outside. They were counseled that they could buy or trade their way to the United States. Many literally sold everything they had, including the family land inherited from the revolution. Others borrowed from local moneylenders at 100 percent interest.[20]

Haitian officials periodically attempted to control the flow. In May 1980, the military commander for the northwest called together all of the area's pastors to inform them that the government wanted to stop the flow. They asked the religious community for their assistance. Indeed, the flow stopped for about a week. But the first boat to leave after the May 1980 embargo departed from directly below the headquarters of the military commander. Residents claimed that the real reason for stopping the flow was to allow the military commander to consolidate a monopoly on kickbacks.[21] Within and outside Haiti, rumors were rife that government involvement reached directly into the presidential palace.[22]

After much pressure from the United States, the Haitian government in the fall of 1981 began cooperating with U.S. authorities to interdict the boats in Haitian coastal waters. The program significantly decreased the flow, although it did not stop it entirely. In late October 1981, national attention focused on Miami after a boatload shipwrecked a few hundred yards from Florida's coast. Thirty-three bodies washed ashore, bloated from drowning.[23]

Of those who arrive alive, many claimed political asylum. The INS with support from the U.S. State Department has consistently denied Haitian requests for asylum, claiming that they are only economic refugees. Many have appealed for relief to the U.S. Federal Courts where their luck has been at best mixed. Sometimes they are refused again; but in other cases, the courts have found in their favor, asserting that many do have valid claims to political asylum.[24]

The reasons for these inconsistent findings lie within the peculiar conditions of Haitian society. One observer has characterized Haitian society as a "kleptocracy," ruled by a government of thieves,[25] a description that makes the boat people both political and economic refugees. The conditions are rooted in Haitian history, but a history that the Duvalier era has exaggerated and improved upon.

With a per capita income around $260, Haiti remains among the 30 poorest countries in the world.[26] Its per capita income is less than half that of Bolivia, the next poorest country in the Western Hemisphere. Even this per capita comparison masks the dramatic inequality within the country; eight-tenths of one percent of the population have 44.8 percent of the wealth. Two-thirds of the rural population (80% of the total population) have annual incomes less than $40. The infant mortality rate, between 130 and 150 per thousand, is among the highest in the world. Meanwhile, there are more Haitian doctors practicing in Montreal than in all of Haiti.

Over three-fourths of the adult population remain illiterate. There are few schools, especially in the rural areas. Instruction is usually in French, a foreign language to the vast majority, and the "free" education of the Haitian constitution usually costs too much for the common man's children. In per capita education expenditures, the Haitian government spends the smallest amount of any nation in the world.

THE ECONOMY

Haiti is still primarily a land of *minifundia* agriculture. Only 6 percent of the land is irrigated and virtually all of that belongs to the richest families in the country.[27] With the development aid of international agencies, the elite have consolidated productive rice plantations in the Artibonite valley. Meanwhile the peasants' land base is rapidly and steadily deteriorating. Coffee remains the primary export, generating 80 percent of all agricultural receipts and over 40 percent of all export receipts.[28] Yet, coffee yields are the lowest in the world. Efforts to improve them have completely failed with most of the money simply disappearing or going to improve the production of the few coffee producers who have high political connections.[29] Nevertheless, coffee production is taxed at rates among the highest in the world. Taxation policies, focused on those least able to pay, have discouraged and even eliminated production.[30]

The most dynamic sector of the Haitian economy is the assembly plant industries which assemble consumer goods for consumption in the developed countries, especially the United States. With the Western Hemisphere's lowest wages and close proximity to the United States, Haiti offers an unparalleled opportunity for investors. Profits are extraordinarily high (30–50 percent on equity) and capital per worker very low ($700–1,500). The assembly sector contributes more than 12 percent to Haiti's domestic product, at least 35 percent of Haiti's exports, and about 45 percent of Haiti's salaried jobs. Yet, no more than four percent of the working population is involved.[31]

The growth stimulated by this economic activity has been depressingly slow. Between 1960 and 1977, Haiti's annual GNP growth rate was barely one-tenth of one percent, although since 1970 GDP growth averaged 4.1 percent.[32] But inflation averaged 13.3 percent and between 1975 and 1979 food production per capita actually declined.[33] Income disparities between rural and urban areas increased. These depressing statistics were closely linked to the practices and policies of the Duvalier government. Fifty percent of the state's income were in unbudgeted accounts, which, it is commonly presumed, ended up in private hands.[34] Duvalier controlled a vast state monopoly, the *Regie de Tabac,* which had exclusive control over distribution of necessities such as fish, cotton, all types of milk and milk products; plus wine, champagne, whisky, rum, perfumes, dental products, soap, bandages, air conditioning, autos, airplanes, and most electrical appliances. In 1977, *Regie de Tabac* was estimated to have collected about one million dollars, but only 580 thousand reached the public treasury. Allegedly an estimated $10 million to $20 million in revenues failed to appear in the budget each year.[35] Some critics of the unbudgeted sector argued that foreign assistance allowed for the existence of extrabudgetary accounts, since in 1977, $62.6 million in public revenue simply "vanished," the same amount of foreign aid that year.[36]

A few of the scandals have become legend. Luckner Cambrone, when minister of the defense and interior, reportedly built up a private business empire by exporting the blood of poor Haitians to the United States, delivering Haitian corpses to U.S. anatomical institutions, and smuggling heroin from Europe to the United States via Haiti.[37] The minister of trade and industry was dismissed after a postage stamp fraud of $2 million in 1975 and the minister of public works allegedly left after he refused in 1976 to open the vaults of his ministry to plunder.[38]

But even without corruption, the government's policies seemed ill-designed for the nation's massive problems of rural poverty. While 80–90 percent of the population is rural, 83 percent of government expenditures are in Port-au-Prince, the nation's capital, and agricultural expenditures never exceeded 7–10 percent of the budget.[39]

In the northwest and in the Artibonite valley, extensive seizures of peasant land by the *Tonton Macoutes,* loyal to Duvalier, continue to terrorize and impoverish the population. Commenting on this practice, the Inter-American Foundation's 1979 Report concludes: "Since renters and sharecroppers have no security on the land they work, investment is discouraged. Instead they tend to overwork the land to produce a maximum yearly harvest, often at the cost of environmental damage. . . . Facing the very real possibility of appropriation of their land by a *gros negre,* farmers are also discouraged from investing in their land and encouraged to overwork it. There are substantiated reports of land-grabs, of judges bribed to issue competing land titles, of extortion by locally powerful quasi-governmental authorities."

The report continues, "It becomes obvious why changes in the physical infrastructure—roads, irrigation systems, markets—will not benefit peasants if they remain in their present condition of dependency. Indeed, infrastructural change may actually lead to their further underdevelopment. Any improvements to the land itself,

or in access to the land, may well only pave the way for land grab-
bing by the relatively wealthy under a cloak of legality and result in
peasant disenfranchisement from the land."[40]

Nevertheless, Haiti remained a favorite among international aid
organizations. Haiti received $142 million in international aid in
1981.[41] That gave it the highest per capita assistance in the Western
Hemisphere. Sixty percent of Haiti's development budget, or $85
million in 1981, was provided by external sources: 50 percent
through multilateral sources (primarily the UN, World Bank, and the
Inter-American Development Bank), and the remainder bilaterally
with the United States in the lead, followed by France, West Germany, and Canada. In addition, more than 130 nongovernmental
organizations provided an estimated $20 million.[42]

Indeed, in the early 1980s virtually all development agents who
had been in Haiti over a year were completely cynical, with most
concluding that corruption was so extensive that the Haitian people
would be better off if all international agencies abandoned Haiti. One
U.S. official in Haiti complained, "No one knows why we are here,
what our interest is or what we are trying to achieve. By maintaining
a large mission here we are just condoning the practices of the Duvalier government."[43]

Many development experts argued that "more compulsive giving" is not what Haiti needed. The country cannot absorb it and
most is wasted. Indeed most international development agents who
have worked in Haiti recount endless stories of money and goods
simply disappearing.[44] Massive amounts of "Food for Peace" sent
to Haiti in bags marked "Not for Sale" are found for sale in Haitian
markets throughout the country. Much of the food which is not
appropriated for sale is used in "Food for Work" programs, which
many claim are used by wealthy landowners for projects to benefit
them, increase the dependency of the peasants, and work to under-
cut prices and incentives to produce for small agriculturalists.

At the end of 1980, after drifting into a foreign exchange crisis,
Haiti approached the IMF for a budget supplement. On December 5,
1980, IMF granted $22 million to Haiti. Shortly thereafter $20 million was withdrawn from the government of Haiti's account.[45] A
cable to then-U.S. Secretary of State, Alexander Haig, stated that
"about $4 million may have been diverted to the VSN," the *Volun-
taires de la Securité Nacionale,* the official name for the *Tonton
Macoutes.*[46] Many believed the other $16 million went into Duvalier's

personal accounts. IMF bluntly states, "The fund's staff (IMF) attributed excessive unbudgeted spending as the most important cause of Haiti's financial crises."[47] Still, Baby Doc's wife, Michelle Bennet Duvalier, reportedly drew a $100,000 monthly salary for her duties as "Mrs. President." Between 5 and 7 million dollars was spent on their wedding. Yet the U.S. and other international aid establishments felt compelled to continue helping. Even if only a small percentage reached the masses of the poor, they claim their suffering would be worse otherwise. A U.S. State Department cable asserted that if the above IMF funds were not granted, "The country would then have to live from hand to mouth. U.S. dollars, which constitute 25 to 40 percent of currency in Haiti, would disappear. Severe hardships would ensue."[48]

CORRUPTION AND REPRESSION

This remarkable corruption would be difficult to maintain without a repressive apparatus efficiently and effectively stifling dissent. When Jean-Claude Duvalier assumed power in 1971, there were no institutions with even the slightest degree of autonomy from the state. The legislature rubber-stamped the president's bills; the press dared not utter a word of criticism and opposition political groups and labor unions had been banned and mercilessly destroyed. Nevertheless, the worst abuses of Papa Doc appeared to have been curtailed. There were no longer corpses of the regime's opponents strapped to chairs lining the road to the airport, nor were there public executions. In 1977, the daytime abuses of the *Tonton Macoutes* were banned from the streets of the capital of Port-au-Prince. Also in 1977, Haiti ratified the Inter-American Convention on Human Rights. At the beginning of 1978, Haiti invited the Organization of American States to conduct a visit *in loco* to examine human rights conditions. Finally in February 1979 opposition political parties were formed.[49]

Yet terror and repression persisted. In 1975 Ezechiel Abelard of Radio Metropole was arrested. No charges were ever brought against him. He died in prison a year after his arrest. In 1976, the body of Gasner Raymond, a reporter for the Port-au-Prince weekly, *Le Petit Samedi Soir,* was found by the side of a road. Most blamed the government for his death.[50]

Absolutely no constitutional or procedural protections were available to anyone accused of political offenses defined by a variety of security laws. For example, Bernier Pierre returned to visit his homeland after a 12-year absence. At the completion of his visit, just as he was ready to board the airplane to leave Haiti, authorities pulled him out of the line of passengers and detained him. The government claimed he was inciting a revolt, although they lodged no formal charges. He was given no opportunity to contact either a lawyer or his family. The transferred him to the National Penitentiary, where he was treated as convicted and again denied a lawyer. After long, repeated interrogations, the government finally informed him that all his privileges to be in the country had been revoked and he was deported without benefit of appeal. The government offered no explanation.[51]

In 1973, two years after Jean-Claude assumed power, Amnesty International found "Haiti's prisons are still filled with people who have spent many years in detention without ever being charged or brought to trial. . . . The variety of torture to which the detainee is subjected is incredible: clubbing to death, maiming of the genitals, food deprivations to the point of starvation, and the insertion of red-hot pokers into the back passage. . . . In fact, these prisons are death traps . . . [and] find a parallel with the Nazi concentration camps of the past but have no present day equivalent. . . . More than once [Duvalier] informed the press that there were no political prisoners in Haiti."[52]

The U.S. Senate Appropriations Committee concluded in 1974 that although "the grim visible terror of François Duvalier's regime may have subsided, it seems that autocratic rule characterized by an unflinching willingness to suppress people has not."[53] And in 1977, Amnesty International stated, "Political prisoners are still rarely brought to trial. . . . Haiti's prisons have one of the world's highest mortality rates among detainees."[54] And in 1978, "The apparatus of repression established under François Duvalier remains in place under Jean-Claude Duvalier."[55]

The O.A.S. Commission that Duvalier had invited was hardly more flattering. They stated flatly that the "intention of liberalization has not been carried out." During 1975 and 1976, "It has in fact been proven that numerous people died in summary executions or during their stay in prison, or because of lack of medical care. It should nonetheless be observed that there has been a notable improvement as regards this right."[56]

But since 1979, human rights had been repressed considerably. A press law was passed making it a crime to insult the President for Life, his mother, the memory of his father, or Haitian culture. After the appearance of two creole plays which indirectly criticized the government, the government required screening of all films and plays.[57] In November 1980, the government swept away all human rights activists and independent journalists. Many were exiled, some disappeared, and in August 1981 others were sentenced to 15 years hard labor.[58]

On August 25, 1981, the government of Haiti tried and convicted twenty-six individuals charged with arson and plotting against the internal security of the state. About one half the defendants were among those arrested in November 1980. The trial was conducted without any pretence of due process. The defendants were denied access to lawyers before the trial. None had been informed of the charges and while in detention, a number of defendants were harassed, beaten, and intimidated. After considerable international outrage, the defendants were retried and reconvicted.[59]

In late 1982 and early 1983, the Haitian government began a campaign of intimidation against the Catholic Church. A Catholic lay worker, Gerard Duclerville, was arrested just after Christmas of 1982. He was tortured and released after two and a half months' imprisonment, a few weeks before the Pope's visit to Haiti.[60]

In February 1984, Haiti conducted elections for the national legislature. Throughout the six months prior to the election the leader of the best known opposition party, Sylvio Claude of the Haitian Christian Democratic Party, was detained and beaten. Gregorie Eugene, the head of the only other opposition party had been exiled and the Haitian government refused to allow him back into the country before the elections. Of those candidates known to knowledgeable observers, none was considered opposed to or even independent of the Duvalier government.[61] Several days after the elections, the U.S. ambassador was quoted as saying they were not democratic.[62]

A few months later, on May 7 and 8, 1984, the Haitian government decreed that all opposition parties were to be banned.[63] One week later the U.S. government certified that Haiti was making a concerted and significant effort to improve the human rights situation there.[64]

In Haiti repression was not limited to those who engage in organized opposition to the government. "Political prisoners" included those who offend the government in any way. One ex-political prisoner states simply: "Politics and everyday life in Haiti cannot be separated. A man can casually say that he is hungry and that can be misconstrued to mean he is criticizing the governmental mismanagement of funds, therefore leading to his arrest."[65] Jeanton Colas, a major designer of urban development projects in Haiti, was arrested and told during his interrogation that his refusal to support overtly the Duvalier government made him suspect. Fritzer Sidney and Prosper Saint-Louis were arrested for having sung a song with anti-government connotations. Both were held incommunicado and severely beaten. Saint-Louis was detained in prison for four months without the opportunity to inform his paralyzed wife and four children that he was still alive.[66]

In some cases, simply having been abroad, regardless of one's activities within or outside of Haiti, had been sufficient to elicit persecution. Sylvio Romet first fled Haiti in 1967, to Nassau where he worked for the health department for ten years. He returned to Haiti in 1977 to visit his seriously ill brother—after being assured by the Haitian Consul that he would be safe. Upon arriving at the Port-au-Prince airport, a Haitian immigration official found his name in a book and arrested him. While in custody the *Tonton Macoutes* forced him to stand for four days in a 2-by-3 cell. He was so severely beaten that he suffered brain damage. He now stutters and lisps when he talks. He was so thirsty after being consistently refused water that he drank his own urine. Finally, he bought his freedom by giving a prison guard $900 he had sewn into the waistband of his shorts. The guard also smuggled him out of the country. Haitian immigration officials confiscated his suitcase, which contained between three and four thousand dollars that other Haitians asked him to deliver to families they left behind.[67]

The experiences of Merlien Mezius were similar: "I flew back to Haiti on Monday, February 19, 1977, and was immediately arrested at the airport. They immediately confiscated the $1,700 that I had in my wallet for my mother's operation. . . . Then at 6 p.m., after beating me, they took me to a prison on the outskirts of Port-au-Prince that I recognized as Fort Dimanche. At Fort Dimanche, they beat me twice daily on a regular basis, every morning and evening. . . . For six days the beatings were the same; they would come and punch and kick me all over, and hit me with a club. . . . I lost six teeth as a result of these beatings and began to lose consciousness more and more frequently. On Thursday morning just before they entered our cell to beat us, I heard one of the guards say to the other, 'Some of the people here are from Miami, and one is from the Bahamas. They are political, they are against Duvalier and we have to kill them.' "[68]

A former member of the infamous security forces, the *Tonton Macoutes*, stated, "Publicly, Jean-Claude Duvalier said that people who are returned to Haiti. . . .would be allowed to return to their homes without any problem. But . . . he simultaneously gave orders in secret to the military and the *Macoutes* that returning deportees from the United States and other countries should always be arrested. Everyone who leaves illegally and then returns is put in jail. The order is still standing and has never been revoked."[69] Another former *Tonton Macoute* stated that "returnees received 'especially brutal treatment,' being constantly beaten about the head and kept tied up in jail cells."[70]

Edouard Jean Louis was an archivist in the Bureau of the Grand Quartier-General of the Haitian army from 1971 to 1975. In that position he filed confidential documents from leaders of the Security Forces including Luc Desir, Chief of the Secret Police. He stated that: "It was in this capacity that I was able to read a message concerning a group of Haitians deported from the United States and arriving in Haiti labeled as Communists. This message contained the order to send them to Fort Dimanche to be executed and it was signed by Luc Desir."[71]

Daniel Voltaire, a former member of the *Tonton Macoutes*, stated: "Once we were given this order, we knew that this was the way to get promoted, generally further our careers, and to get cash bonuses. If you denounced someone to your superiors or to the Service Detective you often get promotions and money because this means that you are doing your job well. Other times, if you denounce or arrest people like these returnees, you will also get sent back to school or to a military academy because you have acted like a real Duvalierist, a real supporter of the President for Life. So denouncing and arresting returnees or people trying to leave Haiti became a good way to get good promotions, money and career advancement. This was done by many troops in the Presidential Guard and the Leopards as well as the Service Detective because we were told that these people had insulted the President for Life and Haiti, that they were spies, and they are *camoquins* or traitors."[72]

When the interdiction policy initiated by the Reagan administration began in Fall 1981, the Duvalier government assured the United States that no Haitian returned to Haiti by the United States would be persecuted. The United States attempted to follow up on this promise by interviewing returnees. They would drive out to a village in a large four wheel drive vehicle, pull up to the local police station and ask the authorities the whereabouts of particular individuals who had been returned. Frequently the authorities would accompany the U.S. official and interpreter to the individual's home and remain for the duration of the interview. While many individuals could not be found, those who were interviewed all claimed that they had not been persecuted.

In Spring 1983 this author had the opportunity to interview one of the same individuals who had been interviewed by a U.S. official. The story he told me was somewhat different. He had been on the first boat to be intercepted by the U.S. Coast Guard. When he and the others were returned to Haiti, they were met by the Haitian government, the U.S. Ambassador to Haiti, and the international press. The U.S. government reported that after a screening by the Red Cross, the individuals were directly returned to their villages. The person I interviewed said that before returning to their villages they were taken to the security prison located underneath and behind the presidential palace. There they were detained and interrogated by Haitian government authorities who informed them that if the U.S. Ambassador had not personally met them, the Haitian government would have imprisoned, tortured, and eventually killed them.

THE ROOTS OF EMIGRATION

The underdevelopment of Haiti and the consequent propensity for emigration has its roots in the pyrrhic victory of the Haitian revolution. The economy was devastated. The state then came to assume the single purpose of providing those in power with a substitute for the income and wealth lost with the landed estates. But migration was slight until the growth of cane production in Cuba and the Dominican Republic at the beginning of this century. Periodically, with economic downturns in these countries, the pulls turned into pushes and Haitians were blamed for the country's ills, shabbily treated, expelled, and even massacred. Meanwhile, corruption and repression were raised to new heights by the Duvalier regimes. Development and development aid benefited the elite at the expense of the potential improvement of the vast majority. In a tragic paradox, more international aid may have produced more misery and migration as it paved the way for landgrabbing and other forms of increased exploitation.

To support these activities the government quickly and violently repressed any opposition, real or imagined. The Haitian migrants were truly both economic and political refugees. Merchants of smuggling seized the opportunity. Until the beginning of the 1981 U.S. interdiction policy, cash, property, or credit would easily transport any Haitian to the Bahamas or the United States. And in this, too, the government profited. Besides exporting their un- or underemployed and receiving subsequent remittances, they retained a share of the smuggling profits through kickbacks.

Under intense pressure from the United States, the Haitian government agreed in 1981 to cooperate with the United States in interdicting Haitian boats still in Haitian territorial waters. Even this cooperation was reached only with private promises of further U.S. support to the Duvalier government. Given the structure of underdevelopment and its maintenance and furtherance by Duvalier, migration is unlikely to subside altogether. At every point profits were to be made—profits in transport, profits from the Haitians' low wages in the receiving economies, profits in their remittances. When the receiving economies falter or more Haitians arrive than can be easily absorbed, the welcome turns to rejection. The Haitians are batted back and forth, eking out a bare subsistence while searching for freedom, only partially delivered by their revolution.

POSTSCRIPT

At 3:46 A.M., on February 7, 1986, Jean Claude Duvalier and his wife took off from Port-au-Prince, Haiti, in a U.S. Air Force C-141 military transport plane. The plane was bound for France where Duvalier and his family themselves sought refuge, thereby ending 29 years of patrimonial rule. Later that morning, a military-civilian junta, dominated by allies of the Duvaliers, assumed control while people joyfully danced in the streets. Three days later, the U.S.

government announced that the new Haitian regime would continue cooperating with the United States in deterring departure of Haitian boat people bound for U.S. shores. Weeks later, unrest returned to Haiti as discontent with the junta emerged and no group proved capable of establishing order. Haiti's long term underdevelopment created the conditions for massive emigration. The Duvalier regimes exacerbated those conditions and established the mechanisms for that migration. They also successfully eliminated all political alternatives to themselves, thus assuring the instability that followed their political demise.

NOTES

1. There are numerous detailed accounts of Haitian history in English. For the revolutionary period, the best is C.L.R. James, *The Black Jacobins* (New York: Vintage, 1963). Another classic account is James Leyburn, *The Haitian People* (New Haven: Yale Univ. Press, 1966).

2. The best discussion of the American occupation of Haiti and the period immediately preceding it is Hans Schmidt, *The United States Occupation of Haiti, 1915-1934* (New Brunswick: Rutgers Univ. Press, 1971).

3. Shem Grasmuck, "Migration within the periphery: Haitian labor in the Dominican sugar and coffee industries," *International Migration Review* 16 (Summer 1982):368.

4. Ibid.

5. Glenn Perusek, "Haitian emigration in the early twentieth century" *International Migration Review*, 18 (Spring 1984), p. 12.

6. Ibid.

7. Grasmuck, "Migration within the periphery," p. 369.

8. Ibid., p. 368.

9. Dawn Marshall, *The Haitian Problem: Illegal Migration to the Bahamas* (Mona: University of the West Indies, ISER, 1979), p. xvii.

10. Ibid., p. 130.

11. Ibid., p. 132.

12. Jo Thomas, "Sadly, the marooned Haitians return home," The New York *Times*, November 17, 1980.

13. Francis Ficklin, "Haitians in New York: Some notes and observations" (Paper presented to the Applied Anthropology Colloquium, Columbia University, April 1980).

14. Susan Buchanan, "Scattered seeds: The meaning of migration for Haitians in New York City" (Ph.D. diss., New York Univ., 1980).

15. Nina Glick, "The formation of a Haitian ethnic group" (Ph.D. diss., Columbia Univ., 1978).

16. Michel Laguerre, *American Odyssey: Haitians in New York City* (Ithaca: Cornell Univ. Press, 1984), p. 31.

17. Alex Stepick, "Haitian boat people: A study in the conflicting forces shaping U.S. refugee policy," *Law and Contemporary Problems: Duke University Law Journal* 45 (1982), p. 178.

18. Ibid., pp. 178–79.

19. Alex Stepick, *Haitian Refugees in the United States* (London and New York: Minority Rights Group, 1982), p. 11.

20. Ibid.

21. Ibid.

22. Ibid.

23. Gregory Jaynes, "33 Haitians drown as boat capsizes off Florida," The New York *Times,* October 27, 1981.

24. Stepick, "Haitian boat people," pp. 180–81.

25. Mats Lundahl, *Peasants and Poverty: A Study of Haiti* (New York: St. Martin's Press, 1979), p. 357.

26. Statistics on Haiti are notoriously unreliable. The best statistics come from the World Bank and the United States Agency for International Development (USAID). Figures are from USAID Country Development Strategy Statement (FY 1984), prepared by the A.I.D. Field Mission, March 1982.

27. Lundahl, *Peasants and Poverty,* p. 178.

28. Christian A. Girault, *Le Commerce du Cafe en Haiti: Habitants, Speculateurs et Exportateurs* (Paris: Editions du Centre National de la Recherche Scientifique, n.d.), pp. 64–65.

29. Robert Maguire, *Bottom-up Development in Haiti* (Rosslyn, VA: Inter-American Foundation, 1979).

30. Vito Tanzni, "Export taxation in developing countries: Taxation of coffee," *Social and Economic Studies* 25 (March 1976), pp. 66–75.

31. All references in this paragraph from "Opportunities for industrial investment in Haiti" (Washington, D.C.: Inter-American Development Bank, 1979), pp. iii–iv and 278.

32. USAID Country Development Strategy Statement, p. 1.

33. Ibid.

34. These allegations are persistent throughout the international community, although the estimates vary from 33 to over 50 percent. In the beginning of the 1980s, the U.S. Embassy and the International Monetary Fund stepped up efforts to control the process; see USAID Country Development Strategy Statement. The figure here is from Roslyn D. Roberts, "Impediments to economic and social development in Haiti" (Congressional Research Service, The Library of Congress, Washington, D.C., 19 June 1978), p. 18.

36. Ibid.

37. Lundahl, *Peasants and Poverty.*

38. Ibid., p. 345.

39. Maguire, *Bottom-up Development,* p. 23.

40. Ibid., p. 15.

41. USAID Country Development Strategy Statement, p. 2.

42. Ibid., p. 10.

43. Quoted in Jack Anderson, "Baby Doc lives up to Papa's standards," Washington *Post,* March 23, 1981.

44. Andy Rosenblatt, "Haitian government's corruption frustrates development efforts," Miami *Herald,* December 20, 1982.

45. Jack Anderson, "Keeping Baby Doc on the dole," Washington *Post,* March 25, 1981.

46. Quoted in Jack Anderson, "The aid fiasco in Haiti," Washington *Post,* March 24, 1981.

47. Anderson, "The aid fiasco in Haiti."

48. Ibid.

49. Lawyers Committee For International Human Rights, "Violations of human rights in Haiti" (New York: LCIHR, June 1980).

50. Ibid.

51. Ibid.

52. Amnesty International, *Amnesty International Report: 1973* (London: Amnesty International, 1973), p. 86.

53. Senator Edward W. Brooke, "Review of factors affecting U.S. diplomatic and assistance relations with Haiti" (Committee on Appropriations, U.S. Senate, November 15, 1977).

54. Amnesty International, *Amnesty International Report: 1977* (London: Amnesty International, 1977), p. 95.

55. Amnesty International, *Amnesty International Report: 1978* (London: Amnesty International, 1978), p. 76.

56. International Commission on Human Rights, "Report on the situation of human rights in Haiti" (Washington, D.C.: Organization of American States, December 13, 1979).

57. Lawyers Committee for International Human Rights, June 1980.

58. Lawyers Committee for International Human Rights, "Violations of human rights in Haiti, November 1980" (New York: LCIHR, December 1980).

59. Lawyers Committee for International Human Rights, "Report on the August 1981 trial and November 1981 appeal of 26 political defendants in Haiti" (New York: LCIHR, March 1982).

60. America's Watch and Lawyers Committee for International Human Rights, "Election 1984, Duvalier style: A report on human rights in Haiti based on a mission of inquiry" (New York: LCIHR, March 1984).

61. Raymond Joseph, "Coming Haitian elections are just for show," *Wall Street Journal,* February 10, 1984.

62. "Haiti: First you drink your puffer fish," *The Economist,* February 18, 1984.

63. "Haiti bans all political activity," New York *Times,* May 11, 1984.

64. "Political parties banned by Duvalier," Miami *Herald,* May 15, 1984.

65. Lawyers Committee for International Human Rights, June 1980, p. 12.

66. Ibid., pp. 15–16.

67. Ibid., p. 41.

68. Ibid., p. 41–42.

69. *Haitian Refugee Center vs. Benjamin Civiletti,* 503 F. supp. 442 (S.D. FL. 1980), p. 532.

70. Ibid.

71. Ibid., p. 533.

72. Ibid., p. 532.

The Dominican Exodus:
Origins, Problems, Solutions

David B. Bray

Dominicans are the late bloomers of the Caribbean migration legions. Jamaicans and other West Indians have been migrating to work on foreign shores since shortly after the end of slavery in the 1830s. Puerto Ricans began migrating to the United States in significant numbers shortly after the United States claimed the island as a prize of war in 1898, and there were substantial Cuban settlements in southern Florida long before the socialist transformation and accompanying migrant/refugee flows after 1959. The Dominican Republic, however, was an historically underpopulated island that was actually the recipient of major international migratory flows to work in the sugar industry at the turn of the 20th century.[1] From 1929 to 1961 it was held in a social and political insularity by the dictatorship of Rafael Leonidas Trujillo, whose hold over his people extended to tight control on exit visas for international travel.

It was not until 1961, with the assassination of Trujillo, that Dominican migration began in significant numbers. Although political events such as coups, revolutions, and elections have clearly been important stimulating factors in Dominican migration, it is commonly held that economic forces have been paramount in maintaining the flow over the last 20 years. From 1961 to 1981, 255,578 Dominicans are on record as having legally migrated to the United States. (See Table 9.1.) The kinship and friendship ties established by this migratory flow are evident in the figures on "temporary visitors"

Table 9.1: Dominican Migration to the United States, 1961–1981

Year	Number of Immigrants	Year	Number of Immigrants
1953–1960	922 (yearly average)	1971	12,624
1961	3,045	1972	10,670
1962	4,603	1973	13,858
1963	10,683	1974	15,680
1964	7,537	1975	14,066
1965	9,504	1976	15,088*
1966	16,503	1977	11,655
1967	11,514	1978	19,458
1968	9,250	1979	17,519
1969	10,670	1980	12,624
1970	10,807	1981	18,220

*1976 includes an additional three months for a total of 15 months, because the INS changed its enumeration period that year.

Source: Immigration and Naturalizaton Service, *Annual Report,* 1954–1981.

admitted from the Dominican Republic, a number that regularly topped 100,000 during the 1970s.[2] A percentage of these temporary visitors overstay their visas each year, and some observers suggest that there may be as many illegal Dominicans as legal ones in this country. Finally, allowing for the natural increase of the immigrant population, a reasonable guess would put the total number of Dominicans living in the United States in the 500–600 thousand range, making them the third largest Hispanic group in the United States. (Dominican diplomats and newspapers regularly claim over one million Dominicans in the United States, but there appears to be no basis for such a figure.)

The majority of Dominican migrants go to New York City and environs, with the percentage rising in recent years. In 1970, 70 percent of the entrants declared New York as their destination. In 1979, 79.9 percent did so. Puerto Rico has long been the second most popular destination, although the percentage going there has been dropping: from 20.6 percent in 1970 to 10.7 percent in 1979. Increasing numbers of Dominicans have been spreading into other northeastern industrial cities. There are now substantial Dominican communities in Connecticut, Rhode Island, and Massachusetts.

As the volume of Dominican migration has grown, the amount of academic attention it has received has grown correspondingly. Most of the literature has focused on the socioeconomic origins of the migrants, the political and economic forces that created and reproduced the migratory streams, and the nature of Dominican migrant adaptation in the United States. Virtually no Dominican social scientist has made international migration a focus of his or her concern, although they have been both active and acute in their analyses of other aspects of Dominican society; U.S. social scientists, on the other hand, have barely concerned themselves with any other topic in recent years. Why the great disparity in research interests? In the United States, Dominican migration is considered both an academic and a public policy "problem," while in the Dominican Republic international migration is considered a "solution" to a whole set of other "problems."

ORIGINS AND PROCESSES

The first studies of Dominican migration emphasized the rural origins of international migrants, but the evidence from more recent studies strongly indicates that the urban middle sectors constitute the predominant element in the migratory flows. Ugalde, Bean, and Cardenas, drawing on a survey of 25,000 households, concluded that Dominican migration is predominantly an urban and middle-class phenomenon, an assertion that other recent studies have largely confirmed.[3] These conclusions immediately raise two questions: "Why not the rural and urban poor?" and "Why the middle sectors?" who are, by definition, not especially desperate in their present circumstances.

The first question is the more easily answered. The rural and urban poor unquestionably have an intense desire to migrate to the United States. Karl Polanyi, writing on the birth of industrialism and rural/urban migration in late 18th century England, noted that "the distant rumor of large wages made the poor dissatisfied with those which agriculture could afford."[4] It is precisely such "distant rumors of large wages" as well as concrete evidence from return migrants that pervade the Dominican Republic and make migration a widespread ambition. But there are major obstacles in the way of the poor who want to migrate. First is the fact that the Dominican Republic is an island. It is far more difficult to leave an island and enter the mainland illegally than it is to walk across a land border, such as that separating Mexico from the United States. In 1981 it cost 2-3 thousand pesos to be outfitted with falsified documents and/or to be smuggled out of the country.[5] It is difficult for the rural and urban poor to amass or even borrow such sums.

The U.S. Embassy also stands as a stern gatekeeper for those who would try to enter as residents or even tourists. Since the passage of the Immigration and Naturalization Act of 1965, with its emphasis on family reunification, it is necessary to have a close relative who is already a legal resident or citizen in order to enter. Even applicants for tourist visas are closely scrutinized for evidence that they might be candidates to overstay their visas, so documentation of substantial economic holdings in the Dominican Republic must be produced. These financial and legal obstacles are sufficiently imposing that they appear to limit severely the ability of the poor to fulfill their migratory ambitions.

The question of "why the middle sectors?" is more complex and is rooted in the political economy of the Dominican Republic over the last two decades, in what can be called a "middle-class bottleneck."[6] In the Dominican Republic the expansion and consolidation of middle-sector migration occurred during the same period as a significant expansion of the middle sectors themselves, raising a variety of questions about the relationship between international migration and class formation. It is frequently pointed out, for the Dominican Republic and elsewhere, that export agriculture creates proletarianized masses and an elite agro/export sector; that import substitution industrialization creates industrial capitalists and an urban manufacturing proletariat (with both influencing rural/urban migration); and more recently, that export-led industrialization "feminizes" the manufacturing proletariat.[7] However, the impact of these development strategies—along with growing state participation in the economy—on the middle sectors, as well as their impact on international migration, have been less noted, particularly for the countries of the Caribbean Basin. It is therefore important to examine the impact of each of these development strategies—export agriculture, import substitution industrialization, and export industrialization—on the middle sectors and international migration.

Export Agriculture

From 1945 to 1961 export agriculture, primarily sugar, coffee, and cacao, experienced substantial growth, their first since the crash of 1929. Sugar exports more than doubled, while the largest plantations became the property of dictator Rafael Leonidas Trujillo (1930–1961) and his close associates. Coffee and cacao, on the other hand, were rooted in smallholder agriculture and benefited an expanding rural petty bourgeoisie.[8] Export earnings in coffee and cacao were 7–8 times higher by the mid 1950s than they had been at the close of World War II. This period of high prices set off a renewed process of class polarization in the rural Dominican Republic, particularly in the northern valley of the Cibao. One study of a cacao-producing area in the Cibao demonstrated the extent of this differentiation and its impact on the rural middle sectors and international migration. Historical and ethnographic research in this area revealed that the land tenure situation had evolved from a more equitable one at the end of World War II to a situation where, by 1980, 28.9 percent of the households owned 87.2 percent of the land.[9] This privileged group benefited from export agriculture; some became members of the national bourgeoisie, the owners of export houses, and high government officials. The majority of the large landholders, however, became incorporated into the urban middle class as professionals, for whom inherited land is just one source of income.

The majority of the households in this area, however, have not been so fortunate. Over 50 percent have become laborers or have been reduced to a landholding too small to support the family. Migration from this group has been massive. The fragmentation of landholdings through inheritance and the acceleration of capitalist differentiation after World War II created a large supply of cheap wage labor that permitted the emerging petty bourgeois sectors to send most of their children away to get an education, while, at the same time, a percentage of the constantly generated mass of surplus labor was steadily displaced into urban formal sectors. However, from this area, as from most other areas of the Dominican Republic, a certain percentage of these former rural *agricultors* were incorporated into international migratory flows, although the degree of incorporation was heavily influenced by their class of origin. From 1945 to 1980 only 4 percent of all the migrants from the proletariat and semiproletariat of this area were in the United States. However, 14.2 percent from the middle class had emigrated.[10]

Urban residence in the Dominican Republic preceded international migration for nearly all migrants from all classes. Another study of a rural area in the Sierra, west of the second largest city, Santiago, also showed that the expansion of coffee cultivation after World War II activated a process of class differentiation. For the beneficiaries of this expansion, international migration became a strategy whereby they could avoid the fragmenting pressures of inheritance and soil erosion and maintain middle-sector status. The conclusion of this study, therefore, was that "[migration] should be interpreted as a product of local economic development rather than as a symptom of overall rural stagnation."[11]

Thus, the rural petty bourgeoisie has at the same time the greatest opportunity to become incorporated into the urban middle sectors of the Dominican Republic and the highest propensity for international migration. Export agriculture both helps to create a middle sector and limits its further expansion. As we shall see, however, it is members of the urban-born middle sectors who migrate internationally at even higher rates.

Import Substitution and Export-Oriented Industrialization

The expansion of import substitution industrialization in the Dominican Republic was delayed beyond that of other Caribbean basin countries by the five years of political turmoil and revolution that followed Trujillo's assassination in 1961. There had been some development of import substitution in the 1950s, as well as an expansion of the middle sectors in the capital city of Santo Domingo, but the unrest that followed Trujillo's fall led to widespread economic stagnation and a virtual halt to new private sector investments. When elements of the old Trujillo elite tried to regain power in 1965, the "April Revolution" broke out as a response by the Santo Domingo middle sectors, in alliance with the urban masses, to the threatened reassertion of traditional oligarchic economic and political domination.[12]

The insurrection was stalled by an invading force of 23,000 U.S. Marines who encircled the revolutionaries in a middle-class neighborhood of Santo Domingo.[13] In November 1965 the revolutionaries agreed to OAS terms and laid down their arms. U.S.-sponsored elections were held the following spring, and voters elected Joaquín Balaguer who, despite his closeness with Trujillo, promised peace and stability to the battered Dominican people. Balaguer was able to shape a coalition of the old Trujillo elite and other groups who united behind a program that included political and economic repression of the working classes, accelerated expansion of foreign investment, and the creation of an urban manufacturing stratum. His policies fostered the progressive integration of an expanded and deradicalized middle class into capitalist expansion and allowed those who could not be incorporated, due to the "middle-class bottleneck," to migrate to the United States. In addition, radical elements of the working and middle class were implicitly offered the choices of migration or "disappearance." An estimated 650 people were killed or "disappeared" during 1966–1970.[14]

Balaguer's industrialization policies more than doubled the manufacturing labor force from 1968 to 1977 (20,000 to 47,562), and it has been estimated that 348 manufacturing enterprises were eventually covered by new industrial incentive legislation.[15] Of the new manufacturing jobs created, 37 percent were in "free trade zones," areas set up specifically to shelter, under various tax and tariff provisions, industries manufacturing for export. The overall growth rate of the economy rose to over 10 percent during 1969–1974.[16] During this period new houses, apartment blocks, restaurants and movie houses sprang up throughout Santo Domingo, while new car sales boomed as the middle sectors underwent their most dynamic expansion in Dominican history.[17]

But even during the boom in middle-class lifestyles and the expansion of manufacturing employment, international migration continued at significant levels. From 1968 to 1972, during the height of economic expansion, international migration averaged 10,804 annually. As time wore on, however, migration steadily rose, averaging over 15,000 annually during 1973–1981, a more than 40 percent rise.[18] The bulk of this migration originated primarily in the urban areas and, to a lesser extent, among the most prosperous rural classes, precisely those social classes that have been the primary beneficiaries of the economic expansion.

The existence of this middle-sector flow and the middle-class bottleneck that sustains it has been attributed to the failure of industrialization strategies to sustain growth (the economic growth rate declined dramatically after 1977), continued dependence on agricultural exports, corruption, and employment competition from a vast pool of under- and unemployed.[19] On this last point Grasmuck has argued that "it is not the unemployed themselves but the relatively skilled and educated whose wages and security are threatened by the existence of a large pool of reserve labor [who] choose to migrate."[20] She also identifies the phenomenon of middle-sector migration as one of the "paradoxes of uneven development. The Dominican Republic is one of the most developed of the Caribbean nations. Yet in the 1972-1976 period, it accounted for 7.9 percent of all America's migrants to the U.S."[21]

It has been suggested by Piore that such middle-sector migration is "transitional" to subsequently increasing numbers of poorer migrants migrating from the rural areas.[22] But such a transition does not appear to be taking place in the Dominican Republic. Instead, as Portes argued in the Mexican case, such middle-sector population movements appear to be an identifying feature of dependent capitalist development in particular countries.[23] Grasmuck has even argued that "it could well be the case that in the short run even expanded economic growth with redistribution will provoke further [middle-sector] outmigration by enabling more aspiring workers to finance such a move."[24] In summary, it can be said that the Dominican poor do not migrate internationally in large numbers because the existing economic and legal structures do not offer them the choice, while the middle sectors migrate because the prevailing structures offer them no other choice.

INTERNATIONAL MIGRATION: "PROBLEM" OR "SOLUTION"?

Why is international migration such a popular subject among U.S. researchers and so little heeded by Dominican researchers? One major reason appears to be that international migration to the United States is not considered a policy "problem" in the Dominican Republic. (On the other hand, a migration issue that is emphatically considered a problem is Haitian migration to the Dominican Republic.)[25] On the contrary, international migration is usually considered one of the few effective solutions to the deep economic problems that beset the country. Indeed, in a country where unemployment and underemployment are estimated at around 50 percent, where 11.8 percent of all farms have 78.6 percent of the land, where 70 percent of the population has been estimated to suffer some degree of malnourishment, and where the foreign debt is a staggering $2 billion, the phenomenon of hundreds of thousands of Dominicans who have departed in search of what is generally perceived to be economic improvement will not be on anybody's short list of major research priorities.[26]

For U.S. social scientists, on the other hand, Dominican migration is one aspect of a great public policy "problem" of the day: Hispanic migration to the United States, both legal and illegal. In the context of legislative debates over new and more restrictive immigration laws, accusations by labor unions that migrants lower wages and take away jobs from native workers, and a public perception that Latin American and Caribbean countries are releasing domestic economic pressure by shipping their impoverished masses to the United States, Dominican migration becomes a problem to be analyzed rather than a solution to be applauded.

The question of whether international migration is a problem or a solution is, of course, not only associated with Dominican migration but is also debated in the broader social science literature. Here we find intense disagreement over whether these migratory flows represent something positive—simply upward mobility writ on a global scale—or something negative—yet another example of the exploitation and extraction of surplus value from the underdeveloped countries. As one example, John Kenneth Galbraith has called international migration "the oldest action against poverty," while Dixon, Jonas, and McCaughan refer to it as "massive exploitation."[27]

Who is right? Can international migration best be characterized as a manifestation of entrepreneurial vigor or as exploitation? Should Dominican international migration be regarded as problematic or problem-solving? It is, in fact, both problem and solution; Dominican social scientists could benefit from a greater appreciation of its problematic aspects for their own society, while their U.S. counterparts would do well to acknowledge that, for however many structural contradictions it may reveal, international migration is a most effective solution for hundreds of thousands of individuals.

The common Dominican belief—expressed in official views and private conversations, that international migration to the United

States provides an effective way out of the economic constraints of an underdeveloped country—is based on a considerable amount of observational data, even if no formal studies have been undertaken. Virtually every Dominican knows both legal and illegal immigrants who have prospered in the United States and a growing number who are returning to live permanently in the Dominican Republic, having achieved their earnings goals.

Growing numbers of Dominican migrants have persisted in their endeavors, the "20-year veterans," and are now beginning to resettle in or near their home areas and substantially "retire" from the U.S. labor market in order to tend to their investments in the Dominican Republic. The story of Eugenio Castillo is the epitome of the contemporary Dominican migrant success story, a story of someone who went, if not quite from rags to riches, at least from a crumbling and precarious economic base to a seemingly stable and secure one.[28] Eugenio Castillo was 32 years old when he first went to the United States in 1963. Before that he had spent four years in the Dominican army (1949–1953) but had returned to the rural area of La Laguna to work along with his siblings and his father on the latter's 100 acres of cacao and subsistence crops. Eugenio married and established a household on his father's land. But when his father died in 1962, the division of land among 10 children fragmented a relatively prosperous multigenerational and multihousehold domestic economy into 10-acre plots. On 10 acres Eugenio could not reproduce the generally middle-sector lifestyle his father had enjoyed or provide opportunities for his own three children. He already had a cousin, also from La Laguna, who was living and working in the United States, so he decided to go there. He was, as he explained it, "looking for something better, a more prosperous future." It was comparatively easy to get legal residency in those days, and in 1963 he used some savings to buy a house in San Francisco de Macorís, the nearest large town, so his children could go to school there while he went off to the United States. His land in La Laguna was sharecropped by a brother-in-law.

Within two weeks of his arrival Eugenio got a job. His cousin helped him secure work as a janitor at a New Jersey golf club. He stayed at the golf club for two years, sending money back to his family and visiting once a year. In 1965 he switched to a job washing dishes at a restaurant, also in New Jersey. The pay was no better but he could work more hours, up to 10–12 hours a day, six days a week.

In 1966 he was able to bring his wife and three children to live with him. He was also able to rent his house in San Francisco de Macorís to an American evangelical missionary. He had thus positioned himself to maximize his savings. While maintaining only one household in New Jersey they had two, and later three and four incomes to pool, while the income from the farm property in La Laguna and the rental property in San Francisco de Macorís could be banked in its entirety.

In 1970 Eugenio returned to the Dominican Republic for six months, leaving his wife and children behind. His wife continued working, and his oldest son, then 18, started working in a factory. Eugenio returned to buy some land because, he said, "Cash isn't worth anything." He ended up buying, for 10,000 pesos, 25 acres of land already planted in cacao, less than 10 kilometers from San Francisco de Macorís. Eugenio then returned to work in New Jersey, the new acquisition being sharecropped by the same brother-in-law who was taking care of the land in La Laguna. He remained in the United States from 1971 to 1975, except for periodic short visits, continuing the dishwashing job. In 1973 his wife moved from domestic work to higher-paying factory work. During this period his second-oldest son also started working in a factory and later drove a taxi. In 1974 they bought an apartment in New Jersey, giving them urban real estate in two countries. They continued to save small amounts from their U.S. income and to bank all of their income from the now-expanded urban and rural properties in the Dominican Republic.

Since 1975 Eugenio has spent far longer periods of time each year in the Dominican Republic. In 1976 he returned by himself for 10 months and bought another piece of land, 60 acres of undeveloped pastureland on which he planned to raise cattle and coconuts. Also in 1976 he purchased a pick-up truck in the United States and had it shipped to the Dominican Republic. In 1977 he returned to the United States for only three months, this time washing dishes in a different restaurant. From 1978 on he has returned to the U.S. for only a few weeks or a few months at a time, to maintain his residency status and to work long enough to pay for the trip; in 1979 his wife moved back to San Francisco de Macorís permanently. Eugenio now spends most of his time in the Dominican Republic taking care of his farms, while two of his children, now married, live in the apartment in New Jersey and work there. Through 13 years of hard menial labor and several more years of intermittent labor, Eugenio, now 53, has apparently secured his financial future. He is a typical example of what labor economists call a "target earner": he had more or less definite earning goals in mind when he entered the U.S. labor market and was willing to work long hours in hot kitchens because there was an end to this phase of his working life in the foreseeable future. He was able to parlay his access to the U.S. job market and his slender resources in the Dominican Republic into an increase in landholdings of almost 1,000 percent (from ten acres to nearly 100), and has added as well an apartment in New Jersey and a pick-up truck. Eugenio's drive has produced a multinational household, with a consequent diffusion of both risks and investments. Each year Eugenio's story is replicated by other Dominicans. Eugenio's economic journey did not bring him "upward mobility" so much as it allowed him to reproduce the same status his father had; he even has almost exactly the same amount of land his father owned. Within the severely constrained Dominican opportunity structure, the U.S. labor market is one of the few opportunities for a person of modest means and education to reproduce a middle-sector lifestyle.

Even migrants who enter illegally and stay for a far shorter time can have spectacular success, at least in the short run. We see this in another example.

Rafael Peralta was the oldest of six children, the 19-year-old son of a farmer who owned outright about 20 acres of cacao and had a few smaller plots that he sharecropped for relatives. Rafael's father was able to provide a decent living for his family but Rafael, who had not finished high school, had no interest in farming and could not find any work in the Dominican Republic. Because of his father's economic holdings, and with the help of some more prosperous friends, Rafael was able to obtain a tourist visa to enter the United States, ostensibly to visit relatives. After entering the United States Rafael, as planned, overstayed his visitor's visa and went to work in an apparel factory.

Within a year the story came back via a relative that Rafael had already purchased a small apparel shop of his own for $10,000. The story was embellished with details such as that the shop was employing 16 people at wages of $8.50 an hour. It was said that he had accomplished this feat by working overtime, accumulating savings, and borrowing from a cousin. The central part of this story was indeed true. Rafael had purchased a small apparel operation, but he had only around 10 employees and the wages paid were below the minimum. It was, in fact, a "sweatshop," but seen from the Dominican perspective it was a symbol of success.

But there is a darker side to international migration in the Dominican Republic. One of the problems with migration as a "solution" is that the poorest Dominicans are as aware of the benefits that migration can bestow as Eugenio or Rafael, but for most of them it is beyond their reach; if they can raise the money, they must risk terrible dangers to get to the United States. It seems fair to say the rural and urban poor of the Dominican Republic are afflicted with "migration obsession."

The knowledge of the great disparity between Dominican and U.S. wage structures, even if the degree of that difference is greatly exaggerated, creates a great restlessness, particularly among youth in the Dominican Republic. Of many young people it is said, "Están loco para irse," (They are obsessed with the idea of going [to the United States]). They are constantly dreaming up schemes, looking for money; they are walking catalogues on the means of illegal entry. If they cannot hope to do it the easiest way, entering on a tourist visa, they are contemplating arranged marriages with a legal resident or citizen, or even being smuggled out of the country. It is usually the poorest Dominicans who opt for the smuggling alternative and who consequently face the greatest danger. It is not known how many are smuggled out of the country each year, but journalistic evidence suggests that it is widespread. Small launches apparently leave seveal times a week from the eastern coast to cross the Mona Channel to Puerto Rico.[29] Dominican newspapers carry accounts regularly of the police detaining launches full of Dominican "boat people" poised to cross the channel. One well-known organizer of such trips has been arrested four times and released on bail each time.[30]

There are frequent reports of capsizings and drownings in the Mona Channel, but little evidence beyond the occasional body of someone who was known to be planning to go the U.S. washing up on the shore. The nature of the risks run by illegal immigrants who are smuggled out was made disastrously clear in the 1980 Regina Express tragedy.

On September 5, 1980, Dominicans awoke to read in their morning pewspapers just how badly some of their fellow citizens wanted to leave their country. The day before, Dominican port police on the docks of Santo Domingo became suspicious of activities on the Regina Express, a Panamanian-registered cargo ship that plied the waters between Santo Domingo and Miami every 15 days carrying agricultural products to Miami and assorted goods back to Santo Domingo. The officials were about to leave the ship, having found nothing, when they heard a muffled banging noise coming from inside one of the ballast tanks. They ordered the crew to open the narrow access door to the ballast tanks. The crew at first said they couldn't, that it would flood the decks. When the police insisted and the door was opened, they found to their horror 34 people crammed into the tank, 22 of them already drowned. Apparently when the crew saw the guards coming aboard they hustled their illegal human cargo into the ballast tanks for hiding. Then—whether accidentally or on purpose has never been established—someone opened the ballast tanks and let the seawater in.[31]

The tragedy of the Regina Express is a powerful argument that Dominicans should not be complacent about international migration. Migration does indeed provide an answer for significant numbers, but it raises expectations and desires among the Dominican masses that undermine national sovereignty and pride, and forces Dominicans to risk their lives to leave the island.

There are also other reasons why international migration, however much it helps individuals, is not a positive phenomenon for the development of the Dominican economy. With migration the Dominican Republic loses the years of educational training it has invested in each migrant. Further, there is considerable evidence that migrant investments focus on rural and urban real estate and small retailing, thus duplicating existing economic capacity rather than investing in new job-creating enterprises.

THE U.S. PERSPECTIVE

Dominican migration has been seen as problematic because it involves a process of "proletarianization,"[32] that is, independent farmers or small shopkeepers become incorporated into the U.S. economy as wage-laborers in low-paid, menial, repetitive jobs, usually in the service sector or small-scale manufacturing enterprise, particularly the garment industry.

On a more abstract level, these Dominican migratory flows are seen by Sassen-Koob as a part of a "recomposition" of capital on a global scale with "the bulk of the immigrants providing low-wage labor to declining, backward sectors of capital."[33] Sassen-Koob goes on to point out that this assertion is correct, but incomplete. Many immigrant laborers work in the expanding, low-wage service sector, which underwrites lifestyles in the high-wage service sector of places like New York City. Thus, "we need to make a distinction between 'backward jobs'—which they often are—and a declining sector in the economy—which it is not."[34] Due to their marginal low-wage status, Dominicans are seen as being exploited within the context of the U.S. economy and, indeed, many Dominicans are thrust into alienating working and living conditions. Accounts of exploitation tend to center on the truly astonishing work weeks put in by some Dominicans.[35]

Further, a certain percentage of Dominicans can find themselves marginalized from any work at all, whether because of cyclical downturns, restructurings of the economy, or inability to adapt to the rigors of life in New York City. For example, a survey by Gurak and Kritz comparing Dominican and Colombian female migrants found that over half (55.7 percent) of the Dominican women in the survey "were receiving or had received some form of public assistance during the past year" (only 24.8 percent of the Colombian women fell into this category).[36] In addition, they found that 37 percent of all the Dominican households in the survey were headed by women, a category notoriously "at risk" for poverty. There are also frequent reports of Dominicans trapped in substandard housing where heat during the winter is erratic and giant rats roam the hallways.[37]

Thus for some Dominicans, possibly the less educated and skilled in the migrant pool, migration to New York does not secure their economic base but rather converts them into a segment of the welfare-dependent "underclass" of American cities where they are subject to multiple problems of substandard housing, juvenile delinquency, and drug addiction. But this stark reality should not obscure the fact that for many other Dominicans, arguably the majority, their entry into the U.S. labor market is less a process of "proletarianization" than it is a "proletarian strategy" that will eventually allow them to reproduce or secure middle-class status in the Dominican Republic. We have already seen, in the case of Eugenio Castillo, the very positive results that 20 years of dishwashing and household income-pooling can produce. Both the pooling of incomes and "entrepreneurial vigor" in immigrant communities do much to overcome the limitations of what can be objectively described as "cheap labor." Waldinger has described the internal structure of immigrant enterprises that could fairly be described as "sweatshops."[38] He undertook a survey of 90 immigrant firms involved in performing contract work for large clothing manufacturers, 50 of which were owned by Dominicans. He points out that the labor forces in these family-owned-and-operated businesses were primarily recruited through kinship and friendship links:

> ". . . migration chains linked entire factories in New York to a common hometown in the sending country, though this was far more common among the Dominicans (27 out of 50 plants) than among any of the other immigrant groups. Often, origin in small towns located in the Cibao—a northern agricultural region of the Dominican Republic—was the unifying thread. For example, relatives and hometown friends composed the entire workforce in an 18-person factory owned by three brothers from San José de las Matas."[39]

Waldinger also found that immigrant firms were more likely to have reduced expectations about the productivity and skills of newly-arrived migrants as long as the new migrants understood that they were only paid for what they actually produced. Employment in immigrant enclaves also extended beyond normal labor relations, with employers much more likely to act as intermediaries in a variety of social, economic, legal, and immigration problems. Such enterprises can even serve as avenues of self-advancement, with workers eventually becoming entrepreneurs; it was found that 40 percent of the owners had previously worked for an Hispanic owner. We have already seen in the case of Rafael Peralta, the young illegal immigrant, that these "sweatshops" are, indeed, symbols of success.

Beyond providing the basis for the material advancement of individuals and households, migrant communities also provide multiple opportunities for individuals to go into a variety of retail and service activities aimed primarily at their own community. This surge of petty capitalism has been a significant economic force to revive many declining neighborhoods. The image of cheap, exploited labor cannot be sustained without modification in the face of these activities. As Sassen-Koob has pointed out, "[immigrant occupation and investment activities] generate employment for immigrants, they reverse the trend towards housing abandonment and store closings, and they generate cash and tax flows for the city. Many of the immigrant communities containing a large number of small, locally-owned firms, started with the direct investment of the labor and savings of the immigrants themselves."[40]

It is difficult, if not impossible, to state with any precision how many Dominicans are "making it" and how many tumble into poverty. But an undue emphasis on the functional aspects of cheap labor for global capitalism reduces our ability to grasp the reality of immigrant communities and how they can develop and succeed within constraining economic circumstances. They are not simply caught in the currents of capital and labor flows but are able to maneuver themselves through these flows to their own benefit. Within the nooks and crannies of transnational capitalism's dominance, many individuals expand and achieve, and gain their own idea of "independence."

NOTES

1. Bonham Richardson, *Caribbean Migrants* (Knoxville: Univ. Tennessee Press, 1983); Centro de Estudios Puertoriqueños, *Labor Migration Under Capitalism* (New York and London: Monthly Review Press, 1979); Frank Moya Pons, *Raices del problema dominicana* (Santo Domingo, Dominican Republic: 1982); José del Castillo, *La immigración de braceros azucareros en la República Dominicana, 1900–1930* (Santo Domingo, D.R.: Centro Dominicana de Investigaciones Antropológicas, 1978).

2. All immigration statistics are from the Immigration and Naturalization Service *Annual Report* (Washington, D.C.: Government Printing Office, 1954–1981).

3. Antonio Ugalde et al., "International migration from the Dominican Republic: Findings from a national survey," *International Migration Review* 13 (Summer 1979): 235–54. For earlier works emphasizing rural origins see Glen Hendricks, *The Dominican Diaspora* (New York and London: Teachers College Press, 1974); Nancie L. Gonzales, "Peasants' progress: Dominicans in New York," *Caribbean Studies* 10 (1970:154–67; idem, "Migrating patterns to a small Dominican city and to New York," in *Migration and Urbanization: Models and Adaptive Strategies*, B.M. Dutoit and Helen I. Safa, eds. (Paris and the Hague: Mouton Publishers, 1975); idem, "Multiple migratory experiences of Dominican women," *Anthropological Quarterly* 49 (1976): 36–45. For more recent works arguing for middle-sector origins see Douglas T. Gurak, "Women in Santo Domingo: Implications for understanding New York's Dominican population," *Research Bulletin of the Hispanic Research Center* 2 (1979); Sherri Gras-

muck, "The consequences of Dominican urban out-migration for national development: The case of Santiago" (Paper presented at 32nd Annual Conference, Center for Latin American Studies, Univ. Florida, April 7-8, 1983); David Bray, "Economic development: The middle class and international migration in the Dominican Republic," *International Migration Review* 18 (Summer 1984): 217-36.

4. Karl Polanyi, *The Great Transformation* (Boston: Beacon Paperback, 1957).

5. *El Nacional*, January 26, 1981.

6. Bray, "Economic Development," p. 227.

7. On the feminization of the manufacturing proletariat see Helen I. Safa, "Runaway shops and female employment: The search for cheap labor," *Signs* 7 (1981): 418-33.

8. Walter J. Cordero, et al., *Tendencias de la economía cafetelera Dominicana, 1955-1972* (Santo Domingo, D.R.: Editora de la Universidad Antónoma de Santo Domingo, 1975).

9. David Bray, "Dependency, class formation and the creation of Caribbean labor reserves: Internal and international migration in the Dominican Republic" (Ann Arbor: University Microfilm, 1983).

10. Ibid.

11. Patricia Pessar, *Kinship Relations of Production in the Migration Process: The Case of Dominican Emigration to the United States,* Occasional Paper No. 32 (New York Univ.: Center for Latin American and Caribbean Studies, 1982), p. 14.

12. Franklyn J. Francis, *República Dominicana: clases, crisis, y comandos,* 4th ed. (Santo Domingo, D.R.: Editora Cosmos, 1975); Piero Gleijeses, *The Dominican Crisis* (Baltimore: Johns Hopkins Univ. Press, 1978).

13. Gleijeses, *Dominican Crisis.*

14. Carlos Vilas, "Clases sociales, estado y acumulación periférica en la República Dominicana 1966-1978," *Realidad Contemporanea* 2 (1979):31-60.

15. Isis Duarte and Andre Corten, "Procesos de proletarización de mujeres: las trabajadores de industrias de ensemblaje en la República Dominicana," (Universidad Antónoma de Santo Domingo: Departamento de Sociología, n.d.) p. 16.

16. USAID, *Statistical Data Book* (Santo Domingo, D.R.: U.S. Agency for International Development, 1977).

17. Ibid.

18. INS, *Annual Reports.*

19. Bray, "Economic development."

20. Grasmuck, "Consequences."

21. Ibid.

22. Michael Piore, *Birds of Passage: Migrant Labor and Industrial Societies* (Cambridge; UK: Cambridge Univ. Press, 1979).

23. Alejandro Portes, "Illegal immigration and the international system, lessons from recent legal Mexican immigrants to the United States," *Social Problems* 26 (1979):425-37; idem, "International labor migration and national development," in Mary M. Kritz, ed., *U.S. Immigration and Refugee Policy:*

Global and Domestic Issues (Lexington, MA: D.C. Heath, 1983).

24. Grasmuck, "Consequences," p. 42.

25. See Sherri Grasmuck, "Migration within the periphery: Haitian labor in the Dominican coffee and sugar industries," *International Migration Review* 16 (Summer 1982):365–77); Martin F. Murphy, "Similarities and variations in labor utilization strategies on sugar cane plantations in the Dominican Republic" (Paper presented at the Annual Meeting of the American Anthropological Association, Washington, D.C., December 6, 1982).

26. Howard J. Wiarda and Michael Kryzanek, "The Dominican Republic," *Latin American and Caribbean Contemporary Record, 1981–82* (New York and London: Holmes and Meier, 1983).

27. John Kenneth Galbraith, *The Nature of Mass Poverty* (Cambridge and London: Harvard Univ. Press, 1979); Marlene Dixon, et al., "Reindustrialization and transnational labor force today," in Marlene Dixon and Susanne Jonas, eds., *The New Nomads: From Immigration Labor to Transnational Working Class* (San Francisco: Synthesis Publications, 1982).

28. This and other anecdotal materials are taken from Bray, "Dependency, class formation and Caribbean labor reserves."

29. *El Nacional,* October 23, 1980; *Ahora,* September 22, 1980.

30. *El Nacional,* February 25, 1981.

31. *El Sol,* September 6, 1980.

32. Pessar, "The Role of Households," p. 360.

33. Saskia Sassen-Koob, "Recomposition and peripheralization at the core," in Marlene Dixon and Susanne Jonas, eds., *The New Nomads* (San Francisco: Synthesis Publications, 1982).

34. Ibid., p. 97.

35. Pessar, *Kinship Relations of Production,* p. 23.

36. Douglas Gurak and Mary Kritz, "Immigration women in New York City: Household structure and employment patterns," *Migration Today* 10 (1982):15–21.

37. *El Nacional,* June 26, 1980.

38. Roger Waldinger, "Immigrant enterprise and labor market structure" (Paper presented to the American Sociological Society Annual Meetings, September 1982).

39. Ibid., p. 13.

40. Sassen-Koob, "Recomposition," p. 97.

The Central American Exodus:
Grist for the Migrant Mill

Guy Gugliotta

In downtown Tegucigalpa, there is a rooming house/bar where in 1981 50 cents bought you a shot of Honduran *guaro* and as much gossip as you could absorb. It was the usual Central American transient hangout—hot, dusty, not particularly comfortable, with a menu that ran to stringy chicken, salty cheese, tortillas, rice and beans, and the odd hardboiled egg. The guests were an open-necked shirt crowd of straw-hatted drummers and drifters, hustlers and small-time entrepreneurs who came to the city to make a big score—or at least as big a score as Tegucigalpa could offer, which is to say not a very big score at all.

What separated this saloon from 50 others like it in Honduras was that it was half full of Nicaraguan expatriates who were getting glassy-eyed drunk, telling lies, plotting revenge, or longing for the good old days that were lost, perhaps irretrievably, in the mist of recent Central American history. On any given evening, the casual visitor could run into a variegated array of "Nicas." There was a pilot who flew one of the dead dictator Anastasio Somoza's Cessna "push-pull" aircraft, used in June and July of 1979 to attack Sandinista guerillas in the poor *barrios* of Managua. The pilot had a wallet full of credentials attesting to his skills, but was marking time as his licenses expired one by one.

Also present was a 40-year-old Miskito Indian, one of several elders chased across the Nicaraguan border earlier that year when it became apparent that tribal ethos mixed just as badly with *sandinismo*

as with *somocismo*. The Sandinistas nevertheless said that the Miskitos were closet Somocistas plotting the counterrevolution. This was
doubtful then. The elder barely had enough money to buy one meal
a day, and some 1,500 of his brethren down on the border were
worse off. There were indeed plenty of counterrevolutionaries in the
bar, but they were often indistinguishable from the freelance *pisto-
leros*, another abundant class. Many of these, more interested in cash
than ideology, had had distinguished careers with the Sandinistas,
but had moved easily into cattle rustling after the war. Beginning in
1981, with the best of Nicaraguan beef long gone to foreign dinner
tables, they were left to plot new remunerative ventures requiring
them to pontificate rather unconvincingly about the Sandinista's
"sellout" to Cuban communism.

Similar scenes, in surroundings much nicer or much worse, were
played out on sweaty evenings elsewhere in Honduras, throughout
the rest of Central America, in Mexico, and in the southern United
States in 1981 and later. By mid-decade, the talk of Nicaragua's
"sellout" had become louder, and the Somocistas' voices had been
absorbed by the fiercer clamor of many more thousands dissatisfied
with *sandinismo*'s drift. But Nicaragua was only part of a far larger
story. Dissatisfaction—with ideology, with the poor fruits of decayed
economies, with political disagreements turned horrifyingly rancid,
with wars badly waged—had turned most of Central America into a
good place not to be. This was because Central America's gathering
eclipse had, by mid 1984, given the world between 1.2 and 1.6 million displaced persons, with the promise of more to come.[1] There
were Nicaraguan Miskito in Honduras and Guatemalan Quiché in
Mexico. There were poor Salvadoran *campesinos* crossing the border
into Texas and former Nicaraguan National Guardsmen hunting jobs
in south Florida. There were well-to-do, rightwing Nicaraguan exiles
living in mansions in Guatemala City and Miami, and leftwing Salvadoran exiles speechmaking in Mexico and globetrotting in Europe.
Famous, apparently disaffected Nicaraguan revolutionaries were living in Costa Rica or trying to make war at home. Famous, apparently
disaffected Salvadoran reformists were doing the same thing.

In all, the United Nations High Commission for Refugees
(UNHCR) estimated there were 245,500 Salvadoran refugees living in
nine other Latin American countries by June 1984.[2] Other organizations calculated there were over 450,000 more Salvadorans wandering about, homeless in their own homeland.[3] The U.S. General Ac-

counting Office suggested there may have been as many as 500,000 undocumented Salvadorans in the United States.[4] The UNHCR listed nearly 45,000 Guatemalans in Mexico, with uncounted thousands in the United States and elsewhere.[5] The Central American exodus presented about a dozen nations with a host of perplexing problems. Honduras, through the early and mid 1980s, had anywhere between 30,000 and 45,000 refugees, mostly Salvadorans and Nicaraguans, socked away in areas often reachable only by aircraft.[6] In the United States, authorities in the early 1980s were deporting illegal Central American migrants, this despite uncontested evidence that innocents in El Salvador's civil war were being exterminated daily. Unfortunately for the Salvadorans, the United Nations definition of refugee does not necessarily include people who simply are scared. Fortunately for the Salvadorans, however, there were public-interest lawyers willing to delay deportation by bogging down individual Salvadoran cases in perpetual litigation.

In numbers, the Central American exodus was significant in world terms without being overarching. The 2.9 million Afghans in Pakistan (1983), some 800,000 homeless Ethiopian wanderers in Somalia and Sudan (1983), and the 1.13 million Indochinese (1981) who have settled elsewhere are comparable migrations.[7] By 1984 Central America had provided more than ten times the number of migrants as Cuba during the 1980 Mariel exodus, the only other reasonably concurrent large-scale diaspora in the Western Hemisphere. More significant, the spigot showed no signs of being turned off. This was because the principal donor countries—El Salvador, Nicaragua and Guatemala—had at least as much trouble in 1984 as they did five years earlier.

Salvadorans in 1984 comprised 72 percent of Central America's total emigrants, and since the left's once hoped-for popular revolution degenerated in 1980 into a civil war of attrition, the "masses"—a pool of some five million people packed into 8,000 square miles of space and looking for an exit—grew increasingly irrelevant. The left had merely to prosecute the war, while the Salvadoran government had to win it. The left destroyed roads, bridges, electrical installations and vehicles without number to ensure the destruction of infrastructure and the disappearance of jobs. The government, denounced as the purveyor of state terror since 1979, continued a bloody war of attrition. Indiscriminate killings of civilians persisted, and thousands of rootless people hiding and wandering El Salvador's scorched earth could be expected to wander for more months—perhaps years—to come. From the left, then, a loss of jobs and a loss of future; from the right, a loss of trust and a loss of nerve. The inevitable result: migration, to continue even in the unlikely event that El Salvador's agony were resolved. The downslide to economic oblivion would take years to reverse, no matter who "won."

In Guatemala, a struggle between guerrillas and government that dominated the years 1978–1982 quieted in mid-decade, with the government at least temporarily ascendant. This did not resolve the tribulations of more than 45,000 Guatemalans in Mexico and another 300,000 displaced persons inside Guatemala's borders. The large majority of these migrants were Indians, many of whom spoke no Spanish and had no skills and few prospects.

For Nicaragua, five years of revolutionary government resolved nothing. Somoza's rich supporters left for Miami and Guatemala City; his poor went to Tegucigalpa bars or to Sandinista jails. The Nicaraguan masses hitched their collective star to promises made during the long upheaval, but in 1984 the promises were still going begging, victims of U.S. hostility and a tattered economy that supported little beyond the barest minimum. When and if it became clear that promises would remain unfulfilled, the masses could be expected to depart. For the Nicaraguan bourgeoisie, who had something to lose but not enough to cut and run, the wait became increasingly tedious and discomfiting. Their government did not trust them, but respected its commitments to protect them. Should it renege, yesterday's bourgeoisie would become propertyless *lumpen,* more grist for the migrant mill. Meanwhile, the Nicaraguan government, with emergencies at every hand, showed only occasional flashes of competence. It built a magnificent armed force but faltered badly in almost every other sector after initial successes. Increasingly the Sandinistas shrouded their shortcomings in polemic.

MIGRANT OR REFUGEE?

Regardless of what the future could hold, Central America's emigration had already, by mid 1984, presented the Western Hemisphere with a problem seldom seen on its own shores: refugees. Widely, but not always accurately, used to describe migrant types throughout the Caribbean Basin, the word "refugee" can mean all things to all people, or nothing to anyone. Seldom is there a clear-cut case. One man's exile is another's wanted criminal; one man's political refugee is another's economic freeloader. Particular cases are befogged by political considerations in receiving countries that are either unsympathetic or too sympathetic to those seeking succor at the border. Lawyers cognizant of the pitfalls of migrant litigation can juggle a particular problem into a legal twilight zone that makes resolution almost impossible.

The United Nations in 1951 defined a refugee as a person who, "owing to well-founded fear of being persecuted for reasons of race, religion, nationality, membership of a particular social group or political opinion, is outside the country of his nationality and is unable, or owing to such fear, unwilling to avail himself of the protection of that country. . ."[8]

Seen from the Central American viewpoint, the UN interpretation, heavily influenced by the problem of displaced persons in post-World War II Europe, is narrow and perhaps excessively political. While most of Central America's refugees in the mid 1980s had a "well-founded" and oft-expressed "fear of persecution," only a handful fit comfortably into one of the United Nations' specific slots. The great majority—those from El Salvador, Nicaragua and Guatemala—fled not for any specific political reason, but because there was not enough personal security at home to keep them from being killed, either by the right, by the left, or simply because they were in the line of fire. "War," as Vietnam activists used to say in the 1960s, "is hazardous to small children and other living things."

Only the 1910–1917 Mexican revolution in relatively recent Western Hemisphere history offers the same large-scale migration as a result of substantial and prolonged death and destruction at home. The Cuban exodus of the 1960s was a more clearly political migration, qualifying much more easily under the UN definition. The character of the Central American migration presented a number of new and complicated problems for a region traditionally more comfortable dealing with its two most common modes of human movement: economic migration, the classic drain of manpower and skills to areas richer in remuneration and opportunity; and exile, the *noblesse oblige* formula by which Latin American winners allow losers a graceful escape.

Economic migration in the early 1980s continued apace from Costa Rica, Honduras, and Belize, the Central American countries without wars. Hondurans on the Atlantic Coast regard a job on the

New Orleans docks as their birthright; remittances from Belizeans living illegally in New York or London are a necessary source of foreign exchange; Costa Rica's 1980-1982 financial crisis dried up economic activity and prompted movement. Oddly enough, the wars of Central America also may have made it easier for economic migrants from El Salvador, Nicaragua, and Guatemala. Thousands of illegal Salvadorans lived in Los Angeles, San Francisco, and Washington, D.C., long before the apocalypse arrived outside the door in 1980; and Guatemalan Indians made annual trips to Mexico as migrant farmworkers long before village life started becoming intolerable in 1981. Even if there had been no war, the flow would undoubtedly have continued, but chaos at home made it easier to ask political asylum elsewhere. This tactic—of trying to become a political refugee regardless of one's true motives for migration—met with mixed results in the United States and Mexico. The U.S. Immigration and Naturalization Service deported hundreds of Salvadorans as illegal economic migrants. The Mexican government did likewise with many Guatemalans.

In the matter of influential exiles, both voluntary and involuntary, matters proceeded smoothly. Col. Adolfo Majano, who once shared a piece of the Salvadoran reformist junta, took political asylum in Mexico in 1980, one of several chiefs or demichiefs of state to take cover. Other Salvadorans included reformists and former junta members: Ungo (to Mexico and Panama), who became leader of the leftist opposition to the current government, and Mayorga (to the United States), and rightist strongman Romero (United States). From Guatemala there was former vice president Villagrán-Kramer (United States), and from Nicaragua there were the last of the Somozas, Anastasio Somoza Portocarrero (United States), former Somocista president Urcuyo (Guatemala) and former Sandinista junta member Alfonso Robelo (Costa Rica). Famed Nicaraguan revolutionary Edén Pastora, *Comandante Cero,* fell out with the Sandinistas, but was eventually denied entry in Costa Rica because he used that country as a base to foment rebellion against his erstwhile comrades in Nicaragua.

The UNHCR in mid 1984 was administering relief and self-help projects for the homeless of Central America in nine different countries. Each country had political as well as humanitarian reasons for its involvement in migrant activities, and some were more involved than others. Nonrefugee migration had provided headaches for Costa Rica ever since 1978 when the then-exiled Sandinistas were permitted to set up headquarters and training camps in the northern part of the country. With no army and a wide-open society, Costa Rica's credibility as a neutral rested in part on its ability to control the activities of émigrés within its borders. The Sandinista affair showed the government either could not or would not take the necessary steps. Later Costa Rica served as a warm-up room for all sorts of exiles of the right and left. In 1981, for the first time since the anti-Vietnam War days of the late 1960s, Costa Rica had a bombing by domestic terrorists. By 1983 the government had attempted, with a degree of success, to get its militant migrant problem under control, proclaiming official neutrality in the Central American conflict and defending it by declaring Pastora and others *personae non gratae.*

Nicaragua, meanwhile, sheltered many of Central America's leftist leaders, including most of the Salvadoran guerrilla high command, and was openly visited by others. Nicaragua also cared for some Salvadoran refugees, probably relatives of leftist sympathizers.

For Mexico, traditional stopping place for the trendy left since Leon Trotsky's arrival in the 1930s, the Central American exodus presented special difficulties. Normally docile newspapers vilified the government of former president José López Portillo as "elitist" for deporting poor, mostly illiterate Guatemalan Indians down on the southern border, while showing an open door to the likes of Trotsky, Peru's Victor Raúl Haya de la Torre, Cuba's Fidel Castro, and El Salvador's Majano. Mexico, like the United States with the Salvadoran migrants, first claimed that the Guatemalans were cross-border laborers who overstayed their welcome. Later, however, it acknowledged that the Indians fit the definition of Central America's refugee/migrant. Most were either in or around their villages when guerrillas came by to hold political meetings, then watched when security forces arrived later to take reprisals for the villagers' supposed complicity with the guerrillas. The massacre of Guatemalan Indians in such incidents became a story told so often that it was a cliché. Its usual outcome was the villagers' departure, usually to Mexico. Mexico eventually opened a camp to relocate the Guatemalans near Campeche, then ran into another typical problem in that the refugees did not wish to stray from the border. This led to clashes between the Indians and Mexican security forces in mid 1984 and more bad blood. Honduras, basically hostile to Salvadorans, had the same difficulties relocating Salvadoran refugees away from the Salvadoran border. For Mexico, however, confrontation with migrants, political or otherwise, was doubly sensitive, damaging its credibility in the battle to obtain greater rights and more lenient treatment for illegal Mexican migrants in the United States.

Beginning in 1981, Mexico also opened camps to accommodate large numbers of Salvadorans in transit to the United States. Some were picked up and deported once they crossed the Rio Grande, others were put in Texas holding facilities, and others were led into the desert to die by Mexican *coyotes* (guides) as in the Ajo, Arizona, debacle of 1980. The Salvadoran illegals presented a problem Washington would have liked not to have, but the administration of President Ronald Reagan used the migrants and the possibility of more to come as a political club to encourage Democratic congressmen in the Southwest to vote more aid to the Salvadoran government.

Different problems were posed by the uneasy presence of exiled rich Salvadorans and Nicaraguan Somocistas in Miami. Salvadoran moderates and U.S. opponents of Washington's policies accused Miami's Salvadoran émigrés of financing and equipping right-wing death squads in the early and mid 1980s. These denunciations were not immediately substantiated, but they did little to enhance the Reagan administration's bargaining power in gathering aid for El Salvador between 1980–1983. The inauguration of moderate Salvadoran President José Napoleon Duarte in June 1984 made El Salvador more acceptable in congressional eyes.

HONDURAS: CAUGHT IN THE MIDDLE

More useful for conservatives in Washington were the Nicaraguan expatriates. Many of these had old friendships with the Cuban exiles of south Florida who had launched the ill-fated 1961 Bay of Pigs invasion from Nicaragua with Somoza's blessing. The Nicaraguan expatriots were thus able to drop handily into Miami's Casablanca-like atmosphere of plotting and intrigue. Between 1979 and 1981, the connection served primarily as an exercise in propaganda, designed to upset a Sandinista government constantly worried about counterrevolutionary cabals. By 1982 propaganda had become reality, and Miami had become a convenient jumping-off and provisioning point for CIA-funded anti-Sandinista groups, which in mid 1984 numbered more than 10,000 armed insurgents.[9] The anti-Sandinistas between 1982–1984 trained and lived in Honduras and worked—and sometimes lived—in Managua. Those involved in this activity claimed at first that the Honduran camps were "clandestine," but like the Costa Ricans with their Sandinista protégés in 1978, it was difficult to believe that military maneuvers could be conducted without the acquiescence, if not the outright help, of local authorities.

This was one migrant-caused focus of Honduran-Nicaraguan friction. Another was the presence of thousands of Nicaraguan Miskito Indians in Honduran refugee camps down on the border. The Miskitos' communal habits and way of life ran afoul of the Sandinistas' efforts at national integration early in 1981, and a series of confrontations resulted in the springtime departure that year of up to 3,000 Miskito officials and youngsters, most of them "soldiers" in Nicaragua's literacy brigades. Vocal, but at first helpless, the Miskito marked time in refugee camps, trying to decide whether their differences with *sandinismo* could be resolved. By 1983, however, continued conflict had fed Miskito intransigence to the point where a rapprochement with the Sandinistas appeared impossible. Loose alliances with the non-Indian Nicaraguan insurgents put guns in the hands of Miskito youngsters. Further confrontations between Indians and Sandinistas on the Nicaraguan side of the border deepened Miskito bitterness and rage. By mid 1984 the Miskito migrant population in Honduras had swelled to 20,000.[10] The exodus had created embarrassment for the Sandinista government, unable to cope with the complaints of a significant number of Nicaragua's rural poor, those for whom the revolution had been intended.

The philosophical differences and mutual suspicion existing between the Sandinistas and Honduras' elected civilian government gave incidents on the Nicaraguan border a much higher profile than those on the frontier with El Salvador, where a similar migrant drama unfolded. Beginning in the spring of 1980, Honduras played host to between 20,000 and 30,000 Salvadoran refugees, who lived first in private homes, later in fever-infested small towns, and by mid 1983, for the most part, in healthier camps with fairly safe water supplies.[11] Most of these refugees were middle-aged or elderly people, or women, many of them sympathetic to the Salvadoran left. The gender and age of the camp population suggest that most of the refugees belonged to guerrilla families. On at least three occasions between 1981 and 1983, Salvadoran troops either entered the camps in

Honduran territory or attacked refugees as they crossed rivers separating the two countries. The Hondurans, despite protests, let the Salvadorans get away with it. Each time it happened, relief agency officials complained and were told about the possibility that refugees were using relief supplies to provision guerrillas across the border. Like Miami exile support for Salvadoran death squads, this accusation was neither proven nor disproven. Among other things, however, the incursions and their results indicated a sympathy for the Salvadoran army cause on the part of their counterparts in Honduras. Also, they reflected Honduras' deeper concern about the presence of thousands of Salvadoran nationals in their territory.

In 1969 Honduras and El Salvador fought an inconclusive war, picturesquely attributed by some to a dispute over a soccer game, but actually rooted in Tegucigalpa's distress over the encroachments of landless squatters from crowded El Salvador across the border to relatively vacant southern Honduras.

The conflict resulted in the closure of the frontier and an 11-year state of war, lifted late in December 1980 after a peace treaty was concluded. Honduran leaders later said frankly they were concerned that Salvadorans might use the treaty as an excuse to start settling permanently in still-vacant southern Honduras. There is little sympathy for Salvadoran migrants in Honduran official circles, still less among the poor Honduran *campesinos* competing for sparse services in hardscrabble border towns.

ATYPICAL MIGRANTS

While it is still too early to make judgments about the ultimate intentions of the Central American migrants, it is possible to draw some interim conclusions, even though in 1984 the conflict was in an extremely fluid stage. It is possible to ascertain why the migrants left, but impossible to ascertain what they will do. In most cases the conditions that led to their departure still exist.

It is certainly clear that the Central American exodus derives little from the migration pattern common to the Caribbean Basin in general. The shared characteristics are geographical and economic. Like the Caribbean islands, the Central American countries are poor nations close to a rich metropolitan power; scarcity of opportunities at home encourages migration to lands of greater opportunity. But the typical Central American migrant had modest ambitions before the wars began. Miskito Indians habitually crossed the Nicaragua-Honduras frontier to visit relatives, seldom, if ever, even bothering to recognize the existence of the border. Guatemalan Indians crossed into Mexico for seasonal work.

Beginning in 1978, however, with the Sandinista sympathizers' departures to escape the wrath of the Nicaraguan National Guard, migration has been conditioned by political events in the country of origin. But unlike the archetypical political refugee as defined by the United Nations, the overwhelming majority of Central American migrants were only vaguely involved with those events (the Salvadorans and the Miskito in Honduras) or not involved at all (Guatemalan Indians in Mexico). In most cases, there is no one at home waiting to kill, torture, or imprison the migrant because of his political or religious beliefs. Instead, combatants in the country of origin have rendered that country uninhabitable for poor citizens who live on the margin even in the best of times. The migrant/refugee tends to identify or sympathize with those who are battling the "oppressor" government of the home country, but this has not meant that the refugee automatically becomes a militant (it is still impossible to determine how politicized a refugee becomes after he migrates, but such a process has indeed taken place among, for instance, the Miskito in Honduras).

Once across a national border, Central American migrants have shown a reluctance to relocate permanently, preferring to stay on the frontier, either to be able to take immediate advantage of changes in the political wind, to be closer to loved ones fighting at home, or simply to remain in reasonably familiar surroundings. The exception to the rule, at least in part, has been the success in relocating the Nicaraguan Miskito in Honduras. Not insignificantly, perhaps, the Indians tend not to regard their homeland as "Nicaragua" or "Honduras," but as "Miskitia," which straddles the border.

Whether the refugee/migrants will eventually become economic migrants is unclear, but the indications are they will not. Again with the partial exception of the Miskito in Honduras, Central Americans uniformly express the desire to return home and have done so whenever the political climate has appeared to moderate. Relative peace at home brings an immediate decline in refugee populations abroad. It is, however, reasonable to assume that the desire to return home will abate as time passes. This, however, is the great imponderable. For the Central Americans, as with refugees everywhere, the most important question is "how long?"

NOTES

1. The figure is arrived at by adding numbers from several sources and should serve as a reasonable assessment of displaced persons for mid 1984. The figures include: 468,000 displaced persons inside El Salvador (Lawyers' Committee for International Human Rights), Americas Watch, *El Salvador's Other Victims; The War on the Displaced* (New York: Americas Watch, 1984), p. 12; 300,000 displaced persons inside Guatemala (United States Department of State), "Country reports on the world refugee situation: Report to the Congress for fiscal year 1984" (August 1983), p. 100; 245,000 Salvadorans elsewhere in Central America (United Nations High Commission for Refugees [UNHCR]), "Number of refugees as of 31 May 1984," *Internal Work Sheet* (Washington, D.C. 1984; restricted distribution); 100–500 thousand Salvadorans in the United States (United States General Accounting Office, "Report to the Congress of the United States, Central American refugees: Regional conditions and prospects and potential impact on the United States" (20 July 1984), p. 32; and 43,000 Guatemalans in Mexico (UNHCR, *Internal Work Sheet*). The figure does not include significant numbers of Salvadorans in Mexico and Guatemalans in the United States.

2. UNHCR, *Internal Work Sheet.*

3. Americas Watch, *El Salvador's Other Victims,* p. 12.

4. U.S. General Accounting Office, "Central American Refugees," p. 32.

5. UNHCR, *Internal Work Sheet.*

6. Ibid. The figure changes depending on political developments in donor countries. The number of Nicaraguans grew steadily from 1980 to 1984, while the number of Salvadorans rose sharply in 1981/82, declined slightly, and then stabilized in 1984.

7. U.S. Department of State, "World refugee situation," pp. 5, 53, 101.

8. United Nations, *Protocol* (31 January 1967, Art. 1. Para. 2, 19 U.S.T. 6223, T.T.A.S. No. 6577, 608 U.N.T.S. 267. n).

9. Juan O. Tamayo, "CIA cash gone. Anti-Sandinistas ask private help," The Miami *Herald,* July 11, 1984.

10. UNHCR, *Internal Work Sheet,* note c.

11. Ibid. The figure of 20,000 in May 1984 began to rise again with camps swelled by youths crossing the border to escape forced recruitment by the Salvadoran guerrillas.

Exodus Elsewhere

Caribbean Migration to Britain and France: From Assimilation to Selection

Gary P. Freeman

Migrants from the Caribbean who journey to their European "mother countries" of France and Britain occupy a distinctly ambiguous position at the intersection of several contradictory roles. They are, first of all, caught up in the aftermath of colonial/metropolitan relationships in which their status is clearly inferior and subordinate. This is exacerbated because they are also persons of color in predominantly white societies. They are, however, part of what is essentially a migration of manpower undertaken for economic motives. In this regard, they constitute a relatively unskilled and marginal complement of labor, located at the bottom of the occupational ladder of the highly industrialized countries to which they move. The roles of ex-colonial dependent, racial minority, and immigrant worker have different characteristics, but they reinforce one another as subordinate statuses.

Nevertheless, migrants to Britain and France from the former colonial possessions in the Caribbean also have had certain rights and privileges not normally claimed by foreign workers. Because of the complex political ties between the metropolitan and peripheral territories, the majority of Caribbean migrants to Europe have, until recently, enjoyed the full range of citizenship rights.[1] In practice, citizenship has amounted to little more than the right to vote and freedom from deportation. Still, it introduces a degree of leverage that is missing in the situation of more typical foreign workers. Although migrant citizens have not themselves exercised their rights in the political arena to any great degree, the fact of citizenship has tempered the policies of the European states. It confounds their immigration control policies, it affects their treatment of West Indians once admitted, and it sharpens the tension between their universalistic rhetoric and the selective and discriminatory policies they pursue.

The significance of citizenship rights for Caribbean migrants may be waning, however. The British have recently moved to abrogate citizenship rights for most immigrants. The French, under the leadership of a socialist government, have strengthened the rights of immigrants, reducing the distinction between citizens and other persons in France. Nevertheless, the government's policy toward the future status of the overseas *départements* may eventually result in the loss of French citizenship rights for their residents.

DECOLONIZATION AND IMMIGRATION

The large-scale immigration of former colonials into Europe has been the ironic and unanticipated legacy of Western expansionism. Former French Prime Minister Pierre Messmer once lamented: "This is a trap set by history. We in France and Europe have been accustomed to colonizing the world. Now the foreigners are coming here to us."[2] Nothing has more severely strained the British and French approach to decolonization or their dreams of racially and nationally pluralistic political associations than the influx of peripheral populations into the center.

As Britain and France went through the difficult process of decolonization, former colonies were granted independence while their subjects were given extraordinary rights vis-à-vis the mother country. It must have seemed at the time a costless gesture toward the old ideals of Empire. It was surely a concession designed to avoid a total break by the new independent states. Under the British Nationality Act of 1948, residents of the newly independent Commonwealth nations could claim citizenship in the United Kingdom and Colonies.[3] Among other things, this status until recently guaranteed free entry into Britain and the full exercise of citizenship rights once there. France followed similar policies toward her former possessions in Africa, though the details of arrangements differed from country to country and actual citizenship was not involved even though individuals were in fact treated as citizens for many purposes, including immigration.[4] With respect to the Caribbean possessions, however, France chose a policy of *départementalization*, that is, integrating the island territories into the French state itself.[5] Residents of Guadaloupe, Guiana, and Martinique (the *départements d'outre-mer*, or D.O.M., in the Caribbean) are citizens of France and may vote in French elections. They have the right to enter the mainland without restrictions and are not regarded by French law as foreigners.

The legal fiction that it was possible to extend British citizenship over large parts of the globe quickly began to unravel under the pressure of immigration from the Commonwealth. Few officials had foreseen that more than a handful of Commonwealth residents would actually come to Britain and, in fact, rights of free entry were not really exploited until the late 1950s. The first sizable immigration was from the Caribbean, principally Jamaica, but as the years passed large numbers arrived from the Indian subcontinent as well. It is estimated, for example, that in 1955 there was a net movement of 27,550 West Indians into Great Britain, compared with 5,800 Indians and 1,850 Pakistanis. The contingent from the Caribbean fell no lower than 15,000 annually over the next six years and the figures for Indians and Pakistanis held steady or increased.[6] The mushrooming concentrations of nonwhite manual workers and their families in British cities stimulated an outcry against unregulated immigration. Although there is evidence that the flow of immigrants was at least roughly linked to employment conditions in Britain, many persons feared that the country was being inundated by a flood of blacks. The outbreak of racial violence in London, Nottingham, and elsewhere in 1958 and after helped bring the issue to a head.

In 1962 the Conservative government responded to these pressures and ended free movement. The Commonwealth Immigrants Act set up a voucher scheme under which small numbers of workers and their dependents might be admitted for specific jobs and strictly limited periods.[7] This act, as implemented by a Labor Government White Paper in 1965 and as supplemented by legislation in 1968 and 1971, effectively ended significant new immigration for work. Actual immigration remained high, however, because of the large number of dependents who joined relatives already in Britain, because of an unascertainable number of illegal entrants, and because of crises in Kenya and Uganda that compelled many U.K. passport-holders to seek admission.[8]

Though there had been a net movement of 66,300 West Indians into Britain in 1961 in anticipation of the introduction of controls, the figures dropped sharply after the coming to force of the Commonwealth Immigrants Act.[9] Net movement fluctuated between a high of 14,848 in 1964 and a low of 688 in 1969 until 1971, when there was for the first time a net movement of West Indians out of Britain (-1,163). This occurred again in 1973 (-2,130).[10]

If control legislation was successful in reducing net immigration, it was devastating with respect to new immigration for work. Only 2,077 work permit-holders from the West Indies were admitted in 1963, 322 in 1970, 61 in 1972, and 10 in 1975.[11] This leaves the entry of dependents of Commonwealth immigrants legally resident in Britain as the most sensitive issue in contemporary British immigration politics. The number of dependents entering the country from the West Indies fluctuated between 2 and 11 thousand annually until 1971, when it fell to 539.[12] Although it is estimated that the number was still as high as 579 in 1979,[13] given the very small number of new immigrants and the fact that many West Indians are leaving the country, it is simply a matter of time until the "dependents" problem ceases to exist.

Faced with a public clamor for strict regulation of new entrants and for the repatriation of those already in the country, successive governments have embarked on an increasingly rigid and racially discriminatory immigration policy. The Commonwealth Immigrants Act had been clearly directed at the nonwhite residents of the Commonwealth and had specifically excluded the Irish from its provisions. The Immigration Act of 1971, the product of the Tory government of Edward Heath, employed the transparent device of a grandfather clause to enable white Commonwealth residents to evade its controls. Under this law persons who had a parent or a grandparent born in the U.K. are considered "patrials" and are granted free entry. Throughout the 1960s, British immigration policy ignored the country's manpower requirements and was designed almost entirely to slow down the influx of nonwhites. The official justification for this policy was to allow sufficient time for the absorption of newcomers, but the practical objective was to placate indigenous resistance.

FROM ASSIMILATION TO SELECTION

French immigration policy has been, on the surface, very different from that of Britain. Though the British economy has in fact suffered from labor shortages in certain sectors throughout much of the postwar period and the government has even actively recruited workers from the Commonwealth on occasion, the prevailing view has been that the country is overcrowded, chronically threatened by unemployment, and embarked on a long-term decline in its economic fortunes. It cannot, therefore, afford to accept additional responsibilities. The French, on the other hand, were troubled by fears of a declining birthrate and by the implications of the enormous population losses of the Second World War.[14] In the early years of the Fourth Republic there was significant support for an activist policy of permanent immigration. The institutional apparatus to administer such a program was created in 1945. The National Immigration Office (ONI) was to coordinate the entry of immigrant workers and their families. Enjoying a formal monopoly over immigration, ONI was unable to carry out its mandate in practice. Most immigration to France took place "spontaneously" or illegally. The government tacitly endorsed this situation by "regularizing" the status of unsanctioned immigrants after the fact. In 1968, for example, over 80 percent of all official new entrants had recourse to regularization, while only about 20 percent came under the auspices of ONI.[15]

France, therefore, adopted a very tolerant attitude toward immigration after the war, both encouraging it in certain forms (through a series of bilateral agreements with countries of emigration, especially former colonies) and passively accepting it in others. The outcome of this policy was a very large movement of workers into the country. In light of the fact that they obviously underestimated the true size of the phenomenon, the official figures published by ONI are fairly impressive: from 30,171 in 1946, they rose to 65,428 in 1956 and then swelled to over 100,000 annually during 1962-1971.[16] Drawn primarily from the EEC and Spain in the beginning, migrants came increasingly from North Africa, especially Algeria. In 1970, the EEC accounted for about 22 percent of all immigrants living in France, with Italians making up 18 percent of this total. Spain and Portugal contributed about 19 percent each, but the North African countries of Algeria, Morocco, and Tunisia together made up 28 percent.[17]

Although French policy was on the surface haphazard and unplanned, it was extremely well-suited to the requirements of the domestic economy. Immigrant workers made up a crucial element of the French labor force and filled important positions that might otherwise have gone begging. As an official in the government of Prime Minister Pompidou frankly admitted in 1966: "Without clandestine workers, we might lack the manpower we need."[18] Disorderly and unorganized immigration was an irritation the French were willing to tolerate at least in the short-term.

Two developments converged to force the government to alter its laissez-faire approach to immigration. The most immediate was the decided shift of the source of immigration from European to non-European countries. The large and growing proportion from North Africa was especially troublesome, given native French attitudes toward Arabs and the bitter feelings generated by the Algerian War. As early as 1969 a report to the Social and Economic Council proposed a "selective" policy that would limit non-Europeans to temporary work permits and reserve permanent immigration of families to persons of European stock.[19] The report's argument that there were strict sociological limits to the ability of any social system to accept alien intrusions (the threshold of tolerance) amounted to a frank repudiation of the idea that French culture had infinite assimilative capacity.

It cannot have been coincidental, however, that the first really serious efforts to put an end to spontaneous immigration were taken in 1972 and after, just as the French economy began to experience the dislocations which persisted throughout the decade. In 1974 France unilaterally halted all new immigration (with the exception of the EEC, of course). This measure was eventually annulled by the Council of State, but subsequent actions have greatly tightened the procedures for obtaining work permits and for bringing in families. Furthermore, in 1975 the government instituted a program of grants to encourage migrants to return home.

Since 1972, then, French immigration policy has become, like that of the British, more and more restrictive and racially selective. From 1973 to 1978 immigration of non-EEC permanent workers fell by 97 percent. The total number of permanent workers and dependents admitted in 1976 was 82,962. This figure declined each year to 56,695 in 1979. Moreover, in just three and one half years 39,000 applications affecting 76,000 persons were filed for assisted repatriation.[20] Taken together, British and French policies have created a framework within which new immigration from non-EEC sources will be very difficult. The implications of British policy for the Caribbean are fairly clear. However, it is necessary to explore the French-Caribbean connection more closely. One of the most striking characteristics of French immigration policy is its extreme heterogeneity and specificity. The overseas *départements* are not normally affected by a more general immigration law, though the actual movement of persons from the D.O.M. to metropolitan France is affected by the larger economic and political context.

Consistent with the desire to attract new workers for the French economy, the overseas departments were seen initially as reservoirs of potential migrants. Their demographic and economic structure encouraged this view. Guadaloupe, Guiana, and Martinique had a combined population in 1974 of over 700,000. For France as a whole only about 30 in 100 persons were 20 years or younger. The comparable figures were 53 in 100 in Guadaloupe, 48 in Guiana, and 52 in Martinique.[21]

The French government took steps to encourage and organize the movement to the mainland of large numbers of its citizens in the D.O.M. In 1963 it set up the Bureau for Migration from the Overseas Departments (BUMIDOM) to exercise a monopoly over such transfers. Operating under the Ministry for the Economy and Finance and the Secretary of State for Overseas Departments and Territories, BUMIDOM has been amply funded, having for example a budget in 1974 of 29,388,250 francs.[22] The agency has the authority to select immigrants, to train them at centers set up for that purpose in France, to place them in jobs through branch offices in Nancy, Rouen, Lille, Lyon, and other major industrial cities, and to house them through intermediary associations that are sponsored by BUMIDOM itself. In all, the BUMIDOM arrangements amount to the only really organized immigration France has managed to achieve.

It is not easy to gather precise statistics on the size of the Caribbean population in France as they are considered citizens and separate figures are collected only irregularly by the census. According to the 1975 census there were 115,465 persons residing in France who had been born in Guadeloupe or Martinique. If one adds unmarried children under 25 residing in the same household, the figure climbs to 163,945.[23] Given the chronic unemployment in the D.O.M., there has been a steady flow of persons out of the islands. Guadaloupe experienced a net loss of about 6,500 persons in each of the years between 1969 and 1978. Martinique had, on the average, a net outward movement of 6,000 persons annually during the same period. Only Guiana had more people coming into the country than leaving it, though the margin has been small.[24] Between 1962 and 1980 BUMIDOM sponsored the immigration of 82,321 persons from Guadeloupe and Martinique, annual levels declining only after 1978.[25]

French immigration policy as a whole has been contradictory to its specific policy toward the overseas departments. First of all, the relaxed attitude toward unorganized immigration from North Africa and elsewhere has served to ease labor shortages, which might have otherwise compelled a more vigorous recruitment policy toward the D.O.M. That is, the government took the easiest course, which was to accept workers arriving on their own rather than to arrange the movement of workers from the overseas departments and territories. It is probable, nonetheless, that about as much immigration as was practicable has occurred from these sources, but in the absence of large-scale migration from other places workers from the D.O.M. would have been in a much more favorable market position. Secondly, the shift to a racially exclusive policy after 1968 is inconsistent with the continued formal right of free entry for the D.O.M. (to say nothing of the more general and ambitious policy of departmentalization) though this contradiction is avoided in the technical sense because residents of the D.O.M. are not officially recognized as immigrants at all.

MIGRATION AND EUROPEAN CAPITALISM

Migration has been a crucial element in the postwar growth of European capitalism. It has helped reduce labor-supply bottlenecks, diminish inflationary pressures, and enhance countercyclical stability. Though it is less well understood and more difficult to document, it also seems true that the importation of a large foreign labor force has served to weaken the market and political bargaining position of European labor movements. This has enhanced the legitimacy and power of ruling coalitions, as has the role immigrants have played in cushioning indigenous workers against the effects of unemployment and recession.

The recourse to a policy of massive immigration was fraught with danger, however. Maximum economic advantage could be achieved only insofar as effective control over entry and exit was maintained and so long as relative social peace persisted. The imperatives of colonial policy prevented making immigration decisions purely on the basis of the requirements of the domestic labor market. Caribbean migrants to Europe, because of their youth, high rates of activity and mobility, and their willingness to perform manual tasks, have made a significant contribution to the French and British economies. Nevertheless, political and social considerations have greatly complicated what might otherwise have been, from the point of view of the metropolitan powers, a very satisfactory relationship.

Labor shortages may be real or contrived. They are real when insufficient workers are available to perform all necessary tasks. They are contrived when certain jobs go wanting even when workers are otherwise unemployed. Migrants can reduce both types, but they are especially useful in dealing with contrived shortages. The distribution of migrants across industries and skill levels demonstrates the extent to which they have filled those industrial sectors abandoned by European workers.

West Indian migrants to Britain have been overwhelmingly concentrated in manual occupations. The 1966 Sample Census reported that 94 percent of Jamaican males and 84 percent of men from the rest of the Caribbean were in manual jobs. For women, the proportions were somewhat lower: 74 percent and 58 percent, respectively. There were heavy concentrations of Jamaican males in metal working (9 percent), the engineering and electrical goods industry (12 percent), construction (14 percent), and transport and communications (14 percent). The comparable figures for immigrants from the rest of the Caribbean were 8, 11, 10, and 20 percent. Jamaican women tended to be located in professional and scientific services (30 percent), clothing and footwear manufacturing (13 percent), and miscellaneous services (10 percent).[26]

It is difficult to obtain reliable statistics on the occupational activities of migrants to France from the overseas departments. It is safe to conclude, however, that they are heavily concentrated in manual and unskilled jobs. For example, of 2,088 women admitted to France through BUMIDOM in 1971, 693 became domestics, 382 managers and skilled workers, 297 hospital workers, and 261 municipal employees. Another 151 entered job training centers, 145 enrolled in courses in nursing and midwifery, and 91 became students at reception centers. The remaining 68 were unaccounted for.[27] One study reported that of 645 men admitted to a particular training center in 1971, 29 percent eventually became metal workers and 65 percent went into construction.[28]

The actual impact of immigration on the French and British economies is a matter of serious debate among academic specialists. Nevertheless, there are several generalizations that seem justified by the available evidence and are agreed to by most observers. The first point is that British squeamishness over immigration, their failure to pursue an economically-oriented control policy, and high emigration by native Britons, reduced many of the potentially useful economic consequences of immigration. This means that immigration has had, over the whole postwar period, an indecisive net effect on the British economy. It has certainly helped to ease the pressure of tight labor markets, especially in the early 1950s and 1960s, but its overall impact on wage levels, inflation, and stability has not been pronounced. Purely from the point of view of the economy, therefore, one may say that Britain has experienced all of the social and political dislocations that accompany immigration while denying itself many of its advantages. It is important to understand the perversity of the British immigration experience. Along with racial animus, it was the fear that immigrants were taking jobs and resources away from the indigenous population that fueled the battles over controls and severely disrupted the British political system. Yet it was precisely this grassroots resistance that precluded the kind of immigration policy that might have significantly aided the country in achieving steady growth and in securing the jobs of British workers.

France did much better on this score. Migrant labor has been central to the achievement of the growth and productivity targets of the successive five-year plans. According to the Employment Commission of the Sixth Plan, migrant worker wages were 10–20 percent below those of national workers with the same qualifications, despite formal guarantees of equality.[29] They have undeniably served, as then Prime Minister Pompidou said in 1963, "to create détente in the labor market and to absorb social pressure."[30] The failure of the French government to take steps before 1972 to master the spontaneous and clandestine movement of workers contributed to their economic utility. Illegal workers, bereft of rights of residency and subject to prompt arrest and deportation, were easy targets of unscrupulous employers who used them to do shift work at wages often far below the norm.

It was the wretched and well-publicized living conditions of foreign workers that, as much as anything else, roused liberal opinion in France behind a more orderly and controlled migration. Once it is necessary, however, to house immigrants and their families properly, to provide them with job training and language instruction, and to compensate them at the same level as native workers, their net contribution to productivity, growth, and profits begins to decline, if not yet for individual employers, then for the economy as a whole. Ironically, then, progress toward equality in the labor market has been bought at the cost of reducing the propensity to recruit and employ foreign workers.

RACIAL CONFLICT AND SOCIAL INTEGRATION

Any discussion of the social situation of West Indian immigrants must proceed from the observation that the scale and seriousness of the problem is so much greater in Britain than in France that it requires a separate analysis. West Indians, and especially Jamaicans, constitute one of the three major non-European minorities in Britain and they have been the focus of the most intense racial conflict there. In contrast, immigrants from the Caribbean overseas departments have not, as a group, become a serious object of anti-immigration agitation or violence. It is not possible, therefore, to generalize with much assurance about French race relations policy toward migrants from the D.O.M., although BUMIDOM has made modest efforts to ease their transition into French jobs and housing.

The British response to racial conflict, once the initial period of disbelief and disavowal had passed, can be called a "community relations approach," involving the creation of an elaborate race relations structure. The 1965 and 1968 Race Relations Acts excited considerable opposition despite their limited scope and weak enforcement provisions.[31] The second law extended the coverage of the first—which had applied to places of public accommodation and service only—to the areas of housing, employment, insurance, and credit. But it was the institutional framework set up by the acts to carry out their provisions and to promote "harmonious race relations" which was the heart of the British policy toward discrimination. The central pieces of this structure were the Race Relations Board, the Community Relations Commission, and the local Community Relations Committees. The first two were national bodies of leading figures from business, education, and the church. The Race Relations Board had the authority to hear complaints about discrimination and to order the parties to attempt conciliation. The Community Relations Commission was responsible for the activities of numerous local committees of volunteers and local professional Community Relations officers whose duties were vaguely defined as promoting community relations.

In general, the British perceived racial conflict in individual terms and sought to deal with it by changing attitudes and promoting understanding between the races. The 1976 Race Relations Act, which collapsed the old Board and Commission into the Commission for Racial Equality and gave it significant new powers to initiate proceedings on its own and to issue nondiscrimination notices enforceable in the courts, does not represent a departure from the old assumptions in any important way and is widely regarded as ineffective.[32]

Though British race policy may have provided some reassurance to individuals, discrimination is still widespread. Immigration has been the source of a new and ugly chapter in British political history. There have been periodic outbreaks of violence in cities with high concentrations of West Indians. The most serious episodes occurred in Brixton in the spring of 1981 and in Hull, Liverpool, Bristol, Nottingham, Manchester, Wolverhampton, and other cities in July 1981. Renewed violence broke out in 1985 in the Handsworth district of Birmingham and in the Brixton area of London. One of the political consequences of the fears immigration has touched off has been the resurgence of neofascist political movements on a scale not seen since the 1930s. This threat was attenuated in part by the efforts of the leftwing Anti-Nazi League and in part by the British voters' lack of interest in extremist movements, but the major political parties are unable to handle race and immigration questions with much skill.

After the Conservatives took the initiative by the closing of free entry in 1962, the Labor Party attempted to establish an inter-party consensus on race by embracing the need for restrictions while at the same time pushing for a vigorous program of antidiscrimination efforts. This consensus broke down temporarily in 1968 when Mr. Enoch Powell, a Tory MP from Wolverhampton, launched a spectacular campaign against immigration. His unprecedented and demagogic behavior cost him his position in the leadership of the Conservative Party, but for several years he dominated public debate over the "color" question. Although both parties were busy enacting more and more stringent legislation to keep non-Europeans out of Britain (the law that is arguably the most straightforwardly discriminatory, the 1968 Kenyan Asians Act, was the work of the Labor Government),[33] neither made any overt attempt to use the issue for electoral purposes until 1983 when Mrs. Thatcher warned the country it was in danger of being "swamped" by aliens. What is probably more surprising is that they also failed to mobilize immigrants behind their banners. A large majority of all immigrants vote Labor, but they have not been concentrated in sufficient numbers to have more than a marginal effect on any election to date. Immigrants have not become a significant part of either party's electorate, nor have they been able to develop much political force on their own. Immigrant organizations have tended to founder on the rivalries and divisions within the West Indian community itself.

The race relations problem for the government today is no longer the adaptation of new immigrants to the strange and inhospitable setting of industrial Britain nor the preparation of the indigenous population to receive them. Rather it is the integration of the large numbers of "second generation immigrants," those young persons born in Britain who have known no other home. In 1981 there were some 519,000 West Indians in Britain, 163,000 of whom were 15 years old or younger.[34]

These young persons constitute a festering problem, the seriousness of which is evidenced in the continual jousting between West Indian teenagers and police. Under the notorious "sus" (arrest on suspicion) law, police can routinely stop and search individuals whom they suspect of carrying weapons or of being likely to commit a crime. Many West Indian leaders have charged that being black seems to constitute a strong presumption of criminality in the minds of the police. In any case, massive sweeps of immigrant communities have been carried out and have resulted in hundreds of blacks being stopped and frisked on the sidewalks. Such an operation precipitated major rioting in Brixton in 1981. A report written by Lord Scarman in the wake of the disorders was critical of the police and recommended a number of procedural reforms.[35]

In the wake of renewed rioting in the late summer of 1985 it was clear that most of Scarman's proposals had not been implemented, particularly his call for more minority police officers. Conflict between the races, whatever its roots in the misunderstanding and prejudice that is the concern of the race relations apparatus, is tied to the opportunities available to immigrants in the job and housing markets, the educational system, and the other social services. It is difficult to get reliable figures on immigrant employment but it is beyond dispute that unemployment among West Indians is very high.

One source gives the rate of unemployment among West Indian males born in the U.K. as 21 percent in 1977/78, compared with 5.3 percent for white males. It was even higher for West Indian females (24.1 percent). Rates were slightly lower for West Indians born outside the U.K. (7 percent and 10.5 percent, respectively).[36] Unemployment has gotten worse since 1978; one estimate claims that black unemployment in Britain quadrupled between 1973 and February 1980. By 1985, most estimates placed it between 40 and 50 percent in the central areas of cities in the Midlands.[37]

The British have been hesitant to develop programs to aid immigrants out of fear of indigenous resentment of special treatment for foreigners and out of a liberal fastidiousness about nonuniversalistic welfare measures. The government's initial position was that the existing services of the British welfare state could adequately care for the needs of immigrants, as it did for those of native citizens. Any temporary problems of adjustment could best be handled through voluntary channels. Eventually, however, limited moves were made toward programs of positive discrimination, at least so far as additional funding was made available to areas thought to have been especially affected by immigration.

The French have been less active than the British in the race relations arena. The government has supported or endorsed an active immigration policy for economic purposes. Because the outbreak of racial hostilities might have constrained their ability to look the other way on massive clandestine immigration, public officials have tended to deny that any serious problem exists while extolling the benefits derived by native Frenchmen from the efforts of foreigners. There have been sporadic outbreaks of racial violence in France throughout the postwar period. These became especially virulent during the years of the Algerian War and its aftermath. In general, French public opinion is more negative about North Africans than any other ethnic community. Civil rights organizations and the trade unions have taken the lead in defending the rights of immigrants, but they have been powerless to do much more than march in the streets in protest against exploitation and discrimination. It was not until 1972 that the National Assembly passed legislation dealing with racial discrimination. The law concentrated on racial incitement rather than discrimination per se, placed such behavior under the criminal code, and created no special enforcement agencies.[38] The widespread acceptance of the "threshold of tolerance" has led to a kind of fatalism about the possibility of multi-racialism, an odd development in a country well-known for its claims to a universalistic culture and language. As much as anything else, the conviction that it would be impossible to assimilate non-Europeans led the government to embrace a policy of racial selection.

Unlike the British, French officials have typically developed specialized agencies and programs to assist immigrant groups. The most important of these is the Social Action Fund (FAS), a quasi-public agency created by the state but exercising programmatic autonomy and enjoying independent access to funds. FAS has devoted most of its energies to building housing for migrant workers, though it provides other forms of assistance as well. BUMIDOM carries out most of these functions for migrants from the overseas departments and in general provides a broader range of services than are available for persons coming from other areas.

THE FUTURE OF CARIBBEAN MIGRATION

The economic crisis of the 1980s radically altered the environment in which immigration decisions were being made. There were no longer any compelling economic reasons for large-scale immigration, given the high unemployment among indigenous European workers and given that those sectors most markedly infiltrated by foreign workers were in severe slumps, as for example construction and metalworking. The combination of the recession, the growing belief that the long-term dependence on foreign labor was detrimental to the productivity and modernization of the economy, and the continuing racial conflict has led to a situation in which there was strong opposition to any significant new immigration for work in the foreseeable future.

The recession reduced sharply the numbers of those seeking to move to Europe and increased the rate of return of those immigrants already there. Nevertheless, very high birth rates may actually increase the total size of the population of Caribbean origin in Britain and France over the next several years.

The impact of the recession was not limited to immigration policy, of course; its effects were felt in the domestic policy field as well. The climate appeared to be most unfavorable to a sustained and vigorous attack against the problems faced by immigrants, and especially their children. Economic dislocation and increased competition for jobs is likely to intensify racial hostilities and turn immigrants into convenient scapegoats. The pressure of inflation and budget crises has taken its toll on ameliorative social services in both countries.

This grim situation was made even worse by legislative developments in Britain. Mrs. Thatcher's Tory administration was more forcefully committed to ending immigration than any of its predecessors of either party. Changes in the nationality law pushed through with great difficulty in 1981 created a framework in which even more stringent policies can be justified. Before 1962 persons living in the Commonwealth enjoyed British citizenship and the rights of free entry and permanent residence. After that date they lost the prerogative of free entry but if they managed to secure residence, could still exercise the rights of citizenship. The new law that went into effect in 1983 removes most of their rights of citizenship as well. It creates three categories of British nationality: (1) British citizenship, which is no longer based on birth but on complex notions of descent and immigration status; (2) citizenship of British dependent territories; and (3) British overseas citizenship.[39] It is in the last category that persons living in the Caribbean fall. Rights accruing to each status are sharply differentiated and unequal. Both the Labor and Liberal parties opposed this legislation and are pledged to repeal it should they obtain office, but it must be observed that Labor's record has been only marginally more sensitive to the plight of immigrants than that of the Tories.

The experience of the Socialist government in France suggests just how narrow the limits to immigration policy are, no matter what party is in power. Mitterrand pursued a two-pronged strategy. On the one hand, he took measures to shut off new immigration more effectively than was the case already. This involved prohibitions on all new immigration for work, efforts to halt clandestine entry (which include penalties for employers who recruit illegals), and financial incentives for voluntary repatriation.[40] These policies differed modestly if at all from those of previous governments. On the other hand, the Socialists moved impressively to strengthen the political and civil rights of foreigners already in France. They suspended the expulsions that had reached epidemic proportions in the last months of Giscard d'Estaing's administration, established the right of association for immigrants on the same terms as for nationals, and placed executive actions toward immigrants under judicial oversight.[41] The general thrust of these reforms is to move from the concept of the rights of citizens to the rights of persons. Although it is too soon to assess the consequences of these changes, it is clear that they are in marked contrast to the British effort to reserve the full privileges of citizenship to the "old British." Ironically, these positive changes may not apply, ultimately, to the Caribbean overseas departments. The socialists hope to promote self-determination through referenda in the D.O.M.[42] If they succeed, the residents of newly independent Caribbean states may in the future lose the citizenship that has heretofore guaranteed their right to immigrate and, however imperfectly, contributed to their social protection in France.

The days when the tug of colonial obligations could take precedence over immediate national interest in regard to immigration are rapidly passing. The end of the great period of economic expansion that was the most remarkable characteristic of European life in the last thirty years removes the pressing need for labor that was the premise of contemporary immigration to Europe. It may, however, be premature to close the book on this saga, and not only because a reinvigorated European capitalism would again require foreign labor to make it work. British and French society have been basically and permanently transformed by immigration. No recession, however severe, and no program of repatriation, however attractive or heavyhanded, will remove their sizable minority communities. Arguments over immigration controls are for the most part matters of the past. Learning to live with the permanent populations immigration has produced will preoccupy policymakers in the years ahead.

NOTES

1. For an extended discussion of the development of citizenship rights within the French and British empires, see Gary P. Freeman, *Immigrant Labor and Racial Conflict in Industrial Societies: The French and British Experience, 1945–1975* (Princeton: Princeton Univ. Press, 1979), pp. 36–39.

2. *Le Monde*, May 9, 1973.

3. Nicholas Deakin, "The British Nationality Act of 1948: A brief study in the political mythology of race relations," *Race* 11 (1969). Canada, Australia, and New Zealand make up the "old Commonwealth." All other members are commonly referred to as "new Commonwealth" nations.

4. Freeman, *Immigrant Labor*, p. 37.

5. Victor Sable, *Les Antilles sans complexes: une experience de décolonisation* (Paris: G. P. Masonneuve & Laine, 1972).

6. Ira Katznelson, *Black Men, White Cities: Race, Politics, and Migration in the United States 1900-30 and Britain 1948-68* (London: Oxford Univ. Press, 1973), p. 34.

7. Nicholas Deakin, "The politics of the Commonwealth immigrants bill," *Political Quarterly* 39 (1968); Freeman, *Immigrant Labor*, pp. 45-52.

8. *Immigration from the Commonwealth*, Cmnd 2739 (London: HMSO, 1965), is the Labor government's administrative response to the Commonwealth Immigrants Act passed by its predecessor. For an account of the problems of British passport holders in Africa, see Derek Humphry and Michael Ward, *Passports and Politics* (Harmondsworth, England: Penguin Books, 1974) and David Steel, *No Entry: The Background and Implications of the Commonwealth Immigrants Act, 1968* (London: C. Hurst and Company, 1969).

9. Home Office, Immigration Statistics, annually.

10. Ibid.

11. See *Commonwealth Immigrants Act, Statistics*, Cmnd 2397, 2658, 3258, 3594, 4327, 4620, 4951.

12. Ibid.

13. Ibid.

14. Alfred Sauvy, "Evaluation des besoins de l'immigration française," *Population* 1 (1946):91-98; Sauvy, "Besoins et possibilités de l'immigration française," *Population* 5 (1950):202-28, 417-34; Xavier Lannes, *L 'immigration en France depuis 1945* (The Hague: Martinus Nijhoff, 1953), p. 9.

15. Pierre Bideberry, "Bilan de vingt années d'immigration, 1946-1966," *Revue française des affaires sociales* 21 (1967); Conseil National du Patronat Français, *Notes et Arguments* 40 (1973).

16. Ibid.

17. Conseil National du Patronat Français, *Notes et Arguments* 26 (1972).

18. Juliette Minces, *Les travailleurs étrangers en France* (Paris: Editions du Seuil, 1973), p. 84.

19. Corentin Calvez, "Le Problème des travailleurs étrangers," *Journal Officiel, Avis et rapports du Conseil Economique et Sociale*, 7 (1969).

20. A. Lebon and G. Falchi, "New Developments in Intra-European Migration Since 1974," *International Migration Review* 14 (1980):539-79.

21. *Annuaire statistique de la France* (Paris: INSEE, 1979), pp. 26, 34. For a detailed demographic analysis of the West Indian departments, see Ivor J. Butcher and Philip E. Ogden, "West Indians in France: Migration and demographic change," in Philip E. Ogden, ed., *Migrants in Modern France: Four Studies*, (Univ. London, Queen Mary College, Department of Geography and Earth Science, Occasional Paper No. 23, 1984).

22. BUMIDOM, Annual Report, 1974.

23. INSEE, 1975 Census, cited in Butcher and Ogden, "West Indians in France," p. 54.

24. *Annuaire statistique de la France*, 1979, p. 64.

25. BUMIDOM, Annual Reports, cited in Butcher and Ogden, "West Indians in France," p. 52.

26. Stephen Castles and Godula Kosack, *Immigrant Workers and Class Structure in Western Europe* (London: Oxford Univ. Press, 1973), pp. 88–90.

27. M. Combes, et al., *La traite silencieuse* (Paris: IDOC-France, 1977), p. 136.

28. Ibid., p. 137. Cf. Butcher and Ogden, "West Indians in France," p. 64.

29. Commissariat General du Plan, *Rapport de la commission de l'emploi*, I (Paris: Documentation Française, 1971), p. 55.

30. Quoted in Minces, *Les travailleurs étrangers*, p. 37.

31. For an extended discussion see Freeman, *Immigrant Labor*, pp. 141–52.

32. Zig Layton-Henry, *The Politics of Race in Britain* (London: George Allen & Unwin, 1984), pp. 122–44.

33. Nicholas Deakin, "Labour Adopts a White Britain Policy," *Venture* 20 (1968).

34. *Social Trends* 13 (London: Central Statistical Office, 1982), p. 179.

35. Lord Scarman, *The Brixton Disorders April 10–12, 1981: Report of an Inquiry*, Cmnd. 8427 (London: HMSO, 1981).

36. Stephen Castles, *Here for Good* (London: Pluto Press, 1984), p. 147.

37. Julian Henriques, Peter Long, and Shanti Patel, "Employment," in *Britain's Black Population* (London: Heinemann, 1980), pp. 64–8. The 1985 statistics come from the New York *Times*, September 11, 1985.

38. Fred Hermantin, "De l'injure et de la diffamation raciste: Etude critique du droit positif français," *Revue des droits de l'homme* 4 (1971).

39. Layton-Henry, *The Politics of Race*, pp. 157–60.

40. Catherine de Wenden, "L'évolution de la politique française d'immigration depuis l'arrivée au pouvoir du gouvernement socialiste" (Paper presented at the annual meeting of the Council for European Studies, Washington, D.C., 1983); Martin A. Schain, "Immigrants and Politics in France," in John S. Ambler, ed., *The French Socialist Experiment* (Philadelphia: ISHI Press, 1985), pp. 166–90.

41. Ibid.

42. *Projet socialiste* (Paris: Club Socialiste du Livre, 1981), pp. 258–59.

Caribbean Migration to the Netherlands: From Elite to Working Class

Frank Bovenkerk

Two years prior to Suriname's gaining political independence in 1975, emigration to the Netherlands reached a peak of 30,000 people a year. A newspaper reporter at the arrival gate of Schiphol Airport was bewildered by the enormous variety of people entering the country. These people didn't fit into the immigration categories the Dutch were used to. The reporter, expecting to write about young, colorfully-dressed, lower-class black males, which was the typical vision the Dutch had of Surinamers, had to change his plans.

Instead, what he saw were large Hindustani families headed by slim, dark-eyed peasants and elderly women dressed in pastel colors and white shawls; flamboyant Creole mothers surrounded by children; people of Javanese descent (something one might have expected 20 years earlier when thousands of Eurasians fled to the Netherlands from the Dutch East Indies); Chinese, Bush negroes (as Maroons were still called in Holland), Lebanese, and even a South American Indian. The reporter decided to interview a random sample and soon discovered that the immigrants had come from all levels of society. They were urban-proletariat, peasants, middle class, as well as well-to-do civil servants and businessmen. How could such an enormous wave of people come from such a small country (population 400,000)?

The Dutch had always considered Suriname to be a provincial corner of their dwindling colonial empire and very few people in the Netherlands were aware of the population diversity of Suriname; a

diversity that has resulted from the constant importing of new laborers to its plantation economy. The poor newspaperman was confronted with a cross section of the Surinamese population come to
Holland during the "ripening" stage of the migration process.

The Dutch government felt itself compelled by this new immigration to develop and execute a reception policy. Several social
science research institutions were assigned to study the needs of this
immigrant group and all of them tried to grasp the complex composition by first paying attention to the history of this emigration.[1] In
these historical accounts emigration from Suriname is compared with
the emigration from the Netherlands Antilles (Curaçao, Aruba,
Bonaire, and three of the smaller Leeward Islands). The latter never
attracted as much attention because their numbers were smaller
(never exceeding 2,000 persons a year) and their rate of return
migration was much higher, averaging 50 percent per year of the
number emigrating.[2]

THE DUTCH CARIBBEAN

Emigration from Suriname and the Netherlands Antilles began
in a manner similar to that of all colonial Caribbean societies. The
children of the elite (white first and then mulatto) were sent to the
mother countries to be properly educated in Europe. Some of them
returned, others stayed. This movement began about two centuries
ago and is still going on. In 1981 more than 2,000 Surinamers and
Antillians were attending institutions of higher learning in the Netherlands. Those who returned were to constitute the administrative and
business elites of Suriname and the Netherlands Antilles. Those who
stayed became university professors, physicians, high school teachers,
and so on. This kind of nonreturn of professionals is one form of
brain-drain. Today more Surinamers are practicing physicians in the
Netherlands than in Suriname.

For more than a century, the people of Suriname and the
Netherlands Antilles have been convinced of the necessity of going to
Holland if one was really to advance socially. This was more so for
Surinamers; for Antillians, studying in the United States became an
alternative of equal merit. Ever since Curaçao and Aruba have housed
American-owned oil refineries (since the 1920s and 1930s), Antillian
cultural orientation has been divided between the Netherlands and

the United States. The number of Surinamers in Holland is now estimated at 190,000; the number of Antillians at 35,000.[3]

Returnees generally, and especially Surinamers, give an enthusiastic account of the Netherlands. If they don't, they are simply not believed. "You tell me such bad things because you don't want me to go, eh?" There was, of course, a strong basis of reality in their optimistic account, especially during the 1960s, once the Netherlands became a welfare state. Returning migrants were reinforcing the favorable attitude toward the mother country created by witnessing the obvious wealth of the Dutch in Suriname and by studying with the missionaries who taught Dutch geography and history in the schools.

After World War II emigration from the Dutch Caribbean exhibited only small increases. During the early 1960s, however, people from a much broader class basis began to participate. Dutch, Surinamese, and Antillian social scientists have speculated a great deal about how this sudden enlargement of the old colonial migration pattern came about. A first explanation is simply that the Surinamese upper-classes expanded.[4] A short economic boom during the war (1942–1945), owing to the exploitation of Suriname's bauxite for the American war industry, had enabled people of new social classes to emigrate to the Netherlands. It was no longer only the doctors, lawyers, managers, and high civil servants who sent their children to Europe; a (mainly Creole) group of school teachers, middle-ranked administrators and nurses left the country as well. This argument does not quite explain the rather sudden rise in numbers, nor the fact that a new category of skilled laborers participated in the migration process.

A second interpretation is popular among politically leftwing Surinamese circles in the Netherlands.[5] They hold that the development of postwar capitalism is responsible for the recruitment of cheap labor from its colonies or former colonies. Hadn't the emigration from the British West Indies to the United Kingdom been triggered by the deliberate recruitment of cheap labor for British industry? During the late 1950s and up until 1963 a small number of Dutch industrial firms did indeed send recruitment officers to Suriname to bring some one hundred skilled workers back to Holland. This experiment, however, ended in disaster. The firms' management seems to have made every possible mistake in introducing their new employees and their white workers protested strongly.[6]

After much trouble, Dutch industry lost interest in Suriname and started to recruit cheap labor of a far more submissive type from the Mediterranean area.

Italians and Spaniards, and later especially Turks and Moroccans were viewed as being more profitable. These Mediterranean *gastarbeiders* ("guestworkers") were recruited on a one-year basis and could be laid off and sent home when economic expansion slowed down. The Mediterranean labor force was supposed to function as a buffer in the economic cycle. Surinamers and Antillians were far less easy to deal with since they were Dutch citizens, which entitled them to the same rights as anybody else. This explanation in terms of direct capitalist exploitation made somewhat more sense applied to migrants from Curaçao and Aruba. For one reason or another, the employment of Antillians was more successful than that of Surinamese labor. It only came to a halt at the end of the 1960s, when the number of skilled workers in Curaçao interested in going to the Netherlands dwindled.

Although labor recruitment for Dutch industry has been quantitatively negligible, its psychological effect was not. The possibility of emigration to the Netherlands came within the horizon of new groups. Emigration was no longer a prerogative for the upper classes alone. From the mid 1960s on, the Surinamese establishment in the Netherlands, a group of successfully assimilated Surinamers, began to protest. The migration of the lower social classes was viewed as a threat to their position.

ATTEMPTS AT DEVELOPMENT

A third argument for the sudden rise in migration figures is no less important; it explains the beginning of the spontaneous emigration of the working classes.[7] From 1958 to 1964, a huge project of economic development was carried out in the form of the construction of an enormous dam on the Suriname River at Brokopondo. This joint project of the American aluminum company Alcoa and the Surinamese government was meant to provide hydroelectric energy for the smelting of bauxite. According to the development doctrine at the time, the building up of an infrastructure was to attract foreign capital; new industries would provide employment. The expected multiplier effect, however, did not occur; foreign investors did not show up and now a big, highly capital intensive Suralco aluminum factory is operating all alone in the middle of a tropical rain forest. This "raft to keep the Surinamese economy floating" provides work for no more than 6 percent of the country's labor force. The workers who built the dam were laid off in 1963 and 1964 and could not find an equally well-paying job anywhere else in the country. And so they took their savings and used it to buy tickets to Holland. The bitter irony of this story is, of course, that an ambitious program for economic development resulted in the loss of a significant portion of the skilled labor force.

From the late 1960s on, there was no stopping it: emigration burst forth in its full magnitude. Ever since the dividing line between elite emigration was eliminated, the internal dynamics of the migration process has been responsible for the departure of ever-growing numbers of people from a widening socioeconomic range. Compared with the poor economy of the remote Suriname, the metropolitan welfare state of the Netherlands is highly attractive, especially to the poorer segment of Surinamese society. The push and pull factors tell the story: (1) The Surinamese unemployment rate has been estimated for years at 30 percent. In the Netherlands of the early 1970s, no more than 5 percent of the labor-productive population was without work, and in the 1980s, 10 percent. (2) The wage level in the Netherlands is three to four times higher than in Suriname. The lower one's place on the occupational ladder, the bigger the difference.[8] (3) Social and economic security in Suriname is almost nonexistent compared with Holland. There is no unemployment insurance, no national system of medical care, and until 1980 care for the old existed only on paper. The people of Suriname were quite aware that one could participate in the welfare state only by emigrating to Holland. Unlike the French colonies of Guiana, Martinique, and Guadeloupe, where the same social security system is in effect as in metropolitan France, Surinamers had to emigrate to take part in it.

It is interesting to note how the respected emigration motive of former days, "education," still works. Several sociological surveys among emigrants, before and after crossing the Atlantic, have shown extremely high responses indicating that education was the motive for emigration.[9] More than 70 percent of the respondents told the interviewers that they went to the Netherlands for their education and that they would return as soon as they were finished. This motive has become generalized and even professed by people whose educational level in Suriname makes it extremely unlikely for them to be able to attend any institution of higher education in the Netherlands.

I remember being the guest of a family in Suriname, where the oldest son Romeo was to leave for the Netherlands the next day. The neighbors and friends who asked about Romeo's plans and prospects were told that he was going to go to high school. Six weeks later, I was in the same home when one of the neighbors came to ask his mother: "Did Romeo already find a job?" These people saw no contradiction between the two emigration motives.

The development of the ethnic and socioeconomic composition of the migratory flow reflects the emancipation of the various groups in Surinamese society in a condensed form. First there were the whites and mulattos, then came the dark-skinned Creoles. The Hindustanis, who had not even completed their urbanization into Paramaribo, were soon to follow. In the early 1960s emigration to Holland could be described as a case of extended urbanization. Surinamers in the Netherlands provided the money for their poorer relatives to buy the much-desired ticket to Holland, a process typical of chain migration. For the Royal Dutch Airlines the route between Paramaribo and Amsterdam became lucrative, and flight prices were considerably reduced. Surinamese society fell apart at the seams: employers lost their manpower, teachers realized that they were educating their pupils for work in another country, shopkeepers saw their turnover drastically reduced. For many people it was not a question of deciding to emigrate but of deciding to stay!

The sharp rise in the emigration curve in 1973 had to do with a major political occurrence in Suriname. In 1973, elections were won by the Creole Party (NPK) and the new prime minister, Henck A. Arron, opened negotiations with the Dutch government concerning independence. The Dutch (Socialist) government jumped at the chance to get rid of this troublesome tropical part of the Dutch Kingdom in an honorable way. For one thing, Suriname's independence would mean the end of the migration, which had been causing growing hostility among the Dutch population. During preparations for independence Hindustani political leaders, and some Javanese as well, raised fervent objections to the prospect of black political dominance in an independent republic. They publicly advised their followers to leave the country to avoid being terrorized by the blacks. The spectacular increase of Hindustani and Javanese, emigration often directly from the countryside, was the response to this political appeal. By Independence Day, November 25, 1975, no less than 150,000 Surinamers had left for the Netherlands.

The two countries agreed that the Netherlands would contribute 3.5 billion guilders to Suriname's development in a period of 10 years. Apart from Israel, this was probably the largest amount of money per capita ever received by a developing country, $4,000 per person. It was to appear that this aid money was too much to digest even in this country with a poor economic and sociopolitical infrastructure: the yearly quota of transfer payments has never been attained. In 1975, however, this seemed like a sound enough economic basis for at least the first 10 years. The new Republic of Suriname started off in an atmosphere of enthusiasm and confidence in the future. The Arron government decided to invest a large part of these funds in a big new project in West Suriname: Kabalebo. As had been the case 20 years before, a big dam was to be constructed as well as a railroad and a new town. It took the Surinamese people two years to realize that the way in which development funds were being spent would bring about neither substantial new employment nor higher salaries. In 1978, when a large part of the railroad was finished, part of the labor force was laid off. They could not find new jobs at the same pay and history repeated itself: they invested their money in tickets to the Netherlands. In the 1975 agreement between Suriname and the Netherlands about "Residence and settlement of each others' subjects," provision was made for the possibility to emigrate to the Netherlands within five years after independence. They went to the Netherlands as tourists; if they could get a job and adequate housing then the migrants were granted residence permits. The dismissed railroad workers showed that this system worked; they used only the first half of their round-trip tickets and thereby functioned as pioneers of a new wave of emigration. Between 1975 and 1980, another 30,000 emigrants left for Holland. The beleaguered newspaperman we met before was at Schiphol Airport again, observing the very same variety of immigrants as five years earlier; another cross section of the Surinamese society was on the move. Had he added several thousands of migrants to other countries (United States, Canada) to the 180,000 now living in Holland, he would come to the staggering conclusion that within 15 years, between one-third and one-half of the Surinamese population had emigrated. At least in part, this did not happen in spite of the former mother country's development aid but because of it.

Since 1980, emigration from Suriname to the Netherlands has nearly ceased. The Dutch government introduced a system of visas and the agreement on passenger traffic between the two countries ended. In the very same year, a small military group seized power. The Bouterse controlled governments that resulted did not affect emigration very much; the route to the Netherlands had already been blocked. During the first few months, after the government had several members of the bourgeoisie killed (in December 1982), emigration figures rose again to several hundred a month. Threatened professionals and a group of students left the country, some of whom were accepted in the Netherlands as political refugees.

Now that the Suriname exodus is over, one may wonder how such a disastrous dwindling of the population was politically possible. Surinamese governments should have all the reason in the world to take emigration as a sign that people lack confidence in their leadership: emigrants "vote with their feet," to paraphrase Lenin. Successive governments understood this differently. Emigrants were accused of being traitors to their country; politicians would not accept any responsibility for their well-being in Holland. Nor would they dare close down the Surinamese frontier, since cutting off the option of settling abroad with relatives and friends would mean political suicide.

During the same period the Dutch government never seriously contemplated closing down the frontier for Surinamers either. This would have meant a violation of international agreements. The Dutch simply waited for Suriname to become independent before settling this question. Had the Dutch people accepted such leniency toward migration? No—yet any suggestion of restricting immigration was immediately labelled as racism and hence as being alien to Dutch political culture.

For the very same reasons, emigration from the Netherlands Antilles is still free—these Caribbean islands still being part of the Kingdom of the Netherlands. There is, however, one all important difference: with a total of 35,000 emigrants, Antillian emigration doesn't amount to the same proportions as does Suriname's. By tacit agreement the possibility of introducing a visa system to keep the Antillians out has not been discussed in the Dutch parliament. Another "beat the ban" episode in Caribbean emigration was thus avoided.

A special social science research project has been carried out to shed light on why so few Antillians leave for Holland.[10] Many of the explanatory factors for Surinamese emigration also hold true for Curaçao, Aruba, and the other Dutch Antillian islands. They have a population of 250,000, the unemployment rate is equally high, salaries are much lower than in Holland, and the system of social benefits, although better than in Suriname, is inferior to that in the Netherlands.

Why do the Antillians exhibit such negligible willingness to emigrate? A first explanation has to do with Antillian cultural identity. The atmosphere there is more cosmopolitan than in Suriname, and the national culture is less exclusively oriented to the mother country. Second, the Netherlands Antilles are not a multiracial society in the political sense that Suriname is. There are no Hindustani or Javanese. The major political cleavage of the present-day Netherlands Antilles is between Aruba and the rest, but up until now this has not resulted in mass emigration. Third, emigration seems far less a definite step for many Antillians than it is for Surinamers. Antillians have a relatively high rate of return. Return migration is not an issue of debate among them.

This is quite different from the case of the Surinamese immigrants. With the exception of a brief period just before and after Suriname gained independence, in the past 15 years their rate of return migration has never been high. It has now sunk to under one percent per year. Surprisingly enough, no single topic is so widely and thoroughly discussed by Surinamers in Holland as the moral and political obligation to repatriate. It is an ideological issue embracing the wish to maintain ties with the native country, and it makes the trials and tribulations of immigration endurable. Where Surinamers cherish a migrant ideology, Antillians practice it.

Public concern in the Netherlands in the 1980s has shifted from the issue of immigration to the question of integration. Surinamers and Antillians insist on not being called immigrants but respected as a new Dutch ethnic group. Where they once demanded the possibility to "live according to their own culture," the problem now is how to get jobs, housing, good schooling and to combat racial discrimination.

NOTES

1. Johannes van Amersfoort, *Immigratie en minderheidsvorming. een analyse van de Nederlandse situatie 1945-1973* (Alphen a/d Rijn: Samsom,

1974); Instituut voor Toegepaste Sociologie, *Surinaamse migranten in Nederland. de positie van Surinamers in de Nederlandse samenleving* (Nijmegen, 1982).

2. Willem Koot and Anco Ringeling, *De Antillianen* (Muiderberg, Coutinho, 1984), pp. 80–100.

3. Philip J. Muus et al., *Retourmigratie van Mediterranen. Surinamers en Antillianen uit Nederland* ('s-Gravenhage: Ministerie van Sociale Zaken en Werkgelegenheid, 1983), Deel II, pp. 1–47.

4. See, for example, Johannes van Amersfoort, *Surinamese Immigrants in the Netherlands* ('s-Gravenhage: Government Printing and Publishing Office, 1969).

5. Fred Budike, *Surinamers naar Nederland. de migratie van 1687–1982* (Amsterdam: Instituut voor Voortgezet Beroepsonderwijs, 1982).

6. A. E. Bayer, *Surinaamse arbeiders in Nederland* (Assen: Van Gorcum, 1965).

7. Frank Bovenkerk, "De Vlucht. Migratie in de jaren zeventig," in *Suriname. de schele onafhankelijkheid.* ed. G. Willemsen (Amsterdam: Arbeiderspers, Synopsis, 1983).

8. Frank Bovenkerk, *Emigratie uit Suriname* (Amsterdam: Antropologisch-Sociologisch, Centrum, 1975).

9. L. Zielhuis, *Migratie uit Suriname* (Paramaribo: Ministerie van Sociale Zaken, 1973), pp. 36–39; Instituut voor Toegepaste Sociologie, *Surinaamse migranten in Nederland.*

10. Willem Koot, *Emigratie op de Nederlandse Antillen* (Diss., Leiden, 1979).

Caribbean Migration to Canada: Prejudice and Opportunity

Frances Henry

Canada, like the United States, has been an immigrant receiving country since its inception. Its earliest settlers (aside from the Native Americans) were the so-called Charter groups—the British and the French. After Confederation in 1867, immigration from European countries, primarily the British Isles, continued. Migration has always accounted for a large component in the growth of the population; this trend likewise continues. In 1975, for example, the Canadian population increased by 354,000 persons; half of this was due to immigration.

The countries of origin of those peoples coming to Canada has changed, however. After World War II, substantial numbers of migrants from southern Europe, Italy, Greece, Portugal and other areas migrated to Canada. Canada's urban population has become even more heterogeneous, complex and pluralistic with the entrance of the so-called visible minority or nonwhite populations, including Chinese, Japanese, South Asians, and West Indians.

Blacks have a long history in the country; there were nearly 4,000 black slaves in New France by 1750 and several thousand blacks arrived with the Empire Loyalists in 1789. Another group sought refuge in 1815. Still others came through the "underground railroad" throughout the first half of the 19th century. By 1850 there were close to 50,000 blacks in Canada, though many emigrated back to the United States once the Civil War was over. By 1941 only 22,000 were in all of Canada, the vast majority descendants of the earlier settlers.[1] During the 1960s and particularly the 1970s, immigration from the West Indies dramatically increased the number of blacks.

Between 1946 and 1982, nearly 222,000 West Indians came to Canada.[2] Another 10,000 can be added to that figure bringing the total to just over 230,000. During the 1960s and 1970s, immigrants from European sources declined from an earlier 76 percent of all migrants to 39 percent; at the same time, total Third World immigration increased to 57 percent, of whom three-fifths are from the Caribbean and Latin America. A word of caution about population figures is necessary. Since the census merely asks for the last country of residence, West Indians who come here via Great Britain—and estimates suggest that there are many such—are counted as British. Additionally, West Indians of Asian origin are sometimes classified as Asians rather than as West Indians, and to further complicate the problem, some studies define ethnicity in terms of blackness or race thereby including Canadian blacks, and American black immigrants with West Indians.

Thus, the best estimates put the numbers of West Indians at about 320,000. The total numbers of so-called visible minority people (excluding the Native Americans) are now slightly more than one-half million people in a nation of 26 million. In percentage terms, this amounts to only about 2 percent of the population but even this moderate number has been sufficient to fuel the flames of racist sentiment. Ontario receives more than half of all immigrants to this country. Toronto and its surrounding regions has the largest numbers of West Indians; smaller numbers are found in the other provinces. Quebec, because of its Francophone policy, has attracted fewer immigrants in recent years and the majority of migrants who come to Quebec are French-speaking. Naturally, substantial numbers of these have come from Haiti and the French Caribbean.

CHANGES IN CANADIAN IMMIGRATION LAW

Prior to 1962, Canada's immigration policy was discriminatory with respect to the social, ethnic, and racial backgrounds of potential immigrants. In 1962, a point system based in the main on educational and occupational qualifications was instituted and this along with increasingly restrictive immigration laws in Great Britain (the traditional recipient of Commonwealth immigration) directly influenced the rate of immigration to Canada. Alarmed by the increase, Canadian authorities tightened their policy. In 1980 a yearly quota on all immigrants was established but this was clearly aimed at curbing the flow of nonwhite migrants. Despite the commonly held stereotypes that West Indians are lazy, slow moving, and uneducated, and Asians are poverty stricken and uncivilized, and that both groups have come to Canada to rip off the welfare and social service system, the majority in both groups are educated, skilled, and in the highly employable age bracket of 20–44 years.[3] This, of course, is an obvious result of the point system, which favors such individuals.

In addition to the effects of increasingly restrictive immigration laws, the economic climate in Canada has been worsening and there has, in fact, been a slight decline in the number of all immigrants and specifically those from the West Indies. From a high-point of 28,000 in 1974, only 12,000 arrived here in 1982. Jamaica, Guyana, Haiti, and Trinidad and Tobago in that order were the countries that sent the largest number.[4] Somewhat more than two fifths of the West Indian population is Jamaican in origin. In fact, "Jamaican" has become the generic term for West Indians in Canada much to the chagrin of those who come from other countries. The majority of West Indians are in the 25–45 age group and a substantial number are dependent children under the age of 16, following the well known pattern of sending for dependent children once one or both parents have become financially and occupationally settled in their new country. Another fairly common pattern, particularly in the 1960s when the government sponsored a female domestic labor scheme, is the initial migration of women who then sponsor their spouses or fiancés as well as children from that union or prior ones.

In the late 1970s, a new scheme for domestics was instituted whereby women were allowed into Canada on work permits for a period of two years. They were to work only as household domestics and their tenure in Canada did not allow them to apply for Canadian citizenship or any other form of government benefit. Early 1984, this scheme was changed after many complaints. Women recruited as domestic workers were henceforth eligible to apply for Canadian citizenship once they have been here for three years.

Most West Indians intend to enter the clerical occupations, closely followed by those in the medicine and health fields (many women hope to enter or train for the nursing profession), as well as those of an entrepreneurial, managerial, or administrative nature.[5] To what extent are West Indians able to realize their job intentions? In 1981, a study suggests that West Indians, in comparison to other ethnic groups, are in low status jobs, earn lower incomes than any other group, and experience more job insecurity. Even when education and skills are controlled, West Indians who, as a group, have higher levels of education and skill than either the Portuguese or Italians, still earn less income and experience more job insecurity. West Indians are more likely to be clustered in low status jobs such as taxi drivers, watchmen, and security guards for men, and domestic and factory labor for women. A small proportion of West Indian men are, however, employed in high status jobs particularly in the medical and health fields but as the study notes: "West Indian men are concentrated in some specific high status occupations but this does not appear to alter their overall income significantly. In fact, West Indians earn even poorer incomes than would be expected on the basis of education and job status."[6] The study further notes that for Italians and Portuguese who also have low job status and are excluded from high status occupations, their lower levels of education and skill account for this; whereas for West Indians, "exclusion from high status jobs occurs for other reasons"[7]—the "other reasons" have, of course, to do with racial discrimination.

Officially employment discrimination on the basis of race, color, religion, and sex is illegal in Canada. Provincial legislation such as the various Human Rights Codes enacted by each province have jurisdictional responsibility for approximately 90 percent of the labor force and the remainder under federal jurisdiction are protected by the Federal Human Rights Act.[8] But many areas of potential discrimination such as housing, health care, and social services are not protected by legislation. Unofficially, subtle forms of individual and institutional discrimination occur regularly. Among both public and private sector employers, indirect and passive forms of discrimination create barriers to members of ethnic and racial minorities. These forms include recruitment such as "word of mouth" advertising, which unfortunately ensures that employers hire persons similar to those already employed and thereby make it more difficult for newcomers to enter certain occupations.

Such recruitment also functions to create and maintain low status job segregation as low wage paying employers recruit and perpetuate their low wage earning labor force. This applies particularly to West Indian women employed in factories in low paying jobs who recruit relatives and friends. Employment agencies used to fill vacancies often accept discriminatory orders for employment. Other forms of discrimination include the use of tests that cannot be passed by newcomers or the use of such screening devices as demanding "Canadian experience" for jobs that, while they clearly require job experience, have no need to require "Canadian experience" at it. Slowness in promotion and lay-offs in a period of economic decline affect ethnic group members most dramatically as they are subject to the "last hired/first fired" principle, often employed as they are in those industries most sensitive to economic constraints. A 1984/85 study by this author focused on racial discrimination in employment in Toronto. Preliminary results indicated that nonwhite job applicants are rejected for employment far more often than are Canadian whites, even when qualifications and prior job experience are controlled. Neither the public nor the private sector has instituted affirmative action programs for nonwhites, though the subject began to receive some attention in 1984/85.

RACISM IN THE CITIES

Racism directed against nonwhites has indeed become a major problem in the large cities of Canada, primarily Toronto, Montreal, Vancouver, Calgary, and others. In Toronto, and elsewhere in the country, a substantial number of racial incidents have taken place. These include assaulting people in the subway, beatings, destruction of South Asian places of worship, harassment of the homes and businesses of nonwhites, complaints of police brutality against nonwhites, physical and verbal conflicts between whites and nonwhites in the school system, and the like. Both West Indians and South Asians have become targets of extremist rightwing groups such as the Western Guard and during the early 1980s there has been a major revival of the Ku Klux Klan, who recruited teenagers in schools among other activities.

In addition to direct physical assaults, racism takes the form of distributing hate literature and propaganda, racial slurs directed against nonwhites, racial grafitti on walls, houses and public building sites, telephone messages such as the "White Power" line maintained by the Western Guard, telling and retelling racial jokes, particularly in the schools, the use of telephone and the mails to threaten nonwhites and, of course, the ubiquitous use of the pejorative term "Paki" to refer to anyone of South Asian origin. While it can be argued that perpetrators of direct attacks on nonwhites are fairly small in number and relatively few persons actually engage in discriminatory behavior, the number of people—that is, members of the white majority—who are attitudinally prejudiced or racist is considerably larger. Using a number of measures of racial prejudice, a large random sample attitude survey conducted by this author in Toronto in 1978 revealed that fully 16 percent (or roughly 250,000 people) of the mainstream or majority group population were very racist in their views of blacks, West Indians, and South Asians. Another 35 percent were "somewhat racist." Although the remainder were classified as either very "tolerant" (19 percent) or "somewhat tolerant" (30 percent), the results indicate that nearly half of the population holds some measure of racist sentiment.[9]

In response to direct and attitudinal racism, a variety of committees and task forces were created by several institutional and governmental agencies during the 1980s. For example, the Metro Toronto city council commissioned a task force, and a special committee chaired by a Roman Catholic Cardinal came to the conclusion that racism was indeed a major problem. Both committees presented a number of serious recommendations to ameliorate some of the problem areas. At the municipal level, each borough's mayorality office has a race relations committee and even the police commission has created a special "ethnic squad" to deal with the ethnic communities. Almost all of the city's school boards have a race relations group and in two cases, reports were released that recommended severe sanctions against students and teachers found guilty of racist behavior. In 1982 the Federal Multiculturalism ministry announced a special allocation of funds to combat racism in the media, and to hold a national symposium to investigate legal solutions to race relations problems.

In 1983 the government established a parliamentary committee to study racism in Canada. Its report, entitled *Equality Now* and released in early 1984, lists 80 recommendations designed to improve race relations in Canada. The recommendations apply primarily to institutional racism and suggest changes in educational institutions, the media, legal reform, employment, and the like. By mid 1984 the only response by government had been a promise to establish a trust fund of $5 million to combat racism in Canada.[10]

Nonwhite community members have mobilized themselves in response to victimization. A number of groups and organizations among both West Indians and South Asians have been created whose primary activities include "soft" responses such as holding public meetings, organizing demonstrations, and the like. A few more militant groups using the Jewish Defense League as a model have also been formed but they have met with little response. A few representatives have advocated violence and race riots such as those that have occurred in the United States and Great Britain. This kind of strategy has been, by and large, rejected by the majority of both South Asians and West Indians because they are basically afraid to upset the status quo and tend to guard whatever progress they have made, but the very fact that such statements have been voiced and picked up by the media indicates that there is considerable unease in both communities.

In addition to the externally imposed pressures resulting from racism, West Indians in Canada have faced a number of social and personal problems peculiar to their community. In the first instance, there has been a considerable amount of segmentation or factionalism amongst them and the term "community" with respect to West Indian ethnicity must be carefully examined. West Indians disassociate themselves from Canadian blacks, particularly those from the Maritimes. They feel superior to Canadian blacks, who are thought to be backward and nonachieving. Canadian blacks, on the other hand, feel that West Indians as newcomers are haughty and arrogant. Canadian blacks, who can trace their ancestry here for generations, feel affronted when they are asked "And what island are you from?" The situation in Montreal is particularly interesting because the black "community" there consists not only of "old time black Canadians" but also of West Indian migrants from both the English- and French-speaking Caribbean. There is some segmentation between all three groups, particularly between Anglophones and French- or Creole-speaking Haitians. Additionally, they are all affected by the larger political and linguistic climate in Quebec.

In Montreal, educated and professional Haitians live in middle class French Canadian areas of the city whereas similarly placed West Indian Anglophones tend to live in the middle class English-speaking areas. Working class migrants from both groups tend to settle in traditional immigrant areas. A considerable number of the 25,000 or so Haitians are professionals; there is, for example, an association of

Haitian doctors and one of Haitian nurses, attesting to the importance of these occupational groups. While Haitians speak the dominant language of Quebec (although there is also the view that working class Creole-speakers are not fully French-speaking despite the prevalence of nonstandard French among French Canadians) their color has set them apart from the Quebecois and they are not as fully welcomed as are French-speakers from European countries.

The treatment of some 2,000 or more illegal immigrants who came here still believing that once in Canada, they could apply for landed immigrant status (that law was changed in 1974) has exacerbated the tensions between Haitians and the Quebecois. The problem was alleviated to some extent with an immigration amnesty. Any illegal immigrant in the country for five years who can demonstrate the ability to cope in the new environment may apply to immigration officials for legal status. Authorities have, however, refused entry to Haitian tourists on the assumption that they would remain here as illegal immigrants.

In 1983, a group of Haitian taxi drivers brought a case of discrimination against two taxi companies in Montreal to the Human Rights Commission. It found in favor of the drivers and the companies were fined and, in addition, told to change their hiring policies.

Haitians as a group cling to their Haitian identity first, although some are sympathetic to the French Canadian struggle for independence. Anglophone West Indians on the other hand tend to remain aloof from that larger political issue since they are particularly affected by the French language legislation and must as other Anglophones first learn French to effectively function in that environment. Relations between Anglophone and Francophone West Indians in Montreal are hampered by the language barriers although some of the former were involved in the fight against the deportation of the Haitian illegal immigrants. Anglophones are more closely linked to friends and relatives in other provinces, particularly Ontario, through visits and telephone calls than they are to migrants from Haiti or the French Caribbean.

The West Indian "community" is further segmented by the remnants of island parochialism. Groups and associations based on common place of origin—say, the Jamaican Canadian Association, The Trinidad and Tobago Association, and others—still function, particularly in Toronto. Increasingly, however, and especially among younger people who attend school and grow up in Canada, blackness rather than place of origin assumes more importance in defining personal identity.

West Indians will continue to be marginal members in a white-dominated society. Total assimilation or integration into the mainstream of Canadian society cannot be expected. West Indians on the whole are highly motivated and achieving people whose integration is hampered by their own internal factions as well as the stressful changes experienced by individuals and families brought about by the immigration process itself and exacerbated by the external or societal forces of racism. As long as individual and institutional racism continues to exist here as elsewhere, even educated and middle class West Indians will be denied full first-class citizenship. Perhaps, however, total integration is an unrealistic goal and in Canada as elsewhere, West Indians and other minorities will be happy to settle for a climate in which there is a more harmonious accommodation between groups and where equal access to desired societal resources are within reach of every individual regardless of ethnic or racial affiliation.

NOTES

1. Robin Winks, *The Blacks in Canada: A History* (Montreal: McGill-Queens Press, 1971), pp. 413–69.

2. *Immigration Canada: Statistics: Employment and Immigration* (Ottawa, 1946–1982).

3. Ibid. See also John Wood, "East Indians and Canada's New Immigration Policy," in G. Kurian and Ram P. Srivastava, eds., *Overseas Indians: A Study in Adaptation* (New Delhi: Vikas, 1983), pp. 3–29.

4. *Immigration Canada*, 1982, p. 16.

5. Wilson Head, *The Adaptation of Immigrants* (Toronto: York Univ. Press, 1983).

6. Jeffrey G. Reitz et al., *Ethnic Inequality and Segregation in Jobs* (Toronto: Univ. Toronto Centre for Urban and Community Studies, May 1981), p. 69.

7. Ibid.

8. *The Canadian Human Rights Code* (Ottowa: Government Printery, 1983); Government of Ontario, *The Ontario Human Rights Code* (Toronto, 1984).

9. Frances Henry, *The Dynamics of Racism in Toronto* (Ottawa: Secretary of State, 1978), pp. 1–2.

10. *Equality Now*, Report of the Special Committee on Visible Minorities in Canadian Society, House of Commons Issue No. 4 (March 1984).

The Implications for U.S. Policy

A Primer for U.S. Policy on Caribbean Migration: Responding to Pressures

Terry L. McCoy

In the late 1970s the presence of large numbers of "illegal" or "undocumented" aliens, designations used for both foreigners who have entered without valid immigration documents and those who have violated or overstayed their U.S. visas, was increasingly viewed with alarm.[1] Estimates of their numbers varied across a range of 2–12 million, and they were blamed for everything from high domestic unemployment to environmental degradation. Many felt that their presence threatened the very nature of U.S. society. In a 1977 New York *Times* column entitled "What Kind of America?" James Reston wrote, "The main fact about the movement of people into the continental United States is that it is out of control. Each year, more illegal aliens come into the United States, and remain here, than legal aliens. Even the official figures and estimates are staggering."[2] In the mid 1980s such sentiments were, if anything, more widespread and intense. Their persistence increasingly generated pressures to strengthen U.S. immigration policy, and a series of comprehensive reform measures were introduced into Congress.

THE CARIBBEAN ROLE

Mexico has been the major source of illegal migration into the United States, a fact that has dominated attempts to reform U.S. immigration policy. Because their numbers were smaller and because, in contrast to the Mexican migrant who surreptitiously crosses a land border in the Southwest, Caribbean migrants enter legally through Miami or New York and then violate their nonresident visas by staying to work, less attention had been paid to the Caribbean migrant, even though after Mexicans the next five sources of illegal aliens are Caribbean Basin countries (the Dominican Republic, Haiti, Jamaica, Guatemala, and Colombia, in that order).[3] All of this changed in the spring of 1980 when the nation witnessed over 120,000 Cubans pouring into south Florida and the daily arrival of dilapidated boats overloaded with Haitian refugees. The Mariel exodus and Haitian boat people redirected concern with U.S. immigration policy toward the Caribbean. The Reagan administration's Caribbean Basin Initiative and foreign policy preoccupation with the region reinforced this orientation.

If U.S. policy on Caribbean immigration is important to the United States, it is of even greater concern to the nations and territories of the Caribbean. If several hundred thousand Dominican or Haitian or Jamaican migrants cause concern in a country of 230 million inhabitants, the impact of their emigration on the Dominican Republic or Haiti or Jamaica, countries with populations of 6.2, 5.2, and 2.2 million people, respectively, is enormous.[4] The fact that a substantial portion of the populations of these and other Caribbean islands live and work abroad has a variety of implications for the sending societies.

Migration has deep historical roots in the Caribbean. With the indigenous population having been decimated soon after its contact with the colonial powers, the area was successively peopled by Europeans, Africans, East Indians, and a smattering of other immigrant groups from around the world. Over the last several decades, however, the flow of humanity has dramatically reversed. It is now emigration that is an integral part of contemporary Caribbean culture, touching virtually every family. For decades emigrants from the British Caribbean went to England in search of jobs and education, but when these doors closed in the 1960s, they joined the Cubans, Dominicans, and Puerto Ricans streaming into the United States.[5] Of the European nations only France, with overseas *departements* in the Caribbean, continues to welcome migrants.

Because overseas migration is so important to the Caribbean, some local governments have de facto policies; none attempts to discourage it (except, of course, the departure of skilled migrants). For densely-populated societies, emigration serves as a demographic release. A study of fertility trends in Barbados found that emigration not only removed people from the island, but it also lowered the local birthrate by drawing off people in the reproductive years.[6] This effect undoubtedly exists throughout the region, as the emigrants are overwhelmingly young adults. They leave societies with high unemployment in search of work. Once employed abroad, they remit a significant portion of their earnings. Overseas remittances not only support extended families at home, but they help cope with unfavorable balance of payments.[7]

Whether we consider the individual migrants to be victims of large, irreversible forces that drive them to move from one country to another, or rational actors consciously seeking to improve their own situation, the fate of hundreds of thousands, if not millions, of human beings is at stake.[8] For them migration is a fact of life and the United States is an extension of their local community. The challenge facing U.S. immigration policy is to balance the domestic and foreign policy interests of the United States with those of Caribbean migrants and countries.

U.S. immigration policy is complex and multifaceted in its composition and application. It is shaped by executive directives, administrative regulations, and judicial decisions, as well as legislation. Consequently, in characterizing policy one must allow for nuances and contradictions. Moreover, although the Western Hemisphere (and thereby the Caribbean) has historically received special treatment, there is, strictly speaking, no separate Caribbean policy. The following sections summarize immigration law, analyze its application in the Caribbean, review recent attempts at reform, and estimate their significance for Caribbean emigration.

THE LAW

For the first century of its existence, the United States threw open its borders to anyone who wished to enter; then in the late 19th century, Congress began to enact measures designed to control immigration. At first these controls were qualitative, excluding criminals, mental incompetents, the seriously ill, and Asians. After World War I, in the face of refugees from war-devastated Europe, quantitative controls were added. The Immigration Act of 1924 instituted a national quota system that limited immigrants from any one country to a yearly quota based on the number of persons of that nationality already in the United States in 1920. A total ceiling of approximately 150,000 quota immigrants per year was also established. Natives of the Western Hemisphere, excluded from the quota, were permitted to enter in unlimited number as a result of "political considerations."[9]

The next major change in immigration law occurred in 1952 with the passage of the Immigration and Nationality Act. Although considerably amended, it is still the basis of immigration policy. While maintaining a national quota system, which once again exempted the Western Hemisphere, the law codified three principles of current policy: family reunification, protection of domestic workers from immigrant competition, and control of alien visitors.[10] In 1965 Congress amended the Immigration and Nationality Act, abolishing the nationalities quota system in favor of annual ceilings. Labor certification was required of all immigrants, except Western Hemisphere parents, spouses, and children of U.S. citizens and resident aliens. But, in contrast to those from the Eastern Hemisphere, nonimmigrant visa holders cannot "adjust status" in the United States.

The 1965 legislation allowed for a three year transition period before it took full effect. Almost immediately in 1968 certain provisions of the legislation came under criticism. Representative Peter Rodino, an interested and influential member of Congress, complained that the Western Hemisphere ceiling of 120,000 was hurting U.S.-Latin American relations.[11] An even more fundamental weakness was the lack of a preference system for selection among Western Hemisphere applicants. Not only was this unfair in comparison with selection procedures applying to the Eastern Hemisphere, but it was slow, cumbersome, and the cause of an immediate backlog of visa applicants. Pressure for 120,000 Western Hemisphere visa numbers was particularly intense because of the flood of Cuban exiles to the United States. Faced with the delay in, or impossibility of, obtaining immigrant visas, Latin Americans determined to migrate to the United States increasingly resorted to fraud and illegal entry.

Confronted with an unworkable system for the Western Hemisphere and the growing influx of illegal aliens, individual Congressmen began in the early 1970s to introduce corrective legislation. Senator Edward Kennedy joined the fight for revision, but no Senate hearings were held until 1976. Both Rodino and Kennedy introduced bills in 1970 that would have created worldwide ceilings, a new preference system applying to both hemispheres, and more flexible refugee provisions.[12] Nothing came of either initiative, for as Senator Kennedy pointed out, "In all candor . . . it must be stated that it remains difficult at this time in our Nation's life—when we are faced with convulsive problems at home and abroad—to concentrate effort and concern on the currently less dramatic aspects of our country's progress and pursuit of justice."[13]

Rodino and Kennedy introduced revised versions of their bills in 1971. A third bill introduced on behalf of the Nixon administration featured a modified preference system, a ceiling of 80,000 immigrant visas per year for the Western Hemisphere plus 35,000 for both Canada and Mexico, adjustment of status in the United States for Western Hemispheric immigrants, except those from Canada and Mexico, and sanctions for employers hiring aliens who are not entitled to work.[14]

By 1972 the illegal alien issue was beginning to assume paramount importance in the immigration debate. Rodino's initiative for that year, which passed the House but not the Senate, included employer sanctions and other provisions aimed at curbing illegal migration; an employer sanctions amendment to the Fair Labor Standards Act passed the Senate. On assuming the chairmanship of the Immigration and Naturalization Subcommittee from Rodino, who moved up to chair the House Judiciary Committee, Congressman Eilberg listed the immigration-related targets of the 93rd Congress as illegal aliens, inequities in the treatment of the Western Hemisphere, clarification of laws governing parole, and low morale and inefficiency in the Immigration and Naturalization Service.[15]

At hearings on these issues, all witnesses supported changes to remove differential treatment of the two hemispheres. State Department officials testified that visa delays and special efforts taken to screen out potential abusers were generating foreign relations problems in Latin America.[16] Once again the House approved a comprehensive immigration bill with employer sanctions, while the Kennedy bill languished in the Senate. In early 1975, President Ford established a Domestic Council Committee on illegal aliens. Senator Eastland's subcommittee finally held hearings on immigration with the Senator seeking approval for a bill that included a provision for importing foreign workers for permanent (rather than temporary) jobs.[17] In late 1976, the Congress finally passed, and President Ford signed, further amendments to the Immigration and Nationality Act.

Although the principal accomplishment of the Immigration and Nationality Act Amendments of 1976 was to eliminate the differences in treatment between the Eastern and Western Hemispheres, Congress was once again unable to reach agreement over how to deal directly with the illegal alien problem.[18] It allowed Western Hemisphere nonresident visa holders to adjust status in the United States as long as they were not holding unauthorized employment, but eliminated the exemption of the parents of U.S. citizen and permanent resident alien children from labor certification.

This last change was potentially of great importance since between 25 and 30 percent of all Western Hemisphere immigrants were parents exempted from labor certification.[19] This exemption had long been opposed by the State Department; consular officials believed that it encouraged aliens to come to the United States on nonimmigrant visas and have a child, which then qualified them for an immigrant visa without being labor certified. Most violated the original visa by working while waiting for their U.S.-born child.[20]

Even before the impact of deleting the certification exemption for parents could be determined, the Democratic Carter administration that took power in 1977 introduced its own proposal to strengthen the nation's immigration policy. In defending the need for additional action, President Carter advanced increasingly familiar arguments: "I am proposing actions that would meet four major needs: First of all, to regain greater control over our own borders. Secondly, to limit employment opportunities of those who are illegally in our country and who are competing with American workers for scarce jobs. Third, the registration and regulation of the millions of undocumented workers who are already here. And fourth, improving cooperation with countries from which these undocumented workers are coming into our Nation."[21]

Carter's proposal was a package composed of six separate measures. The first, and perhaps most controversial, was employer sanctions. Employers who engaged in a "pattern or practice" of hiring undocumented aliens would be subject to civil fines up to $1,000 per alien and possible court injunction.[22] Since Social Security cards would be accepted for identification, the Department of Health, Education, and Welfare was instructed to make it a more reliable indicator of lawful residence but not a "national identification card." Second, the proposal would strengthen enforcement by adding 2,000 new officers on the Mexican border, and the State Department would tighten visa issuance procedures. Third, undocumented aliens who had been in the United States since before January 1, 1970, would be eligible to adjust status to become permanent residents, and those who had been in the United States between 1970 and January 1, 1977 could be granted a five-year temporary resident status with the right to work but not to vote, run for office, serve on a jury, or bring family members from abroad. Aliens in the latter category would not be eligible for public welfare assistance unless state and local governments chose to provide it. Fourth, the United States would enter into negotiations with Mexico and other countries regarding their roles in restricting the flow of undocumented aliens, would offer assistance for labor-intensive development projects and "population education programs," and would increase trade with sending countries. Fifth, the Secretary of Labor was directed to review the current temporary worker program (but not with a view toward reviving the bracero program, which Carter "unequivocally" opposed). Sixth, there was to be a comprehensive interagency study of immigration policy.

Although no action was taken on the major components of President Carter's immigration reform package, most of them reemerged under his successor. In retrospect it is clear that by 1980 a national consensus was emerging on the need for the federal government to stem the flow of undocumented aliens from the Caribbean Basin into the United States. Initially the pressure for action came primarily from within government, most importantly from the commissioner of the Immigration and Nationalization Service. But it began to build outside government in the mid 1970s. Organized labor was prominent in pushing for action. The interagency task force that drafted the Carter proposal consulted a wide spectrum of domestic interest groups,[23] and its final product reflected an emerging consensus on the means necessary to halt the tide of illegal migrants.

As late as the spring of 1980, the problem was still seen as primarily Mexican in origin. However, officials responsible for administering U.S. immigration policy in the Caribbean were aware that it extended beyond Mexico, and it was their opinion that the policy was inadequate to meet the challenge posed by Caribbean emigration.

ADMINISTRATION OF THE LAW[24]

Two government agencies are charged with primary responsibility for controlling the entry of aliens into the United States. The visa office of the Bureau of Security and Consular Affairs, Department of State, issues foreigners the documents, or visas, necessary to enter and remain in the United States. For this and related functions, the Department of State maintains consular posts throughout the world. It is their task not only to issue visas but to determine if the applicant is qualified. A second agency, the Immigration and Naturalization Service (INS) of the Department of Justice screens all persons entering the country at the point of entry and polices migrant affairs within the United States. In addition to the social control functions of these two agencies, the Department of Labor has labor certification responsibilities, and the Social Security Administration provides INS with selected social security information on migrants.[25] Three other agencies—the Customs Bureau, the Department of Agriculture, and the Drug Enforcement Agency—manage the entry of goods and substances into the country. Naturally the participation of so many agencies with differing but overlapping jurisdictions creates ample opportunity for confusion and outright conflict in the administration of policy.

Outside of Mexico the U.S. consular posts in Colombia, the Dominican Republic, Haiti, and Jamaica are perhaps under the most pressure to stem the flow of illegal migration. They are, in the words of one officer, "pressure posts," since each of those host countries contributes an estimated several hundred thousand illegal residents to the United States.

The typical consular post is organized into four sections: an executive office, a visa unit, a citizenship/special consular services unit, and an investigations unit. The consular post in Santo Domingo, a model operation that handles all of the Dominican Republic, had 12 consular officers and a large support staff in 1977.[26] The visa unit is divided into an immigrant visa subunit and a nonimmigrant visa subunit. In Santo Domingo, each had a chief; there were five immigrant visa interviewing officers and only two for nonimmigrants. The investigations unit, with four local investigators, does work for the visa unit.

Officer discretion in the visa-granting process resides largely on the nonimmigrant side. By the time an applicant has made it to the point of applying for an immigrant visa, the consular officer can do little more than see that the law is fulfilled. A degree of individual discretion comes in checking for fraud and in determining if the applicant is likely to become a public charge, but fraud is hard to detect with such a small investigative staff. Furthermore, U.S. law and its interpretation by the courts encourage and legitimate fraud. Since the only way to get an immigrant visa is by having a job prospect and/or close family ties in the United States, it is quite common for would-be migrants to enter on a nonimmigrant visa, get a job in violation of the visa and/or have a child, and then return to their country of origin to request an immigrant visa on the grounds of having a job offer and/or child. The 1976 amendments to the Immigration and Naturalization Act alleviated some of the duplicity by eliminating the labor exemption for parents; however, it became possible for Caribbean immigrants to regularize their status without returning home. The frustration of consular officers forced to grant immigrant visas to people who, they are convinced, violated their nonimmigrant visas, is often intensified by the intervention of lawyers and U.S. Congressmen to expedite the application.

The effort to stop illegal migration from the Caribbean falls on the nonimmigrant-visa officers. Their fundamental task is to screen out potential visa abusers. In pursuit of this objective, the interviewing officer has the authority to deny application for a visa on the subjective grounds that he or she believes the applicant would violate the terms of the visa.

The means used to determine if the applicant is likely to overstay the visa are a brief written application, certain documents, and a 3–5 minute personal interview. All are designed to determine whether the applicant's stake in his native country is sufficient to cause him to return home. Although each post designs its own screening procedure, the routine is similar throughout the Caribbean. Colombian applicants for a tourist visa must present at the personal interview a completed application with the following items: (1) a valid passport; (2) information about employment, friends, and relatives in the United States, and financing of the proposed trip; (3) a photograph; (4) proof of personal income over the past two years; (5) record of banking transactions for the past six months; and (6) proof of employment or school enrollment.[27]

The extensive documentation required of each applicant is balanced by the haste with which the interviewing officer must

evaluate it. It is not uncommon for two or three officers to interview
and process several hundred applicants per day. It is neither an easy
nor rewarding job.[28] The officer is under implied orders from his
government to screen out all potential abusers, while his colleagues
in the rest of the embassy are constantly requesting visas for politically influential applicants.[29] Some consular posts even offer special
treatment for VIP applicants. In general, consular officers are sensitive to the foreign policy implications of their work and realize that
many local people form opinions about the United States on the
basis of how their application for a visa is handled. On the other
hand, they feel constantly besieged by unqualified and undeserving
applicants desperate to get into the United States.[30] Under these
cross pressures, the tendency is to deny most first-time applicants,
up to 90 percent at some posts, but offer them the hope of a subsequent reapplication.[31]

The U.S. government has been reluctant to take up the question
of illegal migration with officials in the Caribbean on a systematic
basis.[32] It is politically sensitive for local governments, since emigration represents a failure to meet the needs of their citizens. At a
more pragmatic level, Caribbean governments maintain that it is our
problem and not theirs. Furthermore, they are quick to point out the
duplicity of U.S. immigration policy—welcoming the skilled, educated immigrant while trying to exclude the unskilled and uneducated.

The U.S. consular officers posted in the Caribbean in the late
1970s saw themselves as an undermanned first line of defense against
an inexhaustible supply of people wishing to get to the United
States. Not only did they feel themselves outnumberd, they also
lacked adequate arms. They were administering a policy that was inadequate for the task. Steps had to be taken to diminish the attrac-
tiveness of the United States to citizens of the Caribbean and increase the penalties for those who insisted on going. The policy in-
adequacy became dramatically evident in the spring of 1980.

POLICY DEVELOPMENTS SINCE 1980

Increased activity under the Nixon, Ford, and Carter administrations indicated that diverse groups were coalescing around a drive
to reform the nation's immigration policy. Although the movement
received a boost from the influx of refugees from Southeast Asia, its

principal preoccupation remained illegal or undocumented migrants from Mexico and the Caribbean. Their accelerated arrival during the 1970s created the growing perception that the country was "no longer in control of its own bordrers," to use a phrase repeated throughout the period. While there were many factors that brought pressure for action on immigration to a head in the mid 1980s, there is little doubt that a watershed occurred in the spring of 1980 when tens of thousands of migrants from Cuba and Haiti landed on the shores of Florida, with officials there helpless to stop them.

In addition to the Mariel and Haitian events, two other developments occurred during the Carter administration that helped fix immigration policy on the agenda of its successor. First, Congress created a Select Commission on Immigration Policy to lay the basis for fundamental changes in immigration policy. Although there had been other study commissions, none was composed of such distinguished members nor impaneled at what turned out to be such a pivotal time. Second, Congress passed, and the president signed, the Refugee Act of 1980. "The new law not only provided an updated definition of refugees consistent with the United Nations protocol on the subject, but also set forth a method by which the president, with the advice of Congress, could prescribe and allocate the number of refugees to be admitted annually."[33]

Although enacted largely in response to the influx of refugees from Southeast Asia, the first test of the new law came from the Caribbean. In April of 1980, the very situation that the new law was supposed to prevent occurred. In the short space of six weeks over 120,000 refugees from one country, Cuba, poured into the United States without prior clearance. It was the beginning of a presidential campaign and the federal government had indeed lost control of the U.S. borders. Whatever else the new Republican administration did, it was going to have to deal with immigration, particularly that from the Caribbean.

Shortly after President Reagan's inauguration, the Select Commission issued its findings and recommendations, thus assuring immigration reform a place on the new administration's agenda. True to its charge of building political consensus for reform, the commission's final report pulled together proposals that had emerged over the past three administrations and that would serve as the key elements of subsequent reform efforts. According to the commission's staff director, "The commission emphasized keeping the 'front door' of legal immigration open, indeed widening it just a little bit by making the system through which immigrants are admitted lawfully more equitable and efficient. But the commission also insisted on closing the half-open 'back door to illegal migration.' "[34] The policy instruments advocated by the commission to accomplish a redress of the balance between immigration through the front and back doors were: penalties for employers who hired persons in the country illegally; a one-time amnesty for illegal aliens who had resided in the United States for a specified period; enhanced border enforcement; increased number of legal immigrants; and a revised immigrant visa preference system.

On March 6, 1981, President Reagan, in an apparent attempt to buy time, established a Task Force on Immigration and Refugee Policy to "review existing practices and recommend ways to strengthen U.S. immigration laws and programs."[35] In July the task force issued its report, and in October the president sent an immigration bill to Congress. Bearing the stamp of the Select Commission, the Reagan bill included employer sanctions, amnesty, enhanced border enforcement, and an experimental guestworker program with Mexico, a provision not among the Select Commission's recommendations.[36] Beyond sponsoring changes in immigration law, the administration ordered U.S. Coast Guard ships into the Windward Passage between Haiti and Cuba to interdict and turn back boats with Haitians headed for Florida. In explaining the move, a Justice Department spokesman said, "We . . . want to send a message, not only to the people of Haiti but to the millions in the Caribbean who would like to come here, that they will be detained and they will be deterred if at all possible."[37] Such statements made it clear that the Reagan administration was determined to restrict the movement of Caribbean peoples to the United States.

In early 1982 Senator Alan Simpson (Rep./Wyoming) and Representative Romano Mazzoli (Dem./Kentucky) introduced nearly identical versions of the Immigration and Reform Act of 1982 into their respective houses of Congress. The major difference between the Simpson/Mazzoli bill and that of the Reagan administration was that the former did not contain a formal guestworker program. Instead it proposed changes in existing temporary worker policy.[38] Despite this difference, the president withdrew his proposal and threw his support behind Simpson/Mazzoli, which then became the focal point of the struggle to reform immigration policy. Given the omnibus nature of the measure, it generated a wide spectrum of interest-group lobbying. Organized labor supported employer sanctions while opposing any expansion of foreign workers. Hispanic organizations, another component of the traditional Democratic coalition, opposed employer sanctions but supported legalization. Elements of the Republican party opposed sections of the measure. Small businessmen objected to employer sanctions and conservatives to legalization.

Such a complex array of interests rendered passage of the bill difficult. It cleared the Republican-controlled Senate in both 1982 and 1983 only to founder in the House, where the Democrats were in the majority. It was clear that the measure represented more of a threat to the Democrats than to the Republicans. In fact, on the second occasion in 1983, House Speaker O'Neill refused to allow it to come up for a floor vote in order to avoid open conflict within his party. In 1984 the Senate again approved the bill, and then, in the face of predictions that it would go nowhere in the House during an election year in which the three leading candidates for the Democratic presidential nomination opposed it, the House brought Simpson/Mazzoli to the floor, debated it, and passed it by the vote of 216 to 211 on June 20, 1984. In the end it seems that the majority in the House succumbed to the attitude expressed by Representative Trent Lott (Rep./Mississippi):

> The immigration problem is a ticking time bomb that must be dealt with now if it is to be dealt with at all in an effective manner. The bill before us is the product of a number of compromises, and I think it is fair to say that nobody is completely happy with all its provisions. If you think our immigration problem is difficult and controversial now, just think how intractable and heated this will be if we fail to tackle the problem at this time.[39]

Once again, however, the measure did not make it to the president's desk for his signature; the Senate and House were unable to work out their differences in a conference committee. Despite this failure it seems probable that Simpson/Mazzoli, or a reasonable facsimile, is on its way to becoming the most important reform of the nation's immigration law since the Immigration and Nationality Act of 1952. With this in mind, we should examine the probable impact of the reform on Caribbean emigration.

The provisions of Simpson/Mazzoli having major implications for the Caribbean are employer sanctions, temporary foreign workers, and amnesty. The premise of the first is that if there were no jobs, then the incentive to enter the United States illegally would diminish. Therefore, penalizing employers for hiring illegals should curtail employment opportunities. The primary flow of Caribbean migrants has been into the service and marginal manufacturing sectors on the East Coast. Under the Simpson/Mazzoli approach, employers in these sectors who hire undocumented workers from the Caribbean would be subject to civil fines (and imprisonment in the case of the Senate version). Enforcement would be hindered, however, by the absence of foolproof identity procedures and, perhaps more importantly, the limited resources of the Immigration and Naturalization Service.

Although the Senate and House versions differed on legal foreign workers, both proposed expanding the number admitted. The Senate bill would have opened up existing policy, whereas the version that passed the House contained a full-fledged guestworker program. Feelings on legal foreign workers run high. Proponents, such as border state agriculture interests, argue that they will be needed to offset the effects of employer sanctions on undocumented workers. The opponents, led by organized labor, retort that foreign workers are not needed if wages and working conditions are adequate; if admitted, they threaten both. On the additional question of the impact of seasonal labor migration on sending societies, there are also disagreements.[40] The evidence from the current largest legal temporary worker program, which supplies 8,500 Caribbean cane cutters to the Florida sugar industry, is mixed.[41] Although the temporary worker provisions of both versions were aimed at supplying Mexican workers to southwest agriculture, they might also bring more Caribbean workers into the Florida citrus and winter vegetable industries. Neither contemplates replacing the undocumented workers in East Coast urban areas with temporary foreign workers.

Amnesty could grant many of the Caribbean workers found in major metropolitan areas of the East Coast legal residence. It could also lead to their expulsion if they arrived after the cutoff date or were unable to demonstrate continuous residence and good character. One other provision of Simpson/Mazzoli, as passed by both houses, that has important implications for the Caribbean is that regulating asylum procedures. It would make it much easier for the government to expel refugees, such as those from Haiti and Salvador, seeking political asylum in the United States.

In the three decades following the passage of the Immigration and Nationality Act, the United States has become the principal destination for Caribbean emigrants. U.S. officials and the American public have viewed this development with increasing concern. The movement to restrict access to the United States was motivated, to a significant degree, by the desire to bring Caribbean immigration under control. However the repeated failure to pass reform legislation does raise the question of whether this country has the political will and institutional capacity to adopt and effectively implement a new policy in the face of the wide variety of interests served by the status quo.

NOTES

1. U.S. White House, Domestic Council on Illegal Aliens, *Preliminary Report* (Washington, D.C.: December 1976), pp. 4–5.

2. Gainesville *Sun*, January 9, 1977.

3. *Preliminary Report,* p. 39. It is interesting, although perhaps not surprising, that the leading sources of legal migration also provide the most illegal migrants.

4. Inter-American Development Bank, *Economic and Social Progress in Latin America: 1983 Report* (Washington, D.C.: Inter-American Development Bank, 1983).

5. By 1964 there were an estimated 300,000 West Indians in Great Britain, or 1.2 percent of the population of Trinidad and Tobago, 8.1 percent of Barbados, 9.7 percent of Jamaica and 31.5 percent of Montserrat; G.C.K. Peach, "West Indian migration to Britain," *International Migration Review* 1 (Summer 1967):34–35.

6. G. Edward Ebanks, P.M. George, and Charles E. Nobbe, "Emigration and fertility decline: The case of Barbados," *Demography* 12 (August 1975): 431–46.

7. The chief U.S. consular officer in Haiti estimated in an interview (Port-au-Prince, June 29, 1977) that the remittances of Haiti's approximately 300,000 illegal migrants prevented a deficit balance of payments. More recently, declines in overseas remittances, because of the international recession, were blamed for a deteriorating economic situation and the internal unrest that resulted in violent demonstrations in Haiti in June 1984; Don Bohning, The Miami *Herald,* June 11, 1984. See also the analysis of remittances by Terry L. McCoy and Charles H. Wood, "Seasonal migration, remittances and development: A study of Caribbean cane cutters in Florida" (Gainesville: Univ. Florida, Center for Latin American Studies, 1984).

8. For a review of competing paradigms of migration, see Charles H. Wood, "Equilibrium and historical-structural perspectives on migration," *International Migration Review* 16 (Summer 1982):298–319.

9. *Preliminary Report,* p. 10

10. Ibid., p. 11.

11. Peter W. Rodino, "New immigration law in retrospect," *International Migration Review* 2 (Summer 1968):59.

12. Peter W. Rodino, "Today's need for immigration revision" and Edward M. Kennedy, "Immigration law: Some refinements and new reforms," *International Migration Review* 4 (Summer 1970):11–15 and 4–10 respectively.

13. Ibid., p. 10.

14. Donald G. Hohl and Michael G. Wenk, "Current U.S. immigration legislation: Analysis and comment," *International Migration Review* 5 (Fall 1971): 342–43.

15. Donald G. Hohl and Michael G. Wenk, "Legislative and judicial developments," *International Migration Review* 7 (Summer 1973):191.

16. Ibid., (Fall 1973):326–27.

17. Donald G. Hohl, "Legislative and judicial developments," *International Migration Review* 10 (Summer 1976):250.

18. Austin T. Fragomen, Jr., "1976 Amendments to Immigration and Nationality Act," *International Migration Review* 11 (Spring 1977):95.

19. Ibid., p. 96.

20. Personal interviews with consular officers in the Caribbean, June–July 1977. Although the officers could identify those who resorted to such tactics, they were legally powerless to deny family reunification visas.

21. U.S. White House, Office of the Press Secretary, "Remarks of the President on reducing and regulating the presence of undocumented aliens," August 4, 1977.

22. U.S. White House, Office of the Press Secretary, *Undocumented Aliens: Fact Sheet,* August 4, 1977. Information for the remainder of this paragraph also comes from the *Fact Sheet.*

23. Interview with White House official, Washington, D.C., August 11, 1977.

24. Information for this section was collected during visits to Colombia, the Dominican Republic, Haiti, and Jamaica in June and July of 1977. I have since interviewed consular officers in the Dominican Republic (1981), Haiti (1983), and Jamaica (1982). For a detailed analysis of consular activities see John Alexander Ritchie, "The consular function: The stepchild of United States foreign policy administration" (Ph.D. diss., Southern Illinois Univ., 1968).

25. Monica Boyd, "Immigration policies and trends: A comparison of Canada and the United States," *Demography* 13 (February 1976):84.

26. U.S. Embassy, Santo Domingo, D.R., "Consular package" (May 1977).

27. U.S. Embassy, Consular Section, Bogotá, Colombia, "Documentos para respaldar la solicitud de visa de turista" (BGT-14, 6/77).

28. Virtually all of the interviewing officers observed in the Caribbean were young and in their first tour of duty. The Foreign Service's use of tracks or cones, which tends to set career patterns, the demanding, repetitive nature of the

work, and the low morale of senior officers tend to cause a high turnover in personnel. I encountered some evidence that steps have been taken to deal with this problem in recent years.

29. Political pressure for a visa can come from many quarters. A leftwing member of the People's National Party in Jamaica, who is a frequent critic of the United States, requested that his residency papers be renewed while serving as a member of the Manley cabinet.

30. Glen Hendericks, *Dominican Diaspora: From the Dominican Republic to New York City—Villagers in Transition* (New York: Teachers College Press, 1974), pp. 55–57, describes an entire industry dedicated to U.S. visa acquisition that has grown up in the Dominican Republic. He also points out that, in addition to getting the holder into the United States, a visa confers immediate economic value based on earning potential and social status.

31. According to the "Consular Packages," the four Caribbean posts studied rejected all first-time nonimmigrant visa applications in FY 1976.

32. The U.S. Embassy in Kingston made visa application rates available to the Manley government to make it aware of the repercussions of its radical political rhetoric. The U.S. government has raised the issue of illegal immigrants with Mexican officials from the president down.

33. Lawrence H. Fuchs, "From select commission to Simpson-Mazzoli: The making of America's new immigration law," in Wayne A. Cornelius and Ricardo Anzaldua Montoya, eds., *America's New Immigration Law: Origins, Rationales, and Potential Consequences*, Monograph Series No. 11 (La Jolla, CA: Center for U.S.-Mexican Relations, Univ. California, 1983), p. 43.

34. Ibid., p. 46.

35. U.S. Department of Justice, "U.S. immigration and refugee policy," July 30, 1981.

36. Wayne A. Cornelius, "The Reagan administration's proposal for a new U.S. immigration policy: An assessment of potential effects," *International Migration Review* 15 (Winter 1981):769–78.

37. The Miami *Herald*, October 1, 1981.

38. Terry L. McCoy, "The ambiguities of U.S. temporary foreign worker policy," (Unpub.), p. 2.

39. The New York *Times*, June 17, 1984.

40. For differing perspectives on Caribbean guestworkers see Franklin W. Knight, "Who needs a guest worker program? They do; we do," and Mark J. Miller and William W. Boyer, "Foreign workers in the USVI: History of a dilemma," *Caribbean Review* 11 (Winter 1982):46–47 and 48–51, respectively.

41. Terry L. McCoy and Charles H. Wood, "Caribbean workers in the Florida sugar cane industry," Occasional Paper No. 2 (Gainesville: Univ. Florida, Center for Latin American Studies, Caribbean Migration Program, December 1982).

The Impact of U.S. Immigration Policy on Caribbean Emigration: Does it Matter?

Robert Pastor

If sovereignty divides the Caribbean, migration connects it. Depending on one's definition, the Caribbean could include anywhere from 16 to 35 nations and dependencies. Almost all of these nations are relatively small and poor with high unemployment and scarce resources and capital. The proximity of so many small and limited nations to the world's richest is a recipe for migration, and indeed, many scholars identify these "structural" determinants as critical for explaining migration from the Caribbean to the United States and more broadly from the developing to the industrialized countries.[1] In addition, the United States and the Caribbean have complementary traditions—the former as a "nation of immigrants" and the latter as a "region of emigrants."

One would therefore expect that the sheer magnetic attraction of the United States would overwhelm any attempt to regulate the flow of emigrants from the region. However, rather than an assumption or a conclusion, this statement about the uncontrollable pressures for migration need be viewed as a hypothesis worth exploring. In this chapter, we will assess the impact of U.S. immigration policies on the region's emigration patterns to the United States. We will examine the evolution of U.S. immigration policy and the extent to which the Caribbean was taken into account by Congress and the president, and then assess the policy's impact on the region. Our purpose is to seek a better understanding of the relative importance of structural pressures as compared with public policies in explaining Caribbean emigration.

EARLY IMMIGRATION POLICY (1882-1924)

Although the first law passed by the United States to limit the number of immigrants came in 1921, the issue was debated practically since independence. In 1797, Rep. Harrison G. Otis of the Commonwealth of Massachusetts implored his colleagues in the House of Representatives to bar the door to further immigration: "When the country was new, it might have been good policy to admit foreigners. But it is so no longer."[2] His colleagues and his successors were unconvinced. During the next century, over 20 million people came to the United States, most of them from Great Britain, Ireland, and Germany.

The fears that Rep. Otis articulated in 1797 were heard periodically through U.S. history, generally with greatest force when the economy was depressed and when the number of immigrants seemed disproportionately large and exotic. In 1882, a record number of immigrants (788,992) arrived, and Congress enacted the Immigration Act of 1882, which set qualitative standards on immigration, excluding certain categories of people such as lunatics, idiots, and "persons likely to become a public charge." These exclusions were expanded over the next two decades, and eventually included geographical and racial criteria. Emigration from the Caribbean to the United States remained small and relatively uncontroversial. In the 19th century, Caribbean immigration to the United States was less than one percent of the total immigration of 125,598 people. In the first two decades of the 20th century, the numbers increased to an average of 11,549 per year or a total of 230,972, but this still only amounted to 1.6 percent of total immigration in that period (see Table 15.1).

To the extent there was any discrimination toward the Caribbean during this time, it was of a positive nature. In 1904, the U.S. Congress exempted immigrants from Cuba and Mexico from paying the "head tax," legislated the year before. Three years later, to address the problem of immigrants who chose to transit these countries to avoid the tax or the immigration restrictions, Congress changed the law to require that they reside continuously in these countries for at least a year. In 1922, this was expanded to five years, and eventually it applied to only those born in these and adjacent countries.

In 1914, a bill was introduced in Congress to place West Indians, because of their race, in the same category as Asians, whose

Table 15.1: Caribbean Immigration into the United States, 1820–1979, by Decade

Decades	Region of Last Residence				Caribbean as a percent of Total
	All Countries		Caribbean		
1820–1860	5,062,414	(123,474)	40,487	(987)	0.8
1861–1900	14,061,192	(351,530)	85,111	(2,128)	0.6
1901–1920	14,531,197	(726,560)	230,972	(11,549)	1.6
1921–1930	4,107,209	(410,721)	74,899	(7,490)	1.8
1931–1940	528,431	(52,843)	15,502	(1,550)	2.9
1941–1950	1,035,039	(103,504)	49,725	(4,973)	4.8
1951–1960	2,515,479	(251,548)	123,091	(12,309)	4.9
1961–1970	3,321,677	(332,168)	470,213	(47,021)	14.2
1971–1979	3,962,675	(440,297)	667,830	(74,203)	16.9
1820–1979					
Total	49,126,313	(307,033)	1,757,830	(10,986)	3.6

Source: U.S. Dept. of Justice, *1979 Statistical Yearbook of the Immigration and Naturalization Service*, pp. 36–38. An immigrant is an alien admitted for permanent residence. The figures in parentheses are the average annual number of immigrants per period. The Caribbean includes Anguilla, Antigua, Bahamas, Barbados, Bermuda, Cayman Islands, Cuba, Dominica, Dominican Republic, Grenada, Guadeloupe, Haiti, Jamaica, Martinique, Monserrat, Antilles, St. Kitts, St. Lucia, St. Vincent, Trinidad and Tobago, the Turks and Caicos, and the British Virgin Islands.

entry was sharply limited. President Woodrow Wilson successfully blocked the bill, and indeed, when other restrictions were passed in 1918 including the requirement of a literacy test, West Indians (and others from the Western Hemisphere) were exempted.[3]

When Congress addressed the immigration issue in the 1920s, immigration from the Caribbean was small, and as the United States attached great importance to the Monroe Doctrine and to good relations in the hemisphere, the central issue pertaining to the Caribbean was whether to treat that region and the entire Western Hemisphere as the rest of the world or better. Until 1952 the prevailing view was that it should be treated better.

The 1921 quota law, which was tightened further and extended to 1924, restricted immigration from those nations in south and eastern Europe eager to send them, and expanded quotas from those in northern and western Europe where the demand was less. The shortfall in labor resulting from the reduced immigration of Europeans permitted increases in immigration from Mexico and the West Indies. Immigration from the Caribbean had averaged about 1,000 per year from 1899 to 1904. From then till 1923 it increased and averaged 3-7 thousand per year. It expanded to 10,630 in 1924.[4] Even more significant to Congress was the record number of Mexican immigrants in 1924 (89,336).

When Congress debated immigration policy in 1924, these increases were noted and to a limited extent evoked a policy response. The major concern, however, was with European migration. The National Origins Act of 1924, which was the product of this debate and concern, revised the formula for designating national quotas so as nearly to eliminate immigration to the United States from Southern and Eastern Europe until 1929, when another formula would come into effect based on the 1920 census. Racism permeated the debate, and an avowed purpose of the law was to maintain the "racial preponderance [of] the basic strain of our people."[5]

The main—but not the only—racial target was Japan. Congress handled the perceived problem associated with the dramatic increase of immigrants from the British West Indies by assigning them the quotas of their mother countries. Some 30 years later, after the McCarran-Walter Act passed, West Indian-American citizens testified to their satisfaction at being considered under the large quotas of "our mother country," Great Britain.[6] But in 1924, the principal motive for deleting the West Indies was racism.

Other than the Caribbean colonies, the rest of the Caribbean and Western Hemisphere was exempted from quotas; unlimited entry was permitted. This special preference was not an accident. There was an extensive debate on the Western Hemisphere exemption. The entire debate, but particularly that on Mexico, had racist overtones. There was also some concern that if we did not set a limit on those coming to the United States from Mexico, others might use Mexico as a transit to enter illegally. Congress's main concern was that illegal aliens from Europe would use the backdoor of Mexico: "Once these aliens land in Mexico, they proceed to the border and almost invariably fall into the hands of the professional smuggler . . . *coyotes.*"[7]

But most of the debate on Latin America and the Caribbean concerned whether we should have a "special" policy for the Caribbean and Latin America and what that should mean. The prevailing view was that in order to maintain good relations with Latin America, the United States would have to give special treatment on immigration. Senator Fletcher expanded on this theme:

> I think we must accord a different treatment, a different code of treatment to South and Central American countries and Canada from what we accord to Europe. Juxtaposition, geographically speaking, makes them different. . . . Ever since . . . the Monroe Doctrine, when we took the position of the big brother, we have had difficulty all along . . . to induce those people to realize that all of our efforts were for their benefit and a protection against intrusion from countries across the sea rather than a selfish purpose. . . . Our duty today . . . is for the "big brother" to show . . . we are not going to do anything selfish that will unnecessarily offend them.[8]

There was also a practical argument for exempting the Western Hemisphere. Although the immigration figures from Mexico and the West Indies had increased sharply in 1921, they were still marginal compared with the flows from the rest of the world. Few worried about Mexico becoming a large source of immigration. "Remember Mexico is not a populous country," said Senator Adams, "It is not teeming with millions of people eager to leave. Those who seek to come are few in number. There will be no great influx if the border is left open."[9] Net immigration for Central America was 725, and for South America, 3,290 in the previous year. Senator Reed insisted that a quota for the Western Hemisphere was "in the first place . . . absolutely unnecessary."[10]

Others, such as Senator Willis, argued that we needed to treat Mexico and Latin America as other nations in the world, but Willis's amendment to include the Western Hemisphere within the quota was decisively rejected 12 to 60. Even Senator Reed, a leading restrictionist, voted against the amendment because of the importance he attached to the "Pan American ideal."[11]

The new law succeeded in restricting European immigration. From 1930 to 1946, the period in which the law was fully implemented, only one-fifth of the 2.5 million numbers were utilized because of little interest in Western Europe. Before the 1924 immigration act, 60 percent of the immigrants were male; afterward, 59 percent were female, reflecting the reduction in the number of independent immigrants and the increase in the number of spouses and families. There was also a sharp decline in the number of immigrants who were unskilled, from over one million in 1911–1920 to under 20,000 in 1931–1940—and those who were agricultural laborers from over one million to under 7,000.[12]

West Indian immigrants could use a very large British quota, which was almost never filled, but for a few years this proved rather sticky. After 10,000 British West Indian immigrants arrived in 1924, only 308 immigrated in 1925, and the number averaged 617 persons a year from then through 1932. Put another way, 102,949 British West Indians immigrated to the U.S. during 1899–1924, at an annual average of 4,118, while a total of 4,933 immigrated during the eight years following passage of the Immigration Act of 1924.[13]

With the Depression, immigration became an issue again. In 1930 there was a concerted attempt to remove Mexico, the independent Caribbean, and Latin America from the quota-exempt category. The debate focused on illegal Mexican migrants taking scarce jobs. The issue was whether to impose a quota on Mexico, and Senators Borah and Swanson of the Senate Foreign Relations Committee insisted that the adverse consequences to our foreign relations would be serious, but their warning went unheeded. On May 13, Senator Harris's amendment to apply the quota to Mexico passed by a vote of 51 to 16. But the State Department, arguing that such an amendment would harm our relations with Latin America and the Caribbean, was able to mobilize sufficient support in the House to defeat it.

THE McCARRAN-WALTER ACT

Congress did not debate these issues again in as comprehensive a manner until the McCarran-Walter bill in the 1950s. During the Depression, the flow of migrants to the United States slowed, and in 1932 was overtaken by the flow of emigrants out of the United States. Nearly 400,000 Mexicans were estimated to have been repatriated. Also, large numbers of Caribbean emigrants returned from the United States and from Great Britain, and even larger numbers from the Dominican Republic and Cuba. Riots occurred throughout the Caribbean between 1935 and 1938, and scholars attribute them to the economic depression as well as the high level of repatriation.[14]

Unemployment, which reached desperate levels in the United States (and elsewhere) during the Depression, disappeared during the Second World War, and the United States even had to recruit agricultural and industrial labor from the Caribbean. In 1942, the United States negotiated bilateral agreements with Mexico, British Honduras, Barbados, and Jamaica for temporary workers, albeit at a much reduced level. At the same time, there was considerable migration during the war to the new bases built by the United States in Antigua and St. Thomas and to the oil refineries in the Antilles.

In 1947, Representative Walter Judd of Minnesota introduced an immigration bill that would limit all immigration from colonies to 100 regardless of the mother country's quota. As West Indians were then immigrating at a much higher rate, Americans of West Indian descent organized and testified against this provision. The bill passed the House but died in the Senate because Senator McCarran had just been charged by the Senate leadership to reexamine all immigration laws, and he insisted that these issues be raised only in that context.

The McCarran-Walter bill emerged from the Senate Judiciary Committees in 1952 with the provision limiting quotas for colonies to 100. Rev. Ethelred Brown, Minister of the Harlem Unitarian Church and Secretary of the Jamaican Progressive League, later said they "were unable to appear at the hearings" to testify against it because they were unaware this provision had been inserted in the bill.[15]

The McCarran-Walter Act was a product of both a long-standing need to modernize the immigration statutes and the security fears of the Cold War. The law codified existing immigration and naturalization statutes and tightened laws to protect the United States against the possible immigration of radicals, communists, or subversives. It also retained the national origins provisions as well as the Western Hemisphere exemption.

The major Caribbean issue—a limit of 100 immigrants per colony per year—was vigorously debated on the floor of both houses. Rep. Adam Clayton Powell of New York, who claimed to represent 150,000 West Indians in his district alone, was the main speaker against the provision: "This section in its impact, discriminates especially against would-be immigrants from Jamaica, Trinidad, and other colonies of the West Indies, most of whom are Negroes."[16] He criticized the bill as racist, and tried to relate the issue in a constructive way to the Cold War motives that were driving the bill:

We are setting up a policy that is not going to help us in our fight throughout the world. Do not think that what you do here is not going to be heard over the world. It is going to be heard in the Caribbean; it is going to be heard where there are people of the dark races. We are going to need them sometime.[17]

Powell was supported by Senators Hubert Humphrey of Minnesota and Herbert Lehman of New York, who introduced a liberal alternative to the McCarran-Walter bill. The Humphrey-Lehman bill explicitly eliminated all racial discrimination and would "leave untouched present immigration from Western Hemisphere colonies."[18] In an advertisement supporting this bill in the New York *Times* on April 24, 1952, 70 distinguished leaders of ethnic groups in the U.S. explicitly noted and endorsed this provision. And an editorial, "The new immigration bill," in the New York *Times* a week later took the same position:

> An entirely new provision limiting colonial quotas is clearly aimed at a drastic cut in immigration from the British West Indies—notably Jamaica—and if the intention is not to exclude Negroes from the Caribbean islands that is unmistakably the effect. It is all the more startling when we consider that there are no quota limitations at all for the independent countries of the Western hemisphere.[19]

These arguments did not move the majorities in Congress. Representative Walter claimed that the provision was not designed to discriminate against Negroes: "It is just a case of equal treatment . . . Haiti and the Dominican Republic all come in without regard to quotas, and they are all colored people . . . if Jamaica had its independence, then the residents of that island would also be quota exempt."[20]

Truman vetoed the bill, but on June 27, 1952, Congress overrode his veto. On September 4, out of anger and recognizing that his term was nearly over, Truman established a Presidential Commission on Immigration and Naturalization to reexamine both the McCarran-Walter Act and current immigration problems, and make recommendations to him by January 3, 1953, before the new Congress was installed. The commission, not surprisingly, issued a strongly worded critique of the act, and it stressed that it harmed U.S. relations in the Caribbean by limiting immigration to 100 per colony (800 total) as compared with 2,500 the year before. The commission observed that the act was "keenly felt . . . as a racial discrimination."[21] Various British West Indian legislatures passed resolutions denouncing the act. Leaders and newspapers from the area protested, as did the British government and the Caribbean Commission (a body formed by executive agreement between the United States, United Kingdom, France, and the Netherlands to plan for the economic and social development of the area).[22]

In hearings before the commission, Walter White, Secretary of the National Association for the Advancement of Colored People, protested the provision's discriminatory features and said he found "many examples of anger mixed with shock" in his recent travels to the region.[23] Secretary of State Dean Acheson testified before the commission and said that the act "causes resentment, weakening the friendship of some of our neighbors, but also causes or emphasizes economic dislocations that weaken those neighbors, whom we need as strong partners and who can furnish us with sites for military bases and strategic raw materials."[24] But the State Department's pleading and the critique and recommendations of the presidential commission were to no avail. The provision remained on the books.

The McCarran-Walter Act did have considerable impact on Caribbean immigration to the United States, though not entirely as intended. Between its passage and the 1965 act, which repealed the discriminatory provision, Caribbean immigration quadrupled over that of the previous decade—221,485 from 1953 to 1965 vs. 53,013 for 1943–1952. (The average annual immigration increased from 5,601 in the decade 1943–1952 to 17,037 in the period 1953–1965.) Caribbean immigration as a percent of total immigration to the United States nearly doubled, to 6.3 percent. The major source of the increase was Cuba and, since 1961, the Dominican Republic. Immigration from the major islands in the British West Indies was reduced, but it still averaged considerably above 200 per year per large island, and in the case of Jamaica, it averaged over 1,000 per year after 1956, and over 2,000 per year after 1961 (see Table 15.2).[25]

In the postwar period, emigration from the British West Indies reached extremely high levels, and when the flow to the United States was reduced by the McCarran-Walter Act, it shifted in direction to Great Britain. One study estimated that before the McCarran-Walter Act went into effect, for every West Indian who migrated to Great Britain, nine went to the United States. After the act the ratio was reversed.[26]

An estimated 300,000 West Indians migrated to the United Kingdom between 1952 and 1964,[27] and just the expectation and

Table 15.2: U.S. Immigration Policy and Caribbean Immigration, 1900-1979

Period	Region of Last Residence				Caribbean as a percent of Total
	All Countries		Caribbean		
1901-1920	14,531,197	(726,560)	230,972	(11,549)	1.5
1921-1924	2,344,599	(586,149)	51,963	(12,991)	2.2
1925-1942	2,371,598	(131,755)	44,724	(2,485)	1.9
1943-1952	1,425,719	(142,572)	56,013	(5,601)	3.9
1953-1965	3,494,554	(268,812)	221,485	(17,037)	6.3
1966-1976	4,309,935	(391,812)	749,742	(68,158)	17.4
1977-1979	1,524,105	(508,035)	285,688	(95,229)	18.7

Source: U.S. Dept. of Justice, *U.S. Annual Report of the Immigration and Naturalization Service for the fiscal year ended* (various). The figures in parentheses are the average annual number of immigrants per period. The Caribbean includes Anguilla, Antigua, Bahamas, Barbados, Bermuda, Cayman Islands, Cuba, Dominica, Dominican Republic, Grenada, Guadeloupe, Haiti, Jamaica, Martinique, Montserrat, Antilles, St. Kitts, St. Lucia, St. Vincent, Trinidad and Tobago, the Turks and Caicos, and the British Virgin Islands.

fear that the United Kingdom would pass a restrictive law impelled over 168,000 West Indians to emigrate in the last two and one-half years before the Commonwealth Immigration Act came into effect in 1962.[28] Three years later, Parliament passed a second law that tightened immigration controls further, restricting total work permits for West Indians to 8,500 per year. As a result, only 257 work vouchers were issued to Jamaicans in 1968, and only 136 in 1969.

When the doors of the United Kingdom closed, West Indians in great numbers shifted direction to the United States—first coming through the side door (as spouses, relatives, and so on), then the back door, and finally, with independence and subsequently the 1965 immigration act, through the front door as well. In increasing numbers, West Indians travelled to the United States on nonimmigrant visas and simply overstayed their visas.

ENDING PREFERENTIAL TREATMENT

The debate on whether to exempt the Western Hemisphere from the natural origins quota system, which had begun with the passage of the Immigration Act of 1921, finally came to an end in 1965. An amendment was introduced to set a quota limit for Western Hemisphere immigration similar to the limit set for the Eastern Hemisphere, but it was opposed strongly by the State Department. The issue, however, was no longer so clear cut, as the New York *Times* noted in an editorial:

> Secretary Rusk urges that Latin American nations remain outside any ceiling [on immigration], as they are now outside the quota system. But this well intentioned position could lead to trouble and ill will in the not so distant future if immigration from Latin America and the Caribbean should grow sharply—as there are signs that it will—and pressures were then built for us to limit a sudden flood of immigrants for which the country was unprepared. While the entire law is being overhauled, it would be better to place all the nations of the world, including those to the south of the United States, on exactly the same footing.[29]

The 1965 immigration law aimed to repeal completely the national origins quota system; remove discrimination based on race or ancestry; create an annual Eastern Hemisphere ceiling of 170,000 with an annual per-country limit of 20,000; and alter the basis of selection to use criteria, like family ties and skills, on a first-come, first-served basis. The Senate insisted on bringing the Western Hemisphere into this new formula, with a ceiling of 120,000 but with no preference system and no country limitations. Instead, immigration would be regulated by a labor certification requirement. The Senate prevailed.

The Western Hemisphere exemption was repealed in 1965 because Congress was more concerned about the increasing numbers of Latin American and Caribbean immigrants since World War II, and the "Pan American idea" was no longer self-evident. One could argue, as the New York *Times* did, that our relations would be improved, rather than endangered, by treating Latin America on an equal basis.

Congress rejected the president's recommendations with some reluctance, as demonstrated by the Senate's decision to delay implementing the 1865 act for three years and to establish in that interim period the Select Commission on Western Hemisphere Immigration to recommend whether to go ahead with it. The select commission completed its report in January 1968, and found that contrary to the fearful predictions of the administration, the passage of the 1965 act "caused little adverse hemispheric reaction . . . [and] no official representations" had been made by Caribbean governments to the

United States.[30] On the principal issue—whether to have a numerical ceiling for Western Hemisphere immigration—the commission was not able to make a final, definitive recommendation. Instead, it recommended delaying the imposition of the ceiling for one year, from July 1, 1968 to July 1, 1969, pending further research. If this was a typical commission recommendation, then Congress responded in its own typical manner: it took no action.

In the short time since the passage of the act, the commission found that the labor certification requirement had effectively restricted immigration from 174,237 in 1965 to 121,877 in 1966. But this is a footnote to the 1965 act, which E. P. Hutchinson accurately described as "a turning point in American immigration policy."[31]

The 1965 act fundamentally changed the pattern of immigration to the United States. The United States opened itself to becoming a Third World nation, and in particular a Caribbean Basin nation. Between 1900 and 1965, 75 percent of all immigrants were of European extraction, whereas 62 percent of the immigrants since 1968, when the act took effect, have been from Asia and Latin America, and by 1978 the percentage had increased to 82 percent. In the past two decades the Caribbean Basin has become the largest source of immigrants into the United States—nearly one-third of all legal immigrants.[32]

Immigration from the Caribbean quadrupled from an annual average of about 17,037 in the period 1953-1965 to an annual average of 68,158 from 1966-1976. Moreover, the percentage of all immigrants who originate in the Caribbean tripled from 6.3 percent to 17.4 percent, and it has increased since then.[33] An analysis based on examining just two years—1965 and 1979—shows how the 1965 Immigration Act affected the composition of the immigrants to the United States. Immigration from Europe declined by 50 percent while immigration from Asia, Africa, and the Caribbean expanded dramatically. Immigration from the islands of Jamaica and Trinidad increased during this time by almost 1,000 percent (see Table 15.3)

While the 1965 immigration act permitted a fundamental change in the composition of immigrants to the United States and brought the Western Hemisphere under a numerical ceiling, as had been the case for the Eastern Hemisphere since 1924, there were still some differences between U.S. immigration policy toward the two hemispheres. Both had numerical ceilings—170,000 for the Eastern Hemisphere and 120,000 for the Western—but the Eastern Hemisphere

Table 15.3: Immigrants Admitted by Country or Region of Birth (Fiscal Years Ending September 30, 1979 and June 30, 1965): The Impact of the 1965 Act

Country/Region of Birth	1979	1965	Percent Change
All Countries	460,348	296,697	+55.2
Europe	60,845	113,424	-46.4
Asia	189,293	20,683	+815.2
Africa	12,838	3,383	+279.5
West Indies	74,074	37,583	+97.1
Cuba	15,585	19,760	-21.1
Dominican Rep.	17,519	9,504	+84.3
Haiti	6,433	3,609	+78.2
Jamaica	19,714	1,837	+973.2
Trinidad/Tobago	5,225	485	+977.3
Other West Indies	9,598	2,388	+301.9

Source: U.S. Dept. of Justice, *1979 Statistical Yearbook of the Immigration and Naturalization Service*, p. 2. The West Indies includes Anguilla, Antigua, Bahamas, Barbados, Bermuda, Cayman Islands, Cuba, Dominica, Dominican Republic, Grenada, Guadeloupe, Haiti, Jamaica, Martinique, Montserrat, Antilles, St. Kitts, St. Lucia, St. Vincent, Trinidad and Tobago, the Turks and Caicos, and the British Virgin Islands.

had a preference system and per-country limits of 20,000, and the Western Hemisphere relied mostly on labor certification requirements as a way to reduce the numbers. Not surprisingly, the waiting period to receive immigrant visas in the Western Hemisphere grew longer and longer. In part because of the new immigration pressures released by the 1965 act, Congress moved in two stages to eliminate the remaining differences.

On October 20, 1976, Congress passed an immigration law that created two essentially equal immigration systems based on a preference system and per-country ceilings of 20,000. However, the ceiling remained at different levels—170,000 for the East and 120,000 for the West. Two years later, Congress finally moved to eliminate the remaining difference; it established a single world-wide ceiling of 290,000.

Two key issues remained: refugees and illegal migration. More than 800,000 Cuban refugees arrived during the last two decades—the largest number of refugees from one source in U.S history. Yet it took the Indochinese boat people to move Congress to pass the Refugee Act of 1980. Ironically the act, which replaced a Cold War definition of refugee with a United Nations definition, and an arbitrary mode of decision making with one that was clearer and fairer, was not able to deal with its first "refugee" crisis, the Mariel mass exodus.

While illegal migration has concerned Congress since the 1920s, it has only recently been viewed as a significant problem. In 1971, the House Judiciary Committee held hearings on illegal migration, and the subject has continued to preoccupy Congress and the president ever since. In January 1975, President Gerald Ford instructed the domestic council to study the problem and make recommendations, which it did in a report in December 1976. The next year, the Carter administration restudied the issue, and in August 1977 it proposed legislation. The principal instrument for reducing illegal migration was employer sanctions. Congress debated the issue, but ultimately dodged it, and instead established the Select Commission on Immigration and Refugee Policy to study the issue again to forge a national consensus on a new approach.

In March 1981 the Select Commission submitted its report to President Reagan. Although estimates of the stock of illegal migrants in the United States ranged from 2 to 12 million, the commission judged that the number in 1978 "is almost certainly below 6 million, and may be substantially less, possibly only 3–5.5 million." Of that, the Mexican component is "almost certainly less than 3 million." The commission also concluded that "an increasing proportion of undocumented illegal migrants appear to come from countries other than Mexico," most of them in the Caribbean, including the Dominican Repulbic, Jamaica, Trinidad and Tobago, and Haiti.[34]

Reagan instructed an 11-member interagency task force to review the report and make recommendations that he would submit to Congress. After the task force reported to Reagan, he unveiled his proposal on July 30. On March 17, 1982, the chairmen of the two Congressional subcommittees on Immigration, Representative Romano Mazzoli and Senator Alan Simpson introduced identical bills, which were closer to the select commission's report than to the Reagan administration's proposals. The Senate passed the bill in August 1982 by a vote of 80 to 19. Mazzoli's subcommittee passed the bill on May 19, but the full committee delayed action until the Senate passed it. During the post-election session, the bill reached the floor of the House, where it died on December 18, 1982, filibustered by the Hispanic-Black caucus.

Both Simpson and Mazzoli reintroduced The Immigration and Reform Control Act of 1983 in the New Congress. Simpson introduced the bill that passed the Senate, and Mazzoli's was the House Judiciary Committee's bill. The two bills gave expanded quotas of 40,000 to Mexico and Canada. All other countries would have ceilings of 20,000. When asked whether the rest of the Caribbean Basin could receive larger quotas—to reflect the fact that the United States was not just a North American nation, but also a Caribbean Basin nation—both Simpson and Mazzoli expressed reservations. But extensive hearings were held on the foreign policy implications of the bill.

The bill suffered a similar fate as in the previous Congresses. The Senate passed it on May 18, 1983, by a vote of 76 to 18. One year later, the House passed its variation of the bill. However, conferees failed to reach agreement on a compromise bill before Congress adjourned.

THE IMPACT OF POLICY

As one surveys a century of U.S. immigration policy and Caribbean emigration, one cannot help but recognize the importance of both structural factors and public policy in shaping the flow of immigrants. One has only to glance at Table 15.1 to recognize that the pressures to emigrate have accelerated in the last three decades when, for the first time, limits on the Caribbean migration were legislated. In the 1940s, Caribbean immigration to the United States averaged less than 5,000 people per year. The level nearly tripled in the 1950s, then almost quadrupled above that in the 1960s, and nearly doubled again in the 1970s. Of the two million Caribbean people who have immigrated to the United States since 1820, 80 percent have arrived in the last three decades, and over half from 1970 to 1980.

On the other hand, the continuing power of structural pressures should not obscure the importance of immigration policy in shaping the composition, numbers, and direction of immigration. A simple illustration of the importance of policy on migration can be seen in comparing Tables 15.1 and 15.2. Both tables cover much the same data—Caribbean immigration from the turn of the century to the present—but the data are organized differently. Table 15.1, which is broken down by decades, does not convey the shifts in immigration as effectively as does Table 15.2, which is broken down by the periods associated with each immigration law. To take just the most vivid example, the decade of the 1960s was a period of large-scale emigration from the Caribbean, reflecting 14.2 percent of total immigration, but the numbers and relative percentage increase if one looks instead at the decade after passage of the 1965 act, and indeed Table 15.3 underscores the impact of that law on the flows of migrants. Also, the 1921 law provided room for expansion of Caribbean immigration at the expense of emigration from southern and eastern Europe.

Even Table 15.2 needs to be disaggregated by country to understand more completely the impact of policy. The McCarran-Walter Act of 1952 did curb migration from the British West Indies and redirect it to Great Britain. But the number of Caribbean immigrants to the United States increased nonetheless—three-fold over that of the previous decade—because of large-scale emigration from Cuba, the Dominican Republic, and Haiti. When the 1965 amendment to the Immigration and Naturalization Act passed, liberalizing immigration from the entire Caribbean and the Third World, the composition of immigrants to the United States changed rather fundamentally. The Caribbean Basin became the largest source of legal migration to the United States—and also of illegal migration.

The public debate on immigration policy almost always reflected some measure of sensitivity to the possible impact on the Caribbean. Even when Congress was insensitive, as in 1914 and 1952, the executive branch compensated. Moreover, the decision to exempt the entire Western Hemisphere from the quota system from 1921 to 1965 reflected a national consensus that the Caribbean and Latin America should be treated better than the rest of the world. It also represented a judgment that the Western Hemisphere was unlikely to become a large source of migration. When, in the 1960s, both judgments changed, the Western Hemisphere was brought into a single, global system.[35]

While the Caribbean was frequently taken into account in formulating U.S. immigration policy, it never played a large role in the debate. It is commonly believed that the decisive factor moving Congress toward new immigration policies is fear—fear of unemployment during periods of recession or depression and fear of a security threat. It is certainly true that economic downturns do generate Congressional speeches to restrict migration and sometimes also result in legislation. It is also true that the fear that radicals or subver-

sives might immigrate was an important factor as Congress debated
immigration policies in 1882, 1921, and 1952. However, as one surveys the whole of U.S. immigration policy, the one factor that stands
out most consistently as being crucial in the debate is numbers—large
numbers of immigrants. When the number of immigrants surges,
Congress restricts. In cases when the economy was depressed and
Congress debated immigration policy, as it did in 1930, but the
number of immigrants was low, Congress did not legislate. Similarly
when security fears were most pervasive, but the number of Latin
American immigrants remained low, as in 1952, Congress had no
problem exempting Latin America and the independent Caribbean
from immigration quotas. In short, economic and security fears
often provide the additional impetus to legislate, but the single most
important factor is the sense that the United States has lost control
of its immigration policy—that the number of immigrants has surged,
and some response is necessary.

Structural pressures to emigrate will remain formidable, but the
destination of the Caribbean emigrant will, to a great extent, be
determined by U.S. immigration policies. One hopes that such policies will be sensitive to the originating country and to the evolving
relationship between the United States and the Caribbean.

NOTES

This chapter draws on my longer paper, "Caribbean emigration and U.S.
immigration policy: Cross currents," which was prepared for a conference on
"The International Relations of the Contemporary Caribbean," sponsored by
the Caribbean Institute and Study Center for Latin America (CISCLA) at the
Inter-American University of Puerto Rico, San Germán, April 22-23, 1983. The
longer paper, together with other conference papers, will appear in a forthcoming book edited by Jorge Heine, Director of CISCLA, and Leslie Manigat. I am
grateful to Jorge Heine for support and comments on that paper.

1. See Alejandro Portes, "Modes of structural incorporation and present
theories of labor immigration," and W. R. Bohning, "Elements of a theory of
international economic migration to the industrial nation states," in Mary M.
Kritz, Charles B. Keely, and Silvano M. Tomasi, eds., Global Trends in Migration (New York: Center for Migration Studies, 1981).

2. Earl G. Harrison, Immigration Policy of the United States (New York:
Foreign Policy Reports of the Foreign Policy Association, April 1, 1947), p. 1.

3. Sidney Kansas, U.S. Immigration: Exclusion and Deportation and
Citizenship, 2d ed. (Albany: Matthew Bender, 1941).

4. Malcolm J. Proudfood, Population Movements in the Caribbean
(1950; reprint, New York: Negro Univ. Press, 1970), p. 88.

5. Robert A. Divine, American Immigration Policy, 1924-1952 (New

Haven: Yale Univ. Press, 1957), p. 56.

6. President's Commission on Immigration and Naturalization, *Hearings* (Washington: 1952), p. 247.

7. 18 April 1924, *Congressional Record*, 68th Cong., Senate, 6622.

8. Ibid., 6622-33.

9. Ibid., 6625.

10. Ibid.

11. Divine, *American Immigration Policy*, p. 52.

12. Harrison, *Immigration Policy*, p. 17.

13. Proudfoot, *Population Movements*, p. 88.

14. Dawn I. Marshall, "Toward an understanding of Caribbean migration," in Mary M. Kritz, ed., *U.S. Immigration and Refugee Policy: Global and Domestic Issues*, (Lexington, MA: D.C. Heath, 1983), pp. 118-20.

15. *Hearings*, 1952, p. 250.

16. April 25, 1952, *Congressional Record*, House, pp. 4435.

17. Ibid., p. 4439.

18. Ibid., pp. 4431-32.

19. New York *Times*, "A new immigration bill," May 1, 1952.

20. Testimony cited in Marion T. Bennett, *American Immigration Policies: A History* (Washington, D.C.: Public Affairs Press, 1963), pp. 190-91.

21. *Hearings*, 1952, p. 54.

22. Ibid.

23. Ibid., p. 55.

24. Ibid.

25. Select Commission on Western Hemisphere Immigration, *Report of the Select Commission* (Washington: January 1968), pp. 40-55.

26. Dennis Forsythe, "Black immigrants and the American ethos: Theories and observations," in Roy Bryce-Laporte and Delores Mortimer, eds., *Caribbean Immigration to the U.S.* (Washington, D.C.: Research Institute on Immigration and Ethnic Studies, 1983), p. 68.

27. Cited in Milton Morris and Albert Mayio, *Illegal Immigration and U.S. Foreign Policy* (Washington, D.C.: Brookings Institution, October 1980) p. A-5-2.

28. Virginia Dominguez, *From Neighbor to Stranger: The Dilemma of Caribbean Peoples in the United States* (New Haven: Yale Univ. Antilles Research Program, 1975), p. 11.

29. "Progress on immigration" New York *Times*, July 17, 1964.

30. *Report of the Select Commission*, 1968, p. 11.

31. Edward P. Hutchinson, *Legislative History of American Immigration Policy, 1789-1965* (Philadelphia: Univ. Pennsylvania Press, 1981), p. 337.

32. Robert A. Pastor, "Migration in the Caribbean Basin: The need for an approach as dynamic as the phenomenon," in *U.S. Immigration and Refugee Policy*, p. 97.

33. See Table 15.2, this chapter.

34. Select Commission on Immigration and Refugee Policy, *Staff Report* (Washington: April 30, 1981), p. 66.

35. Robert A. Pastor, "U.S. immigration policy and Latin America: In search of the 'special relationship,' " *Latin American Research Review* 19 (3) (1984), pp. 35-56.

The American Debate on
Immigration Policy:
Ideology, Politics,
and Citizenship

Anthony P. Maingot

Is the U.S. immigration problem just another of the many difficult issues confronting decision makers and citizens alike, or is it a
special problem? An American dilemma perhaps? Certainly in terms
of persistence it has the features of a special problem; each U.S.
generation seems to need—though perhaps not relish—the debate over
the principles and implications of immigration. Like the "Negro
problem" it appears to be an integral part of the larger complex of
persistent problems this democracy carries over from generation to
generation.

But, if the immigration question is another one of the ongoing
complex of issues, why has there never been anything approximating
a consensus on the precise nature of the problem, let alone a possible
resolution of it? Consensus is used here to mean legitimacy: the belief
by at least a working majority in the essential appropriateness—if not
full righteousness—of a particular policy. The question then becomes: Is the nation any closer today to such a consensus than it has
been in any of the major periods of serious debate on the issue—the
1890s, the 1920s, and the 1950s? Surely one could argue that there
have been periods of substantial consensus on that other American

Reprinted by permission of the publisher, from *U.S. Immigration and
Refugee Policy: Global and Domestic Issues*, edited by Mary M. Kritz (Lexing-
ton, MA: Lexington Books, D. C. Heath and Company; Copyright 1983, D. C.
Heath and Company).

question, of race. Whatever their private feelings and prejudices, the society and its political and judicial representatives have slowly but surely been giving shape to a civil rights thrust that can be slowed down but not reversed.

The argument in this chapter is that no such consensus appears likely on the immigration issue. A comparison with the Negro problem reveals fruitful insights and here one could do no better than to turn to Gunnar Myrdal for guidance. Myrdal is convinced that the United States had developed "the most explicitly expressed system of general ideals in reference to human interrelations" of any Western society.[1] He called this the American creed. It is to this creed that both blacks and immigrants appeal their disputes and claims over rights and privileges. Here the two problems show a similarity: both groups appeal ot the American creed specifically, and to the conflicting values of the majority white society generally. This is a very important aspect since, from that commonality flow similarities in the manner in which the arguments, claims, and grievances are articulated and in the mechanisms utilized for their redress. The American creed is upheld by utilizing the whole gamut of legal and political avenues.

Once the similarity is established, however, the differences begin to reveal themselves more clearly. Perhaps a closer review of these differences will throw some light on the lack of consensus on the immigration problem. This is so because, in a fundamental way, these differences reflect the attitudes and postures of the white majority to the race problem and the immigration problem, respectively. The black-white relationship has a firm moral infrastructure and the resulting dilemma has a heavy content of historical guilt. The immigration dilemma, while also ideologically related to the American creed, is more political and secular. Given this secularity it engenders the good sociological analysis or court brief, but is incapable of the purely righteous and moral indignation of a Harriet Beecher Stowe's *Uncle Tom's Cabin.* At no time has the immigration question produced the poignancy of a Richard Wright's *Black Boy,* or the passion of a James Baldwin's *The Fire Next Time.* That lack, in turn, has meant that the kind of excruciating and guilt-laden response of a Norman Podhretz, "My Negro Problem, and Ours" has been absent. "Special feelings about color," confessed Podhoretz,[2] "are a contagion to which White Americans seem susceptible even

when there is nothing in their background to account for the susceptibility." It is the collective guilt of a nation that still has to conquer
racism, yet has to deal with a system of explicitly expressed general
ideals, as Myrdal noted. This historical guilt—part of the underpin-
nings of U.S. black-white relations—is lacking in the immigrant problem. These special feelings are reserved for the only group in the U.S.
mosaic that did not come voluntarily, that cannot identify historically with a single particular country, language, or religion.

Immigrants and immigration, on the other hand, were concep-
tualized quite differently. At a practical, immediate level, the white
majority's interest seldom stretched much beyond the proper concern over that all important initial opportunity: the foreigner's right
to be here in the first place, the privilege of entry. Since the immigrant came voluntarily, it was the immigrant who was supposed to
have the special feelings of gratitude and satisfaction.

At a broader and more ideological level, immigrants were sub-
sumed under an overarching view of nation-building. Immigrant and
native alike were perceived to be parts of an ongoing process in which,
as Frederick J. Turner[3] put it, self-determination, self-restraint and
"intelligent democracy" were creating something new and original.

The well-researched history of the travails of each new immigrant group as they attempted to become a part of the experiment
warns us against too ready an acceptance of this widely held view. But
the fact is that even though that belief—like Turner's own theory of
frontier—may have been more myth than reality, it certainly was the
kind of myth that, through the process of the self-fulfilling prophesy,
lent itself to the creation of other myths. In the process of ethnic bargaining that accompanied the immigration process, perceptions about
a new group's contributions to U.S. democracy were very important.[4] In other words, the battleground was that of power and the task
at hand was to gain membership in the community as a competitor.

Because it appeals to the American creed, the immigration problem clearly has a moral dimension, but it is the dimension of moral
accountability rather than of moral obligation. What is absent, thus,
is the kind of moral consciousness that constantly activates the white
majority's sense of guilt. Lacking this, the immigration dilemma
takes on the dimensions of a high-order secular problem. It is of high
order because it does have a moral content that appeals to the American creed, and yet it is secular, that is, a political problem that is
defined and given shape and direction through an ongoing and ever-
changing process of societal bargaining.

This being the case, one can well understand why the overriding concern in the white majority's constant struggle with the immigration problem has been limited to periodic attempts at achieving politically acceptable procedural justice at a given time, as distinct from, for instance, the pursuit of a general policy of equality that transcends space and time. Power (or perhaps disparities in power), not historical guilt, is the key to understanding why in immigration policy the only consensus has been (can be?) that there should be periodic reviews and revisions of policy and procedure. The issue of reparations to the descendants of the Japanese incarcerated during World War II illustrates the point that U.S. society does respond to moral issues, but that in cases of immigrants the process is one of accountability rather than moral obligation.

Illegal immigration and refugee issues have made the immigration problem more complex, more unpredictable, inasmuch as they have intensified the moral links with the American creed; they have not, however, converted it into a new American dilemma. It remains a secular problem, albeit one that will probably come up for review more frequently and involve increasingly more complex issues of political and legal philosophy and procedure. This chapter focuses on this lack of consensus in U.S. immigration policy and hypothesizes that in an age of ethnic revitalization a consensus becomes even more difficult. Given this difficulty, the chapter suggests an emphasis on the nature of U.S. citizenship as an evolving condition. Citizenship as an ongoing experiment might be a way of reorienting the debate in a constructive way, a debate that is presently beyond consensus. Because the concept requires an equal emphasis on the society and on the individual, on privileges as well as obligations, it forces a real assessment of the way in which new members of the community secure truly enduring rights. This appears to be especially important in a society such as that of the United States.

THE DEVELOPMENT OF CULTURE
AND SOCIAL PLURALISM

The preoccupation with race relations, or more specifically, with what U.S. whites have, until recently, called the "Negro problem," has meant that despite the history of immigration, there has not been any fundamental agreement among U.S. scholars on the need to study and document the nature of ethnicity in the process of immigration and acculturation in the United States.[5] Fortunately, not all U.S. scholars have felt this way, since there is a distinct need to understand the parallel developments of cultural pluralism and social pluralism in the United States. The former describes the retention of ethnicity as an organizing principle within groups; the latter scrutinizes the stratification system, the structure of inequality.

The first major systematic exposition of the concept of social pluralism was that of Furnivall[6] in his study of what is today Indonesia. Furnivall's fundamental thesis is that the plural society was not created by fiat, by a series of policies, but rather that historical circumstances, including an evolving economic system, dictated policy. "The plural society," Furnivall wrote, "was not planned; it happened." And it happened because the values and institutions of the society had not been shaped by one group; no one group monopolized power; none had social, economic, or political predominance. "The plural society," he noted, "is in fact held together only by pressure exerted from outside by the colonial power; it has no common social will."[7]

Certainly no one would argue that Furnivall's plural society model fits the United States precisely. Yet in a very fundamental Furnivall manner, the United States was not planned; "it happened." And it happened because after the initial consensus on an open door, on the value of not having an explicit or institutionalized immigration policy, there never was a policy that could be agreed on or, if agreed on, implemented. There was, rather, unplanned and incremental growth.[8] Agreement on that essential aspect of state sovereignty, control over one's borders and the right of exclusion, grew even more slowly. Immigration laws, such as they were, tended to follow population movements; they neither caused them, nor, indeed, totally controlled them. Other factors took care of that. One such factor was the economic cycle. As early as 1926, Harry Jerome[9] hypothesized that, with the exception of a few periods, immigration increased with prosperity and decreased in depressions. The number of departures tended to follow the opposite course.

International politics, especially foreign wars, also had a way of shifting immigration flows and policy. The exemption of Western Hemisphere citizens from both of the restrictive 1924 and 1952 quotas, for instance, responded to both specific national politics as well as foreign policy needs. By the time actual immigration flows and limits were set on Western Hemisphere immigration (the 120,000 ceiling of 1965), events of the Cold War had created new conditions that made ceilings totally unrealistic. The architects of the provisions on anticommunist refugees of the 1952 McCarran-Walter bill had no way of predicting where those refugees would come from.

The constantly changing national political desiderata forced flexibility and constant shifts in immigration policy, as did the role of repeated presidential vetoes of restrictive legislation. Both reflected the different constituencies operating in U.S. politics, with the executive showing more susceptibility to pressures from urban immigrants than the legislature.[10]

By the mid 20th century the United States had become a complex social and cultural plural society and even the most restrictive of policies could not control immigration. The findings of Roney,[11] that between 1953 and 1965 (a period of strict quotas and emphasis on control over immigration flows) only 35 percent of all immigrants admitted to the United States were quota immigrants, are significant. This is especially so when we discover that four-fifths of the nonquota admissions during that period were nonquota immediate relatives of U.S. citizens or natives of Western Hemisphere countries. Additionally, hundreds of thousands were admitted through special legislation.

To understand the growth of U.S. social pluralism, in all its unplanned and uncontrolled dimensions, it is not adequate to ask whether all who wanted to come in did; the question is rather whether large numbers of those whom the restrictionists of the early 1920s and 1950s and other periods wanted to keep out were kept out. It appears that they were.

It is interesting to note how observers during past periods of restrictive immigration policy assumed that the policy would indeed restrict the flows. Writing in the early 1950s, Juznets and Rubin[12] took note of the free market play between capital and labor, but worried that wars and restrictive legislation would curtail not only immigration, but also the healthy patterns of U.S. population growth. Their conclusion was less than prophetic: "Indeed, the change in the whole climate of international relations has been so drastic that it is hard to imagine a return to the unprecedentedly wide and free movement of people in the world. . . . [No longer would they] take advantage of better opportunities and contribute markedly to the growth of their country of destination."[13]

In fact, history will record that during the two decades after the 1965 legislation, immigration reached levels equal to those of 1900–

1910 (between 8 and 9 million). A brief look at the causes reinforces the notion of an unplanned socially plural society: (1) the removal of quotas and an increase in the ceiling of legal immigration by the 1965 amendments to the Immigration and Nationality Act; (2) political changes in Cuba and Indochina leading to a flood of refugees; and (3) the large increase in the illegal immigration of those seeking work.

The first cause—the 1965 act—can be said to have been planned; it responded to the pressures of the new emphasis on civil rights within the U.S. system. In other words, liberalized immigration policy was a direct beneficiary of shifts in national politics. Causes two and three were impossible to predict and thus plan for. How could those who in the 1950s set a limit of 17,400 refugees per year predict that Cuba and Vietnam, not Hungary and Poland, would provide hundreds of thousands of applicants for that new refugee status? Additionally, who could predict that Britain, for instance, would no longer welcome West Indians just at the time when the 1965 amendments opened the doors of the United States to them?

At this point the inner contradiction between an assertion of an American creed and the postulation of a theory of social pluralism (which assumes precisely the absence of any such collective will) becomes evident. A resolution might be found in the admission that major portions of the American creed itself have been flexible and malleable, a product of ongoing bargaining. Each generation, confronted with different problems, assesses the situation and interprets the creed accordingly, thereby adding to it. In this process intellectuals play a significant role.[14] "The writing of American history," says Higham, "has always had . . . an intimate relation to history in the making. To examine the two together is to see the United States in terms of its evolving consciousness of itself."[15] In this process the interpretations of the role of immigration (written, as Fuchs notes, largely by Anglo-Saxon Protestants[16]) have emphasized the exact opposite from the historical guilt evinced toward the Negro problem: a not-undeserved sense of pride in U.S. largesse with foreigners.

> Historically, equality of opportunity was a particularly apt form of egalitarianism for a new, undeveloped frontier country. . . . The best economic benefit which the government could give was to offer a person free access in developing undeveloped resources for his own profit, and this is what America did offer . . . equality of opportunity did become the most highly sanctioned form of egalitarianism in the United States.[17]

The principle of equality of opportunity, especially when produced by guilt and fear, might operate to create a consensus on certain problems; immigration is not one of them. Short of saying "all are welcome" or "none is welcome," opportunities become results of political bargaining combined with innumerable and thus unpredictable events.

Given this unpredictability, policy becomes reactive. This reactive nature of U.S. policy is also evident in the broad sweeps of ideology regarding immigration and ethnic assimilation. Gordon,[18] for instance, admits that Anglo-conformity is probably still the strongest implicit theory of assimilation in the United States; yet he masterfully delineates three major philosophies or "goal systems of assimilation" in U.S. history up to 1960s. The figures show that throughout the years, and regardless of whether the dominant ideology was that of "Anglo-conformity," "melting pot" or "cultural pluralism," to use Gordon's terms, the flow of immigrants continued. In fact, by the 1960s the United States had a population and society that—prodded by the right combination of issues—was ready to enter another ideological phase, that of ethnic revitalization.

The shift in ideologies indicates how an initially dominant majority group had to adjust to new circumstances as pressure from the new immigrant groups, as well as rethinking among intellectual leaders of the majority groups, pressed for changes. These changes do not reflect fundamental shifts in overall power relationships but the differential composition of the majority group and the role of conflict and competition in U.S. life. A continual search has taken place for a policy that best reflects the dominant group's ideas about opportunities at any particular time.

This parallel development of cultural and social pluralism was essential if this new phase (the ideology of ethnic revitalization) was to be possible. It is in the context of this new ideology of assimilation that both Presidents Carter and Reagan have attempted to reformulate immigration policy.

THE IDEOLOGY OF ETHNIC REVITALIZATION

What has been happening since the 1920s, and with considerable force since the early 1960s, is not an historical awareness of an existing state of cultural pluralism or of the plural society, but rather a call for ethnic revitalization. This new ideology is not merely concerned with retaining whatever cultural persistence and diversity might exist; it is also interested in revitalizing dormant ethnic identities and even in creating new ones.

While it is clear that the seeds have been present at least since the early 1900s, it was in part the upsurge in black nationalism—at home and abroad—that gave impetus to a new ethnic revitalism among nonblack ethnic groups.[19] Today the interest in ethnic identities is everywhere in evidence in academic and public discussions. Even the majority group discovers its ethnicity.[20] Glazer and Moynihan have most recently suggested that *ethnicity* seems to be a new term and that the new usage of it reflects a new social reality.[21] In popular U.S. usage, *ethnic group* no longer refers merely to minority and marginal subgroups at the edges of society, that is, groups expected to assimilate, or, at best, to survive as merely exotic elements in the larger society.

Far from creating a consensus, the U.S. immigration problem has tended to draw interest, or at least response, from a wide number of different groups with equally varied interests, involvements, and sentiments. Not only is there no solid, ongoing foundation of affected morality or historic guilt to cement the transition from one ideological phase to another, there is, in addition, the regionalization of the problem. Certainly crucial is the fact that, given the historic concentration of ethnic immigrant groups in a few states, each group tends to agitate in different geographical areas, even though, in the final analysis, they all end up lobbying in Washington.[22]

In such a milieu, what are the prospects for immigration policy on the one hand and racial justice on the other? A tentative answer is that, precisely because of a lack of consensus on policy, expanded immigration is probable but increased racial justice is not. While the ideology of ethnic revitalization may suit the Cuban immigrant well, there is some evidence that the same ideology might be counterproductive to the black ethnic group, as Kilson has warned.[23] The ideology of ethnic revitalization merely adds new elements to the existing process of ethnic and nonethnic bargaining in the system. The search for a consensus on immigration policy in the 1980s takes place within a most difficult context of crisscrossing allegiances, interests, and values characteristic of the era of ethnic revitalization. And yet there are crucial issues of rights (individual and societal), as well as of nationhood (sovereignty and national security), that do call for a consensus (that is, legitimacy) and are profoundly affected by the immigration problem.

DANGERS OF A WEAK CONCEPT OF CITIZENSHIP

In modern, multiethnic societies there is a need to appeal to concepts that transcend all types of division, including class and ethnicity, and that also have specific grounding in law and custom. Such a concept is citizenship.

Since U.S. history has shown dramatic shifts in the general climates of opinion regarding ethnicity and immigration, the concern centers on the role that an erstwhile weak concept of citizenship might play in a new era of backlash, an era in which anti rather than pro attitudes characterize the general mood. In such a negative context there might be a tendency to argue and act instrumentally, utilizing a stark citizen/noncitizen dichotomy as a political weapon, that is, to emphasize only the exclusive rights of citizenship and the delimiting aspects of noncitizenship, or, again, to tend to disregard the citizenship of controversial groups. In such an environment it is to be expected that all immigrants—legal or illegal—and citizens from politically weak (minority) groups might lose.[24] Should such a large-scale violation of rights occur, it is clear that all lose as pluralism and democracy give way to authoritarianism. The question remains, however: Can a consensus be built around the principle and idea of citizenship?

Since T.H. Marshall published his crucial *Class, Citizenship and Social Development,*[25] the sociological study of the role of citizenship has received some impetus. Citizenship can be considered as a resource in the continual bargaining that characterizes all social processes. It is one of many sources of power, but differs from other sources, such as social class or social status, in that, theoretically at least, it does not divide the society. Again, theoretically, it recognizes all under a common definition of citizen. In part this is a result of the fact that, as understood in the 20th century, the concept is comprehensive of all rights and obligations.

In the 20th century struggle between those who favor human rights and those who emphasize property rights, it is the former group that advocates the expansion of the concept of citizenship to make it more inclusive of social and economic rights. This fact has been ignored by students of power, who assume that citizenship, because it is shared by all, no longer has any relevance for the study of stratification. Citizenship, says Lenski, continues to figure prominently in the distributive process: those who lack other kinds of resources, together with those who, for ideological reasons, believe in social equality, "have combined to fight for the enhancement of the value of citizenship at the expense of those resources which generate inequality."[26] What is involved is a process of political bargaining. Since citizenship is no longer perceived as a natural law or political absolute, its definition and its weight as a resource are matters to be bargained and fought for.

This is especially true in plural societies where, as Bendix[27] has noted, the development of the concept involved the parallel evolution of twin ideas and prerogatives: (1) the plebiscitarian idea, and (2) the functional idea. The former is epitomized in the French Revolution's notion of a nation of citizens with no intervening institutions or groups (church, guilds, corporations, and so forth) between the individual and the state. This ideal state, however, did not last long, if in fact it ever existed. What occurred, rather, was that group representation, or as Bendix puts it "the differential affiliation of individuals," became accepted as part of the democratic concept of citizenship. In fact the right to join groups and associations became an integral part of the freedom and privileges of citizenship— thereby ironically perpetuating not just differences but indeed inequalities. "In this sense," Bendix concludes,"the equality of citizenship and the inequalities of social class develop together."[28]

One plural society where this functional approach to citizenship found dramatic expression was the United States. As is well known, the U.S. Constitution speaks not of citizens but of persons: "We the People," not "We the Citizens," and, again, the Bill of Rights speaks of the "rights of the people" to bear arms or enjoy freedom of speech. A major reason for this, Frank George Franklin notes, was that many of the founding fathers (some of whom were non-native born) wished to encourage immigration, a process that might have been restricted by excessively demanding requirements for naturalization and citizenship:

Every point had to be considered with reference to its effects on immigration. The problem was to adjust the naturalization law so as to gain the maximum advantage from immigration with the least harm or danger to republican government and institutions, and to other interests of the country.[29]

At most they insisted that no one—especially in matters of trade—enjoy the privileges of both citizens and aliens. The general sentiment was that the very act of immigration was proof of attachment to and affection for this country. In fact, it was only after the Civil War—in a new political mood in sharp contrast and opposition to that which had excluded the Negro from citizenship—that an authoritative definition of U.S. citizenship was made. Kettner puts it succinctly when he observes how the issue was settled: "Not logic, but force. . . ."[30] Bickel points to the specific political and constitutional needs of that period: The Dred Scott decision had to be effectively, which is to say constitutionally, overruled by a definition of citizenship in which race played no part. In fact the Fourteenth Amendment was born in order to establish citizenship for the newly emancipated black Americans. Beyond that specific, functional need, says Bickel with approval, the concept of citizenship has played a very minor role in U.S. Constitutional history. "I find it gratifying," he notes, "that we live under a Constitution to which the concept of citizenship matters very little, that prescribes decencies and wise modalities of government quite without regard to the concept of citizenship."[31] The emphasis, rather, has been on moral, political, and traditional sources, sources more complex, says Bickel, than the simple contractual notion of citizenship. "Citizenship," he concludes, "is at best a simple idea for a simple government."[32]

Rather than providing a consistent, hard, and fast doctrine of guarantees and prerogatives to those that hold it, definitions and applications of the U.S. concept of citizenship have depended on the temper of the times and on the outcome of the competitition for power of those groups functioning in the system. Unfortunately the results of this person- rather than citizen-stressed functional approach have not always been that "balance between order and liberty" that Bickel posits. Two characteristics of U.S. society and form of government delayed the full realization of the ideal of "one people." Aside from the issue of whether "the people" meant one sovereign community or many, there was the issue of the black man in U.S. society. Kettner notes that the universal attitude of color prejudice was one of the major obstacles to settling the questions about "the extent, the shape, and the inclusiveness of the community of citizens."[33] It is clear that, driven in part by the force of historical guilt, attitudes toward the black man have changed. It is a fair question to ask how other immigrant groups fare in this respect.

Lacking any sense of moral dilemma about immigration, U.S. citizens, it appears, never believed that the opportunity given immigrants to enter the United States had to be carried over into other areas of social relations. As early as 1928 Bogardus showed that while U.S. citizens of all races were quite willing to allow a large number of immigrant groups into the country and, indeed, to become citizens, this right to citizenship did not translate into rights as friends, club members, neighbors, employees, and, even less, spouses.[34] Interestingly enough, Bogardus found that U.S. whites seemed as ready as Jews, and certainly more than blacks, to admit other ethnic groups to citizenship.

In a way, this distinction between the rights of legal citizenship and the benefits to be expected therefrom might be an additional explanation of why some groups with great horizontal mobility do not acquire U.S. citizenship, or do so for strictly strategic reasons. While one could argue that such an instrumental usage of the right denigrates its significance and weakens the sense of nation, the problem is that U.S. governing elites themselves have so used the concept.[35]

A case in point is Puerto Rico where, through the Jones Act in 1917, the United States granted citizenship as a reward to the "loyal" Puerto Ricans. The Puerto Ricans were preferable to the "ungrateful" Filipinos, who were granted independence. But, as Cabranes notes, this was an opportunistic and politically expedient use of citizenship: "Congress did . . . impose severe restrictions on the citizenship conferred on the Puerto Rican people. . . . For the first time in history, citizenship was granted to a people without the promise of eventual statehood and without the full panoply of rights guaranteed by the United States Constitution."[36] The real purpose was an expedient one: "Congress felt free to grant a limited citizenship to the Puerto Ricans and thereby indefinitely extend the island's colonial status."[37] It is not surprising that the arguments advanced to grant this citizenship initially, and to modify and expand it subsequently, should both have been grounded in particularistic considerations: the considerations at both times were argued in terms of race and ethnicity. These have traditionally been the most persuasive of the functional approaches in the conflict over the U.S. definition of citizenship. It was to be expected, therefore, that the argument in favor of granting Puerto Ricans citizenship was based on the idea that the people of Puerto Rico are white and European and, therefore, quite different from the Filipinos. It was this appeal to ethnicity that carried the day for the Jones Act.[38]

As the national and international role of race and ethnicity in political bargaining changed, so did the arguments concerning Puerto Rican citizenship. An appeal to the other end of the ethnic scale became more useful in making the political case as the Puerto Rican Cabranes notes: "Citizenship of the 'second class' in a colonial setting was destined to fall into disrepute in the era of decolonization and the reassertion of claims to equality by long-oppressed racial minorities in the United States."[39] The battle for first-class citizenship will be fought along functional alignments and not so much on constitutional tradition or principle. As such, pressures from national civil rights groups and international decolonization movements will be crucial elements in the process. With a weak concept of citizenship to fall back on, the outcome will depend on climates of opinion on race, ethnicity, civil rights, and decolonization among decision-making elites, which in turn depend on the influence of national and international forces on that climate of opinion. At this point the battle could go either way in Puerto Rico. Ironically, "rewarding" the Puerto Ricans with independence (as with the Philippines) certainly remains a U.S. option despite the fact that they are now, and have been since 1917, U.S. citizens.

It was during the early stages of World War II, however, that this country witnessed a most glaring abuse, which might have been mitigated somewhat by a stronger political and constitutional concept of citizenship: Executive Order 9066, which led to the discriminatory exclusion and detention of Japanese Americans. The Japanese represent a significant example of U.S. pluralism in the Furnivall sense. Few groups have had more restrictive measures taken against them, yet not only did the group increase in numbers, the number of U.S. citizens among them also increased. Approximately two-thirds of the Japanese detained under Executive Order 9066 were U.S. citizens. Given the racial and ethnic tradition in functional alignments and the anxious climate at that time of war, it was not at all surprising that German- and Italian-American citizens and aliens were exempted from the order. As a group of U.S. scholars has noted:

> The Supreme Court, in fact, dealing with broad problems of the war power of the military over civilians within the country, the degree to which the courts would review exertions of that power, and questions of racial classification under the Fifth Amendment—which speaks only of "persons"—found little occasion to emphasize any constitutional distinctions between citizens and aliens.[40]

The functional rather than the plebiscitarian prerogatives of citizenship appear to dominate in U.S. history. As a consequence, it appears that the weight of citizenship as a resource in the U.S. political system has varied very much with the overall political climate in which competition takes place.

Traditionally, race and ethnicity have figured prominently in debates surrounding the role of citizenship, although the extent of their influence has varied over the course of U.S. history. In the past two decades, however, the impact of race and ethnicity has been dramatic and has served to weaken the role of citizenship as a resource. In such a context of ethnic revitalization certain groups do make relative gains, at least in the short term. Such is the case with any group of illegal aliens that shares an ethnic identity with any significant native group that chooses to support its claims. The question remains, however, whether these short-term achievements made during a period of ethnic revitalization are sufficient to anchor the long-range rights of the new group in the body politic. The rights of the working class, for instance, resulted from a gradual process of citizenship-building, that is, integration and incorporation of this class into the political system, into full community membership. With this full membership in the community goes the sharing of the rights and also duties of securing and perfecting the basic human equality that such a membership promises. This is not to say that citizenship promises the abolition of social inequality; it only opens the way for the systematic and constructive challenging of those inequalities. In large part it does so by creating a legitimacy (consensus) around its requirements. As such, citizenship is not a natural law principle, it is a developing principle, that is, it requires the active promotion of the rights and duties that are its essence. Citizenship-building is like community-building in that they both require full membership and participation in the enterprise.[41] T.H. Marshall is worth quoting at length here:

There is no universal principle that determines what those rights and duties shall be, but societies in which citizenship is a developing institution create an image of an ideal citizenship against which achievement can be measured and towards which aspiration can be directed. The urge forward along the path thus plotted is an urge towards a fuller measure of equality, an enrichment of the stuff of which the status is made and an increase in the number of those on whom the status is bestowed.[42]

If the functional idea of U.S. citizenship has tended to create the idea of people being mere citizens, then the hope is that an emphasis on the developmental idea will change that to the idea of fellow citizens. To the extent that the pursuit of ethnic grievances inhibits the growth of community, it also obstructs the development of the fellowship of citizens. The process begun with the Fourteenth Amendment has to be continued. As Kettner notes, "It made a difference—both to him and to the wider community—whether Dred Scott was legally a citizen. It makes a difference still."[43]

CONCLUSIONS AND PROPOSITIONS

In the socially and culturally plural society, especially in an era of ethnic revitalization, there can be no consensus on immigration policy. The increasing complexities of U.S. society and the legal system of due process present a real problem for any policy that seeks a consensus on equal opportunity of entry. What is justice and fairness of opportunity in a complex world where millions would enter the United States every year if given the opportunity? Is it not a matter of "Right versus Right," as Teitelbaum[44] has put it? In a complex, ethnically plural world, there always exists the danger that in the process of bargaining these groups create a zero-sum situation, a situation in which their own particular ethnic lobbying results in their checkmating each other.

When an ethnic group argues for its particular right above and beyond a general right, that is, as distinct from that of all other groups, it contributes to a possible backlash to all such special rights when broad ideological climates change. How then to handle the question of rights in the context of immigration policy?

It is the central conclusion of this chapter that this issue of rights cannot be decided in the context of immigration policy formulation alone. It has to be considered as a separate issue, subordinate to the matter of general constitutional, legal, political, social, and economic privileges and obligations. In other words, the argument has to be put in an arena where there is at least a probability of achieving a political mandate, if not a consensus. As such, a discussion around the rights of citizenship might be in order. The following two propositions are advanced as contributions to that debate:

1. The well-meaning attempts to put citizens, aliens (legal and illegal), even prospective immigrants on the same plane of rights are detrimental to the growth of an operational concept of citizenship. Once in the United States, they have these rights only in theory or in part so that their vulnerability contributes to the perpetuation of those inequalities already present in the system.

Around the world, nation after nation is either closing its doors to newcomers, making it a one-way movement out, or setting racially based criteria of admission. The two traditional liberal ideals of freedom of movement and transferability of civil and human rights from one country to the other are under serious attack everywhere. One way to safeguard their continued existence is to understand that neither right has ever existed in pure form. Invariably and traditionally they have been qualified or modified. These modifications have been in the form of laws and regulations governing the entry and exit of individuals, and immigration laws governing more lengthy or permanent settlement. The days when mere physical presence in a state's territory secured all rights are long gone. Today those rights should be secured through a process similar in many ways to the establishing of a stake, a process in which legal and customary responsibilities, obligations, and requirements often precede some rights. To ignore these procedures is to further weaken and threaten what remains of the respect for freedom of movement and settlement with rights.

The notion of equality of opportunity in immigration has to follow, not precede, the notion of the full rights of citizenship. This idea is premised on the simple logic that no nation that fails to pursue the rights of all its citizens will be much disposed to pursue them for immigrants, not legal immigrants and certainly not illegal ones.

2. The prospect of increasing numbers of permanently resident noncitizens has serious implications for both the institutional and

cultural dimensions of national politics. Aside from the very real issues of sovereignty and national security, there is the issue of the threat to an evolving social democracy (that is, citizenship). The United States finds itself in the singular geographic position of bordering large populations of quite different social and economic conditions. Changes in the occupational distribution of the foreign-born reflect the shifting origins of new immigrants. Illegal workers in the United States are more easily manipulated than are social conditions at home, such as labor unionization and general pressures for higher wages. It is this vulnerability of status that makes plausible Burnett's somewhat harsh assessment that the acceptance by certain U.S. sectors of the flow of employable illegal immigrants shares some similarities with the homelands policy in South Africa.[45] If, as Forbes asserts, "Naturalization is a necessary, though not the only, condition for full civic participation,"[46] then one has to be terribly concerned about, for example, the U.S. resident Mexican population's low rates of naturalization and, consequently, civic participation. While ethnic politics and lobbying achieves some gains for these noncitizens (especially during a stage of ethnic revitalization) it could hardly be the long-range answer to their generalized lack of power as a group.

There is real need, therefore, to begin linking research on race and ethnic relations to immigration and naturalization questions. Within the broad parameters of Marshall's developmental concept of citizenship, the following questions take on importance:

1. What are the rates of naturalization among different ethnic-immigrant groups? How have these rates varied over time?
2. What are some of the obstacles to the acquisition of citizenship, in the society and in the group itself?
3. How do the two fundamental rules governing citizenship, by place of birth and by parentage, operate to enhance or retard the development and protection of individual and societal rights? Which rule is most suited to a world of increasing population movements accompanied by heightened nationalism and ethnic identifications?

No policy can long elevate a particular issue into a very high-order problem without eventually having to deal with it. The longer the delay the greater the danger of a harsh response. The immigration problem in the United States is very much in this category. A new approach might lead to the necessary consensus that today appears beyond our reach.

NOTES

1. Gunnar Myrdal, *American Dilemma* (New York: Harper & Row, 1944), p. 3.

2. Norman Podhoretz, "My Negro Problem, and Ours," *Commentary* 35 (1963):93–101.

3. Frederick J. Turner, *The Frontier in American History* (New York: Holt, 1920), pp. 281–82.

4. A good illustration is the benefit derived by the 19th century immigrant German population from the generally held, but erroneous, belief that their vote elected Abraham Lincoln in 1860. The significance of showing that they "voted right" was an important sign that the immigrants "owed" their new nation something for the privilege of entry. Joseph Shafer, "Who elected Lincoln," in Lawrence H. Fuchs, ed., *American Ethnic Politics* (New York: Harper & Row, 1968), pp. 32–49.

5. Lawrence H. Fuchs, "Immigration, pluralism, and public policy: The challenge of the *Pluribus* to the *Unum*." in Mary M. Kritz, ed., *U.S. Immigration and Refugee Policy*, (Lexington, MA: D.C. Heath, 1983), pp. 289–315.

6. J. S. Furnivall, *Netherlands India: A Study of Plural Economy* (Cambridge, MA: Macmillan, 1939).

7. J. S. Furnivall, "Some problems of tropical economy," in Rita Hinden, ed., *Fabian Colonial Essays* (London: George Allen & Unwin, 1945), p. 168.

8. This in part explains why the United States has experienced none of the ethnic xenophobia or secessionism of other new nations. The incremental expansion of U.S. territory, from the original 13 colonies to the 50 states, did not involve the incorporation of large populations that were ethnically different. There were 200,000 inhabitants in the whole of the Mexican territory that was incorporated by the United States in the mid 19th century.

9. Harry Jerome, *Migration and Business Cycles* (New York: National Bureau of Economic Research, 1926).

10. Lisa Smith Roney, "The present immigration system: Its origins and operations," in U.S. Select Commission on Immigration and Refugee Policy, *U.S. Immigration Policy and the National Interest: Staff Report* (Washington, D.C., 1981), pp. 295–351; Fuchs, "Immigration, pluralism, and public policy," pp. 289–94.

11. Roney, "The present immigration system," pp. 321–22.

12. Simon Kuznets and E. Rubin, *Immigration and the Foreign Born* (New York: National Bureau of Economic Research, 1954), chapter 4.

13. Ibid.

14. This partly explains how L. Coleman ("What is American: A study of

alleged American traits," *Social Forces* 19 (1941):492–99) could survey a very large body of literature on the American character and discover that, at one time or the another, authoritative writers attributed virtually every known value, custom, and cultural trait to the Americans.

15. John Higham, ed., *The Reconstruction of American History* (New York: Humanities Press, 1962), p. 10.

16. Fuchs, "Immigration, pluralism, and public policy," pp. 294–96.

17. David M. Potter, "The quest for the national character," in Higham, ed., *The Reconstruction of American History*, p. 215.

18. Milton M. Gordon, *Assimilation in American Life: The Role of Race, Religion and National Origins* (New York: Oxford Univ. Press, 1964).

19. Theodore Draper, *The Rediscovery of Black Nationalism* (New York: Viking Press, 1970); Cynthia Enloe, *Ethnic Conflict and Political Development: An Analytic Study* (Boston: Little, Brown, 1973); Wendell Bell and Walter E. Freeman, eds., *Ethnicity and Nation-Building: Comparative, International, and Historical Perspectives* (Beverly Hills, CA: Sage Publications, 1974).

20. Perhaps the most representative statement of this new attitude is contained in Michael Novak, *The Rise of the Unmeltable Ethnics* (New York: Macmillan, 1971). Interesting also are the various projects of the American Jewish Committee's Institute on Pluralism and Group Identity. Great impetus was given to this new ethnic consciousness by the funding of the Ethnic Heritage Studies Program as part of Title IX of the Elementary and Secondary Education Act by the federal government.

21. Nathan Glazer and Daniel Patrick Moynihan, eds., *Theory and Experience* (Cambridge, MA: Harvard Univ. Press, 1976), p. 5.

22. Lawrence H. Fuchs, ed., *American Ethnic Politics* (New York: Harper & Row, 1968); Charles McC. Mathias, "Ethnic groups and foreign policy," *Foreign Affairs* 59 (1981):975–98.

23. Martin Kilson, "Blacks and neo-ethnicity in American political life," in Glazer and Moynihan, eds., *Ethnicity: Theory and Experience*, pp. 236–66.

24. In recent decades the world has witnessed dramatic backlashes to erstwhile "privileged" immigrant groups, many of them citizens of the countries in question: the Portuguese and Italians in Venezuela after the fall of the Pérez Jiménez dictatorship (1957); the East Indians in East Africa; ethnic Chinese in Southeast Asia; and West Indians in some Central American countries.

25. T.H. Marshall, *Class, Citizenship and Social Development* (New York: Doubleday, 1964).

26. Gerhard Lenski, *Power and Privilege: A Theory of Social Stratification* (New York: McGraw-Hill, 1966), p. 83.

27. Reinhard Bendix, *Nationbuilding and Citizensip: Studies of our Changing Social Order* (New York: John Wiley and Sons, 1964), pp. 89–126.

28. Ibid., p. 94.

29. Frank George Franklin, *The Legislative History of Naturalization in the United States* (New York: Kelley, 1971, reprinted from Chicago: Univ. Chicago Press, 1906), p. 38.

30. James H. Kettner, *Development of American Citizenship, 1608-1870* (Chapel Hill: Univ. North Carolina Press, 1978), p. 351.

31. Alexander M. Bickel, *The Morality of Consent* (New Haven: Yale Univ. Press, 1975), pp. 53–54.

32. Ibid., p. 54.

33. Kettner,, *Development of American Citizenship*, p. 351.

34. Emory Stephen Bogardus, *Immigration and Race Attitudes* (New York: Ozer, 1971, reprinted from Boston: D.C. Heath, 1928).

35. One can cite the attitude of Puerto Rican communist leader Juan Mari Bras, who maintains that he has no attachment to his U.S. citizenship but could not function without it (*El Mundo*, 20 September 1981).

36. José A. Cabranes, *Citizenship and the American Empire* (New Haven: Yale Univ. Press, 1979), pp. 98–99.

37. Ibid., p. 99.

38. Ibid., pp. 82–101. Gordon K. Lewis adduces another expedient reason for the 1917 granting of citizenship: the United States "felt obliged to prove her liberalism as against Imperial Germany," in *Puerto Rico: Freedom and Power in the Caribbean* (New York: Monthly Review, 1963), p. 3.

39. Cabranes, *Citizenship and the American Empire*, p. 101.

40. Jan Ten Broek, E. Barnhart, and F. W. Watson, *Prejudice, War and the Constitution: Causes and Consequences of the Evacuation of the Japanese Americans in World War II* (Los Angeles: Univ. California Press, 1954), p. 311.

41. The people of Massachusetts knew already in 1779 that citizenship had to be earned. Listen to their constitution: "No man, nor corporation, or association of men, have any other title to obtain advantages, or particular and exclusive privileges, distinct from those of the community, than what arises from the consideration of services rendered to the public; and this title being in nature neither hereditary, nor transmissible to children, or descendants, or relation by blood. . . " (Act VI).

42. T.H. Marshall, *Class, Citizenship and Social Development*, p. 92.

43. Kettner, *Development of American Citizenship*, p. x.

44. Michael S. Teitelbaum, "Right versus right: Immigration and refugee policy in the United States," *Foreign Affairs* 59 (1980):21–59.

45. R. Burnett, "Illegal aliens come cheap: South Africa's homeland's policy," *The Progressive* 43 (1979):44–46.

46. Susan S. Forbes, "Doing well by doing good: The impact of illegal immigration to the United States," in U.S. Select Commission on Immigration and Refugee Policy, *U.S. Immigration Policy and the National Interest*, pp. 221–94.

Index

Acheson, Dean, 250
Alcoa Aluminum Company, construction project, Suriname, 207-8
aliens: illegal, 67, 69, 72-3, 225, 228, 229, 230, 274; undocumented, 9-10, 84, 225, 231
American creed, 261, 262, 263, 266
amnesty, 10-11, 80, 88, 238
Arab receiving states, 53
Aruba: emigration, 51; as sending/receiving country, 53
assimilation, ideologies of, 267
Audubon, James, 50

Bahamas: emigration, 22; as receiving country, 25; as sending/receiving country, 53; size, 16
Baldwin, James, 261
banana plantations, factors in migration, 20, 21
Barbados: emigration, 17, 18, 19, 20, 21, 22, 25, 28, 48, 51, 59, 61, 226-7; fertility rate decline, 23, 226-7; independent status, 26; as sending/receiving country, 53; temporary labor, importation of, 53
Belize, 5
Bendix, Reinhard, 270
Bermuda, migration to, 20
Bickel, Alexander M., 271
Bishop, Maurice, 58
boat people (*see* Haitian migration)
Bogardus, Emory Stephen, 272
Bracero Program, 24-5, 75
Britain: citizenship rights for migrants, 185-7; decolonization and immigration, 186-8; economic impact of immigration, 194; immigration control legislation, 187-8; immigration policies, 26-7, 187-8, 197, 200; mass Caribbean emigration to (1950s), 26-7, 187-8; racial discrimination, 26-7, 195-8
British Guiana, migration to, 15, 17, 18, 19
British Nationality Act of 1948, 186
British West Indies, emigration, 23, 187, 188, 250
Brody, Richard A., 112
Brown, Rev. Ethelred, 248
Burciaga, José Antonio, 8
Bureau for Migration from the Overseas Departments (BUMIDOM), 191, 193, 195, 199
Bureau of Security and Consular Affairs, 232
Burnett, R., 277
Bustamente, Jorge, 87

Cabranes, José A., 272, 273
Cambrone, Luckner, 140
Canada: black history, 214-15; cross section of immigrants, 215; domestic labor, migration program for, 216; employment discrimination, 217-18; Human Rights Codes, 217; immigration policy, overview, 27-8, 215-18; migration to, countries of origin, 214-15; mobilization of nonwhite communities, 220; 1976 Immigration Act, effects of, 28;

About the Contributors

Robert L. Bach teaches sociology at the State University of New York at Binghamton. He is the coauthor with Alejandro Portes of *Latin Journey: Cuban and Mexican Immigrants in the United States* (1985).

David B. Bray is Foundation Representative for Paraguay and Northern Argentina for the Inter-American Foundation. He has taught at Tufts University, Tulane University, and the University of Florida. He has written on Caribbean Basin Export Agriculture, migration and industrialization.

Frank Bovenkerk teaches cultural anthropology at the University of Utrecht in Holland. He has published on urban ethnography, immigration in the Netherlands, and anthropological research methods. A recent book, *Italiaans Ijs* (1983), is about the social history of Italian ice cream vendors in the Netherlands.

Charles V. Carnegie, a Jamaican, did his Ph.D. in anthropology at Johns Hopkins University. He has taught at Bates College and the University of Florida and is at present Visiting Research Fellow at the Institute of Social and Economic Research, the University of the West Indies, Mona, Jamaica.

Gary P. Freeman teaches political science at the University of Texas at Austin. He is the author of *Immigrant Labor and Racial Conflict in Industrial Societies: The French and British Experience, 1945–75* (1979), and numerous articles on comparative social policy and the welfare state.

Guy Gugliotta covers the Caribbean and Latin America as a journalist for the Miami *Herald*. He has held both a Nieman Fellowship (Harvard 1982–1983) and an Alicia Patterson Fellowship (Argentina, 1985).

Frances Henry teaches anthropology at York University in Toronto. She has worked extensively in Trinidad, Guyana, and the Dominican Republic, where she is conducting a study of the European Jewish settlement in Sosua. The West Indian community in Canada is one of her main interests.

Barry B. Levine teaches sociology at Florida International University., He has taught at universities in the United States and Latin America. He is the author of *Benjy Lopez: A Picaresque Tale of Emigration and Return* (1980), editor of *The New Cuban Presence in the Caribbean* (1983), and coeditor of *Problemas de desigualdad social en Puerto Rico* (1972). He is editor and cofounder of *Caribbean Review*. Presently he is finishing a manuscript on capitalism and poverty in Puerto Rico.

Anthony P. Maingot teaches sociology at Florida International University. He is presently on leave at the Rand Corporation in California. He has taught at universities in the United States and the Caribbean and has written extensively on the Caribbean and Latin America. He is presently working on a manuscript entitled *The Caribbean as Modern Conservative Societies.* During 1982–1983 he served as president of the Caribbean Studies Association.

Dawn Marshall is a research fellow at the Institute for Social and Economic Research, University of the West Indies, Cave Hill, Barbados. She was counterpart chief technical advisor to the "Man in the biosphere project: Studies on population, development and environment in the Eastern Caribbean" and edited the four project reports. She is project coordinator of the Institute of Social and Economic Research longitudinal eastern Caribbean migration project. Her publications include *The Haitian Problem: Illegal Migration to the Bahamas* (1979), *Tourism and Employment in Barbados* (1978), and *Migration as an Agent of Change in Caribbean Islands Eco-Systems* (1982).

Terry L. McCoy is director of the Center for Latin American Studies at the University of Florida. He also holds appointments in the departments of political science and sociology. Together with Charles H. Wood, McCoy carried out a comprehensive study of the use of Caribbean workers in the Florida sugar industry.

Robert Pastor teaches political science at Emory University in Atlanta and directs the Latin American and Caribbean Program at the Carter Center. In 1985-1986 he was Fulbright professor of U.S. Foreign Policy at El Colegio de México in Mexico City. He was senior staff member in charge of Latin American and Caribbean Affairs on the National security Council from 1977-1981, and the Executive Director of the Linowitz Commission on U.S.-Latin American Relations from 1975-1976.

Aaron Segal teaches political science at the University of Texas at El Paso, and is author of four books and many articles on the Caribbean, including *Haiti: Political Failure, Cultural Successes* (1984) and *Population Policies in the Caribbean* (1975). He is currently visiting professor at the Air War College in Alabama.

Alex Stepick teaches anthropology at Florida International University. He has written extensively about the Caribbean and Latin America and is presently engaged in research concerning the urbanization and social structure of Mexico.